Ganges River

Jamuna River

Narmada River

KATHIAWAD

Calcutta
Kharagpur

Bombay

INDIA

Arabian Sea

Bay of
Bengal

Madras

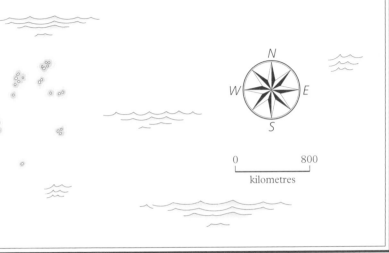

INDIAN OCEAN

N

W   E

S

0   800
kilometres

Shards of Memory

Shards of Memory

Woven Lives in Four Generations

PARITA MUKTA

Weidenfeld & Nicolson
LONDON

First published in Great Britain in 2002
by Weidenfeld & Nicolson

© 2002 Parita Mukta

A CIP catalogue record for this book
is available from the British Library.

For permission to reprint the following we thank:
'Winter Song', Hull, © BMG music publishing; 'Fog on the Tyne', Hull, ©
Charisma/EMI music publishing; 'Bury My Body', Price, © Dash Music/EMI;
'A Woman's Heart', Brady, © Darte; 'Pancchi Kahe Haut Udaas' & 'Ek Bangla
Bane Nyara', K. L. Saigal/Kidar Sharma, 'Nayanhinko Raah, Prabo', © Hindusthan
Musical Products Ltd; 'Pannchi Banoon Udti Phiroon' & 'Pyar Kiyaa To Darna
Kya' & 'Ho Gore Gore, banke Chhore' & 'Teri Shehnai Bole', © Gramaphone
Company of India Ltd; 'A Woman Writing' is reprinted courtesy of the
Victoria and Albert Picture Gallery.

ISBN 0 297 60728 6

Typeset in Joanna MT by
Selwood Systems, Midsomer Norton

Printed in Great Britain by
Butler & Tanner Ltd, Frome and London

Weidenfeld & Nicolson

The Orion Publishing Group Ltd
Orion House
5 Upper Saint Martin's Lane
London, WC2H 9EA

in memory of
and homage to
my father.

CONTENTS

Acknowledgements   viii
Family Tree   xii
Map   xiv
Introduction   xv

PART ONE: BA
Ba and I   3
Archive Odyssey: Dhankor's Story   21
Voices that Rise from the Past   29
Journeying On   35
Arriving   40
Migratory Birds   42
The Passage   53

PART TWO: HARSHAD
Hunger Stories   61
Witnessing Hunger   87
Every Day a Diwali   95
The Magical Conjuring of Food   100
The Hues of the Sky   103

PART THREE: RAJ
Raj   117
Popat Bhukiyo Natthi, Popat Tarsio Natthi   130
Catherine Cookson Country   132
Haba   142
The First Father to Britain   151

PART FOUR: SONPARI
Ladli Sonbai   159
The Muse of History, A Woman Writing   175
The Magic of a Child   182

Notes and suggested reading   199
Glossary   213

ACKNOWLEDGEMENTS

I have been fortunate in having a community of open and enquiring minds around me that has encouraged me to explore moments, which, while being specific to a historical time, have been lived in profoundly personal ways. I would like to thank my father first and foremost. My father journeyed with me throughout this writing, read the different drafts (including that entitled 'Ladli Sonbai'), bore my questioning with fortitude and encouragement, and above all lived out his faith in honest, critical enquiry to open up a non-injurious way of being. His departure on 18 November 2001, just a week before the final proofs reached me, has left a deep void. I have decided to retain the writing which relates to my father in the main part of this book in the present tense.

My mother and my grandmother bear my appreciation and love for showing me the value of the inner life; my sister Bindu, my niece Suchi and nephew Moonie as well as my brother-in-law Nebiyu for being with me; my aunt Tara for winging messages across the distance; my partner David for his constancy in nurturing me and for the contemporary photographs which appear in this book; my daughter Sonpari for drawing me into a different world.

Many colleagues in the departments of history, law and sociology at the University of Warwick have offered valuable support throughout the period of writing, which has been much appreciated. Others have discussed various issues that have been raised in the different drafts of some of these chapters, and provided important feedback. Of these, I would like to thank

Uma Chakravarty, Gabriele Dietrich, Chris Fagan, Catherine Hall, Tanika Sarkar, Mary Shinn and John Solomos. Mary Kennedy, Ursula Sharma, Esha Shah and Meg Stacey have taken this work to their hearts, and this has warmed my own.

I would like to thank Judith Herrin for an encouraging conversation at the prize-giving reception hosted by Weidenfeld and Nicolson at the Institute of Historical Research, London, on 7 July 2000; Peter Rushton for replying promptly and warmly to queries regarding the town of Sunderland amidst his busy teaching commitments and trade union work; Sumit Sarkar for responding with tremendous insight to an earlier draft of the writing that appears here in Part Two; Carolyn Steedman for intellectual nurturance and her work.

Many members of both my paternal and maternal families have been generous in making available to me personal diaries, letters, photographs, newspaper clippings, songs and much more. Many have also shared their own memories with me, in relation to which I have measured my own. Each of them bears my thanks. While all have had their own struggles and achievements in different walks of life, I would like in particular to pay tribute to my aunt Madhu in Ahmedabad, as well as my maternal aunt Kantamasi who worked throughout her life as a schoolteacher in various small towns of Kathiawar. Kantamasi reached out (and often) to widowed women around her to provide them with the training that would enable them to earn an independent living.

My uncle Sharad introduced me to John Macbeth, as well as to Ashwin and Heather Thakkar in Sunderland. I am grateful to them as well as to Mukundbhai Jasani for enabling me to write the 'Raj' chapter in a textured way.

I have benefited greatly over the years through conversations with Khodidasbhai Parmar whose beautiful 'Sonbai' painting is reproduced here (Plate XIX), and which provided vivid colours to a well known fairy-tale. I owe a debt to the late Moham-medbhai for taking photographs of family members, *gratis*, between the years 1948–54. The family of Mohammedbhai's younger brother was housed by my grandfather when it first migrated from a Kathiawadi village to Nairobi in the late 1920s. I have held close the photographs taken by Mohammedbhai in his studio (those that have survived and have come to me) during the writing of this book, knowing that in the cycle of remigrations, this is a debt that I may not be able to repay through different forms of gifting.

There are two individuals who I would like to say a very special thanks to: Chetan Bhatt who has been there since 1998, and Jennifer Lorch. Chetan has provided that rare mix which combines a real understanding of the knot of family living together with a mind which is able to soar high above it; and Jennifer who took great pains to step in, with a quiet and practical warmth, at a particular point in the writing cycle.

My editor at Weidenfeld, Michele Hutchison, picked up my manuscript with wonderful efficiency and grace, put thought and care into it, and saw it to completion in good time. Anita Noguera and Lesley Austin assisted me, with enormous enthusiasm, in the last stage of the writing by chasing up text, music and photo copyright permissions, for which I am grateful. Finally, I would like to thank Michael Downes, the copyeditor, for his contribution to the aesthetics of the layout of this book.

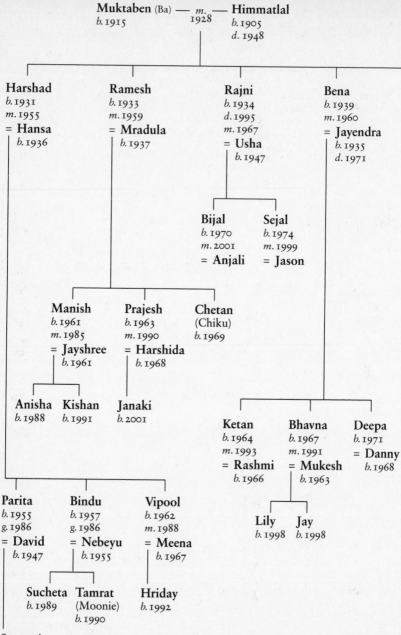

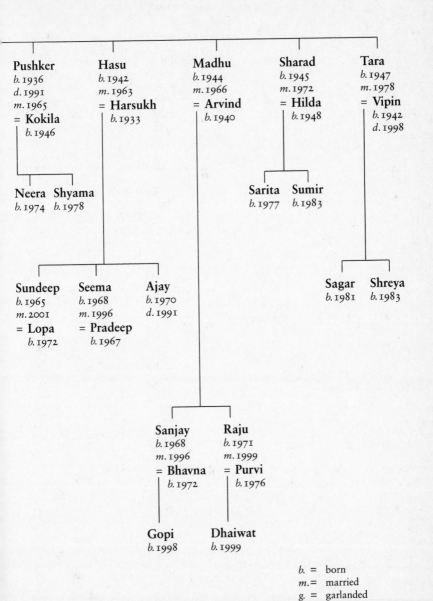

Pushker
b. 1936
d. 1991
m. 1965
= **Kokila**
b. 1946

Hasu
b. 1942
m. 1963
= **Harsukh**
b. 1933

Madhu
b. 1944
m. 1966
= **Arvind**
b. 1940

Sharad
b. 1945
m. 1972
= **Hilda**
b. 1948

Tara
b. 1947
m. 1978
= **Vipin**
b. 1942
d. 1998

Neera **Shyama**
b. 1974 *b.* 1978

Sarita **Sumir**
b. 1977 *b.* 1983

Sundeep
b. 1965
m. 2001
= **Lopa**
b. 1972

Seema
b. 1968
m. 1996
= **Pradeep**
b. 1967

Ajay
b. 1970
d. 1991

Sagar **Shreya**
b. 1981 *b.* 1983

Sanjay
b. 1968
m. 1996
= **Bhavna**
b. 1972

Raju
b. 1971
m. 1999
= **Purvi**
b. 1976

Gopi
b. 1998

Dhaiwat
b. 1999

b. = born
m. = married
g. = garlanded
d. = died

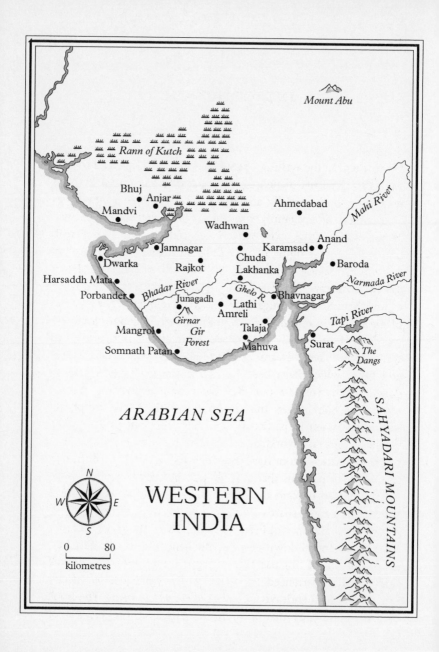

Mount Abu

Rann of Kutch

Bhuj

Anjar

Mandvi

Ahmedabad

Mahi River

Wadhwan

Anand

Jamnagar

Karamsad

Chuda

Lakhanka

Baroda

Dwarka

Rajkot

Narmada River

Harsaddh Mata

Bhadar River

Ghelo R.

Bhavnagar

Porbander

Junagadh

Lathi

Tapi River

Amreli

Girnar

Talaja

Mangrol

Gir

Forest

Mahuva

Surat

The

Dangs

Somnath Patan

ARABIAN SEA

N

W   E

S

WESTERN

INDIA

0   80

kilometres

SAHYADARI MOUNTAINS

INTRODUCTION

I embarked on the writing of this book because I wanted to give words to the lives of people with whom I have lived in close proximity, both spatially and imaginatively. These are the lives of members of my family who do not find their faces reflected in the images that exist within the public world, which is dominated by the figure of a South Asian (usually male) migrant for whom making a fast buck is the be-all and end-all of life. Say 'East African Asian' and the pictures conjured up are those of merchants, traders, sugar-barons forced to flee the persecution of the Idi Amin regime because they had *made themselves hated*. No member of my family has succeeded in being rich; none has wanted to. Their dreams contain colours which are varied and deep, which have been handed down from generation to generation to create a rainbow that is visible over the arch of time. This book charts this, beginning with the weave of life between women in particular, and extending out to the public world of jobs and workplaces.

I have written about lives that are woven together, of threads that bind, of patterns that are stamped in the cloth of our very being, that go beyond the call of history, obligation, loyalty. I have written about shards of memory, as history inflicted wounds on those caught up within its embrace. These shards of memory have been handed down between the generations, and have cut, deep, but out of this has also emerged a fine understanding of this world, experienced by many, which continues to occupy our professional endeavours and intellectual concerns. The book tells of the bonds that have been forged in the process of migrations, dispersals and (re)settlements. It follows the move of my grandparents in the early 1920s from the princely region of Kathiawar in western India (in present-day Gujarat) to Kenya Colony. It tells the story of the children, grandchildren and great-grandchildren of these migrants from Kathiawar as they built their lives first in East Africa and (from the 1970s onwards) in the cities of London, Ahmadabad, Miami, Toronto. It describes the cultural jostling between a peasant world-view and that of an unbridled financial system.

However, if history is 'about' anything, then it is about the pasts which we all bear within ourselves; the weight of memories which we carry and which affect our lives in such capricious ways; the impossibility of building a future that is shorn of the traces of that-which-has-gone-before. The reader is thus asked to enter into the interior life of this family, in a story that contains the everyday hopes and tragedies recognisable in so many families throughout the world.

The story and the telling of the tale are perhaps unique in two ways. Firstly, this is not a chronological account of migration. Nor have I wished to go to the other extreme and transmute the lives I write about into a fictional form. I want the people that I have grown up with to be known as real, embodied people who have acted in this world and made their own unique mark in it. I have written pen portraits of significant members of my family, and if these remain in the minds of my reader and become familiar to them, like people they have come to know, then I shall be happy.

At one level, then, I have been moved to convey the endeavours of individual family members – my grandmother, my father, my uncle, my daughter. They are individuals that I love deeply, even though two of them are no longer on this earth. Furthermore, having been brought up in a culture where the universe spun through magical tales was as tangible as the everyday material world, I know as an adult writer that the life stories cannot be disentangled from these other stories. The domain of cultural expressions (songs, stories, films, well-loved books) provides all of us with the imaginative landscape within which we place our lives. I have chosen to anchor the lives of those family members that I write about here within the folds of these cultural expressions, utilising stories and songs to deepen and enhance the book's landscape. I hope my readers will enjoy the different types of stories.

The final (and ever-shifting) layer of the story is the historical one, which proverbially slips away, like sand. I have delineated that epoch which can broadly be described under the rubric of colonialism–decolonisation–globalisation. This is the broad canvas upon which the colours dance, wherein the deep and vibrant hues of peasant cultures fuse into the technicolour of the digital age, scarred by the growing strength of militarism and organised violence. While I am convinced that the contestations surrounding the story of industrialised progress remain unresolved in a world which continues to be divided in terms of riches and goods, I write less in this book about the workings of the political economy than about the cultural history of widowhood and hunger, and the ways in which certain men are typecast as 'effeminate and emotional' so that the caring and nurture they pour into creating a family life is devalued and unrecognised. I tell a history of being bereft and of a specific kind of childhood: of a father–daughter relationship that frayed at one point, only to be rewoven, more tightly, on a stronger thread. Above all, this book is suffused with the call of the cuckoo, associated always and for evermore in the culture with a longing for the Beloved, when the rainbird calls out '*pee-kahan, pee-kahan*', 'Where is my Beloved?' For you then, who must have heard this plaintive cry at some time in your life.

Part One
BA

By the shores of Gitche Gumee
By the shining Big-Sea-Water,
Stood the wigwam of Nokomis,
Daughter of the Moon, Nokomis...

There the wrinkled, old Nokomis
Nursed the little Hiawatha,
Rocked him in his linden cradle,
Bedded soft in moss and rushes
Safely bound with reindeer sinews;
Stilled his fretful wail by saying,
'Hush! The Naked Bear will get thee!'...

And he sang the song of children,
Sang the song Nokomos taught him...
Saw the moon rise from the water
Rippling, rounding from the water,
Saw the flecks and shadows on it,
Whispered, 'What is that, Nokomis?'
And the good Nokomis answered:
'Once a warrior, very angry,
Seized his grandmother, and threw her
Up into the sky at midnight;
Right against the moon he threw her;
'Tis her body that you see there.'

HENRY WADSWORTH LONGFELLOW, Hiawatha's Childhood

BA AND I

Ba always wears a white *sadlo*. There is, however, a photograph that surfaced (as does a piece of flotsam that rises up in the waves of migration) pulling a familiar figure into the swell of the breakers. I fall into the memory of this photograph first held in the hand, long gazing at it, with a curious twist at the heart, for it pertained to a time when Ba did not belong to me. This photograph is the only evidence of a time when she was not attired in the white of a widow's garb. In this studio photograph (Plate I), she sits with her right arm leaning on a table, its soft upper contours encircled by a heavy, gold bracelet. She has a round face and she wears a dark-coloured *khareto* of sheer voile over a petticoat that falls into pleats in a fashionable fan shape. My grandfather, dressed in a suit and tie, stands upright, slightly behind her, the fingers of his right hand bridging the distance created by her shyness at this public viewing. Her face is tilted in his direction, the eyes aware of his presence in the world.

I never knew my grandfather – and thus I saw Ba always in white. As a child, I did not see the white *sadlo* as an insignia of the oppression of widowed women, but as comfort, warmth, and complete acceptance: I could rush to wipe my hands on the edge of her clean *pallav* and would not be rebuffed. The badge of widowhood, still visible to the eye in the towns and villages of Gujarat, as well as on the high streets and buses of major cities in Britain, evokes in me a constant yearning to sit close, be told stories, to bestow warmth and have it bestowed on me. I have learnt though that Ba's generosity of heart and mind, her ability to enfold all those who come in her presence, is a rare one. Being clad in a white *sadlo* does not always envelop the wearer within a pure light that makes effulgent the shadow of widowhood. While Ba appears genuinely to have 'forgotten' the moments of complete darkness that are embodied in the experience of widowhood, I have seen many in situations similar to Ba eaten up by their memories, their faces bleak and hard. The difference must lie in her improved social circumstances, in her spiritual relationship to self and the world, and in her uncanny ability to sift the chaff from the grain, grasping the optimistic potential of a person while paying tribute to the jagged edges and spiky burrs. One comes away from the encounter transformed, shimmering, evanescent.

My grandmother, clad in a white *sadlo*, directed my eyes from an early age not to things on this earth, but to the sky above and the moon beyond. Her fingers mixed the *rotli* with *shak*, dipped this in *dahi* to soften it: the hand was raised high to the sky outside, waved in a circle, and then swooped down. '*Chanda chodi, ghimain bodi, mari Pari na modha main hapuk kodi.*' ('Mixed in the rays of the moon, dipped in ghee, here's a morsel coming for my Pari.') My waiting mouth was opened wide to receive sustenance with a 'hapuk' and a laugh, thinking I was swallowing the rays of the moon with it. There was then our regular joint sighting of the Old Woman who lived on the moon, when we lingered outside, watching her at an immense distance, an outcast visible to the eye of the whole world. She can be seen clearly on the night of the full moon, hobbling along far away from the earth, an Old Woman who had once been a grandmother, thrown up into the sky at midnight.

The stories of widowhood that have now become my familiars bear a close relationship to that of the Old Woman on the Moon. That story opened up a universe in which perverse (or powerless) old women were expatriated to a place that had the capacity to wane and wax according to the needs of the refugees it accepted. No other displacement can compare with this. The moon as a place of banishment, exile, refuge. The Old Woman on the Moon, however, though cold and deprived of human warmth, has a goat tethered to her arm which provides her with milk and thus nourishes her thin frame. That is a luxury denied to many on this earth. But then the earth, unlike the moon, does not contain those impassable craters. Instead, the earth has had cities of marble and sandstone erected upon her, villages clustered around wells and fields, civilisations which boast of ancient trade routes, temples and mosques of immense beauty, dance and music which link one up to the Creator. The Old Woman on the Moon is denied all this: she lives a chill existence.

The memory of our joint observation of the *dosima* living on the moon is significant to both Ba's life and my own. The quiet, shared moments of gazing upwards bound me to the *dosima* close to my side, as well as to the one high up above. It forged an inner world of immense complexity, in which fine, invisible threads of affiliation and disaffiliation were spun into an intricate pattern whose tracery the adult mind continues to replicate. The relationship between the Old Woman on the Moon and my grandmother is defined by the moment when widowhood struck Ba and she experienced being thrown up into the sky at midnight, right against the moon. It is this that makes us, her daughters and granddaughters, circle around her protectively. The year was 1948, the day 11 March in the solar calendar – in the lunar calendar, the third day (trij) in the month of *phalgun sud*. She was thirty-three years of age: her eldest son was sixteen; the youngest daughter, six months old, was suckling at her breast. She became engaged at the age of eleven and a half while living in her paternal village in western India; she was married at thirteen. She took a boat across the Indian Ocean to join her husband in Nairobi at the age of fifteen, and had nine children there. My grandfather, beset with financial worries, and having asked for the loan of her bracelets which were pawned – 'No, it did not help. It was like trying to patch up the sky that has torn asunder,' – had a painful heart attack and died at home in the middle of the night. And yes, the women and men of the community imposed upon her the stigmata of widowhood. Enough.

The date 11 March 1948 remains as a marker against which the family measures all subsequent events, public and private. Seven months after my grandfather died, India and Pakistan became separate, sovereign nation states. Eight and a half months later, Gandhi was assassinated by a sectarian communalist in the grounds of Birla House. The colonial state consolidated its military holdings in Kenya Colony in the same year (1948), ensuring the build-up of arms in the region. Three years before this, the world had witnessed what Robert Oppenheimer described as the destruction of the universe: the first atomic genocide of civilian populations took place, with the dropping of a nuclear bomb on Hiroshima on 6 August 1945, and on Nagasaki three days later. Thus was the order of contemporary world politics established.

I said 'Enough,' when narrating the moment of Ba's widowhood, as a sharp ending, a narrative fracture, for it is too difficult to continue. But it can never rest there. 'Never' is a negative eternity, and I am well aware that my endeavour to grasp her hurt is an unrealisable one. She has maintained an implacable silence on the events surrounding the moment of her widowhood, these having been narrated to me by my aunts, Hasu and Madhu, who bear the burden of witness. It is Ba's silence which propels me to a study of a subjective experience and a historical condition which has entered my pores and seeped into my skin. With Ba's face so close, here by my side, the past is a well-traced landscape whose contours I comprehend as intimately as I do those of the present. The past is here, now, dwelling within her and within me. I read the life stories of widows, return again and again to the nineteenth century social reform movements that took place on the subcontinent. I attend to the debates that have been well rehearsed, cogitate on the compromises exacted in the lives of those who attempted to improve the widows' plight. I chew on the bitter taste, swallow the grief.

Widowhood ruptured Ba's quiet life. It has rendered us, her daughters and granddaughters, mute in the face of this pain. And yet – housebound and family-centred as her life has

6

been, her cosmology embraces the universe. Her world view encompasses peoples of diverse mentalities and finds commonality in all. Her philosophy can be summed up in the following words: the sun shines on everyone alike, the tree provides shade for all. '*Jevi drashti evi srashti*,' she says. Creation is beheld through one's particular vision. Genesis begins in your gaze.

The philosophy of the mature Ba, like her white clothing, consists of many layers, wrapped around one another. Her parents had left the village of Virpur in peninsular Saurashtra (present-day Gujarat) early on in the twentieth century, to migrate to Bengal, which contained the fabulous imperial capital of Calcutta. Her father had given up the life of a tenant farmer, left the land which did not provide adequately for him, and had gone to the town of Kharagpur to work as a cook in the household of a Jain trader. The subsequent setting up of a Gujarati Hotel in Golbazaar was the outcome of a migrant's desire to become independent of his patron. The town of Kharagpur was a major railway junction on the Calcutta–Nagpur line, and the Gujarati Hotel served savouries and sweets to the employees who took a break from their tasks in the workshops of the Locomotive, Carriage and Wagon Departments of the Railway. Ba was born in Kharagpur in 1915, on the seventh day of *vaishakh*, just as the spring was drawing to a close, within a darkened room of a building that adjoined an eating house. Both her home and the Gujarati Hotel bustled with the talk and shouts of the Oriya, Madrasi, Telugu and Bihari workers, migrants all, who slept on the floor of the eating house after this had been cleaned at night. Paltu was at the beck and call of everyone, while Turi sifted the rice grains. The sound of the pounding of grain mixed with the sizzling of fried *nimki*, the seeds of the bishop's weed plant popping in the oil. Ba lost her mother when she was aged eight, but she often talks about the emaciated figure sitting in a chair, enduring the last stages of TB. When I hear of her father taking her up on his lap regularly (where he would put a sweet-ball in her mouth) saying with a laugh, 'Oh ho, so my Mukta has a temperature today. Is that because she has not eaten a *pendo?*' – it feels as if I have reached the child which lies deep inside her, now swaddled by the adult clothing. She is a fragile and precious figure and I fear to touch her, but she looks back at me with dark, sturdy, over-large eyes. Ba considers herself to have been a well-loved child, and the core is well protected.

When Ba reached the age of eleven her father sent her, together with her younger sister Hira, back to the homeland in Saurashtra, to the village of Virpur near the town of Lathi (made famous by the ruler–poet Kalapi[i] and the more ancient Dedo), in order that the two girls learn the craft of home-making from the paternal grandmother and a paternal (widowed) aunt. It was time that the girls were groomed for their future lives, and women were needed to do the tutoring. Ba talks about days spent by the well, chatting and laughing with young girls her own age. Her eyes smile when she describes the day Santokma came to view her as a prospective bride.

One morning, my aunt Ottamfoi told me that a special guest was arriving and that I should be careful about how I talked and held myself. A few days before this Bapuji (my father) and Motamama (my elder brother) had arrived from Khar-agpur and I had been very happy to see them.

I went to fetch some water from the well at the edge of the village, and on my return I saw that someone had arrived at the house while the others were away. She asked for my aunt and without thinking I said that she had gone to get some *ghee* for a guest! You know that *ghee* is a luxury and that it is only obtained on special occasions to serve to guests. Santokma simply smiled and waited. When my aunt Ottamfoi arrived she asked me to feed some *obad* into the fire. Ottamfoi must have wanted Santokma to know that I could do the housework well, and when I asked 'Ottamfoi, what is *obad?*' she pinched me sharply on my arm. Santokma saw this and said, 'Ottamben, the poor girl has come here from a far place, and does not know our ways. Besides, she's a motherless girl. Treat her gently.'

Santokma stayed with us for four days, and on the second from last day of her visit, I was given new clothes and told that this was my engagement day. All I knew was that I was engaged to Santokma's son, who was living somewhere in Africa, and that he was doing well for himself in a far-off place. Perhaps Santokma chose me because I was the daughter of a man who lived in a different part of the country, and she thought I could adjust to a life abroad. She also knew both my maternal and paternal families, so it was all arranged. *Gaud-dhana* were eaten by five elders who acted as witness to the engagement. There was no large feast, or public show. I went around smiling, thinking something big had happened to me. I remember Motamama looking happy and stroking my cheeks. Bapuji was more reserved.

When Ba sketches with quick brush strokes the events that catapulted her into a different world, her voice retains the quality of a young girl who was hardly aware of the tremendous changes that were to take place in her life. She trusted that the decisions that were being made about her future would contribute to her happiness, and that the life that was being mapped out held promising horizons into which she would expand. There is a faith here in the essential *goodness* of all human beings which has formed the mantle that she has woven around herself.

Ba's father (a self-denying, somewhat stern man who had taken quickly to the nationalist political movement led by Mohandas Karamchand Gandhi) clearly thought that a young man who was making good in Africa would be a good match for his Mukta. If he did ask himself whether his daughter would remain friendless in a communal, racially stratified milieu where there would be no member of the natal family around her to turn to (if he was even aware of this), it did not deter him from accepting a son-in-law that he had not set eyes upon. Santokma appears to have been more astute and strategic in her assessment of the situation. She had been widowed while her two eldest sons were studying in the town of Bhavnagar under the patronage of her brother Venilal Upadhyay, who was a pleader in the courts. She knew her second son had acquired a taste for the social liberties and expansive landscape which his life in Bhavnagar, and later his sea voyage to Mombasa, had provided. Santokma was in search of a young woman who would adapt to the desires of the new age, in which young men wanted wives who would accompany them in the public world, while also providing domesticity and the anchorage of a home for her son. She understood that the young Mukta would be malleable enough to attempt both. Mukta could be educated into her different roles – and the family was a respected one.

The engagement lasted a year and a half. Neither had seen the other. There was no exchange of letters. This had to wait till after the marriage, which took place in the month of May, 1928. Ba had not seen a photograph of him, knew only that his name was Himmat. She had spent the time between the engagement and the wedding doing daily household chores in Virpur, in the company of young women of her own age. For his part, he had set his financial affairs in Nairobi on a firm footing, and he set sail for the voyage home, disembarking in Bombay. He landed back in Mombasa on 28 July 1928, now married but without his young bride.

Ba's being is now so suffused with the sheen and transparency of a woman untouched by the hands of a man that it is difficult to ask her about her married life. She retains the shyness of a young girl when she is asked about her life with 'him'. She is reticent about talking of this aspect of her past existence in front of her daughters-in-law and her sons, but the narrator (and the romancer) in her enjoys this part of the story and takes pleasure in it. There is a palpable sweetness in her memories of their life together which has the power to disarm my anger at him for deserting her so early, in such a state.

Ba narrates how she left the village of Virpur on her wedding day in a bullock cart. As she dozed, the veil slipped from her face, and he reached out and took her hands in his gently. She pulled them back, and a female relative who was travelling in the same cart said, 'Have some decorum, Himmatbhai, just because you've come from abroad. You'll shame and frighten the girl.'

The wedding party stayed that night in a field outside a village, with Ba's brother-in-law patrolling the area with a gun in his hand. There was a great fear of bandits at that time. Four days later, when my grandfather took Ba to the town of Bhavnagar to show her his old haunts, while the other women in the village of Lakhanka made remarks about how times must have changed if two people could got out in public unchaperoned, Santokma did not try to stop him. Ba says that they stayed in Bhavnagar for ten days:

> We would go around in a horse and carriage to different places. It was a new world for me, this kind of life, and while it seems a very long time ago, I have a vivid picture of him from this time. He wore a gleaming white European-style topee which he would doff at acquaintances, then put on again. He was confident in his ways and open in his outlook. He also had great affection for me and wanted to broaden my horizons. When, after having spent time together, he had to leave Virpur for Bombay to set sail for Mombasa, I cried. He was sad too, and wanted to take me with him, but I was too young to begin married life then, and I returned to Kharagpur after a while and stayed there for two years.

She remembers the gifts he left for her: writing paper, already addressed envelopes, and a fountain pen filled with ink. He wanted her to communicate across the distance that separated them. Did he know that this would be regarded as a subversive act in the village society and did he deliberately wish to flout convention? Or was he simply too far removed from the intricate cultures that existed within the female domain? The issue would surface sharply when they started a joint life together in Nairobi.

She hid his gifts within the folds of one of her wedding saris. There was consternation in the house when the writing paper and pen came rolling out of a sari while a visitor was viewing the trousseau. My grandfather was keen to nurture a companionate marriage. On Ba's arrival in Nairobi two years later, he had different (male) teachers come to the house to tutor her in spoken and written English. He bought books for her to learn the new language. These were found by a younger female relative and disappeared. The sorority conspired to keep her firmly within the confines of the vernacular language and vernacular knowledge, for adoption of English was thought to lead to an espousal of the mores of this language-community. His efforts to change this view were met with a collective resistance. A battle was waged between the forces of a male-directed modernity and the forces of reaction, within which a section of the women sought zealously to preserve the clearly demarcated female domain over which they reigned supreme.

How young she was – pliable and eager to please! She took care not to invoke the wrath of the sorority. When conflict arose between keeping the peace (which meant ceding to voice raised in loud castigation) and her own desire to reach out in the wide expanding space, to follow that enticing ray of light, she chose peace. She did not wish to fell the gnarled trees that stood in her way, but remained loyal to the teachings of her aunt. She took after her mother, a devout Krishna devotee who had made the bestowal of love in the domestic sphere the essence of her spirituality. Ba attempted to slip in to a new life, far away from her sister Hira, whose head she had stroked on the day of her departure as the latter lay asleep. Hiramasi had woken up and had clung to her: 'Don't go. Don't go.' Ba became involved in nurturing the small shoots which peeped out over the horizon, tugging at her. Four *tapuria* arrived – Harshad, Ramesh, Rajni, Pushkar. Then the birth of a daughter, Bena. It was Yamunatai, a trained midwife who wore a sari draped Marathi-style round her, who brought Harshad into the world. Aasabai came for the second birth, her big capable hands providing the assurance that the event was unextraordinary, a matter of routine. Sheruben presided over all the other births, her skills as a peripatetic nurse providing her with an aura of professionalism. The nurses and teachers – Taraben Apte who taught in the Kutchi Gujarati Girls School, Shantaben Bhagvat in the Arya Samaj Girls School – came from urban centres in western India, cities which, while retaining a close link to rural life, had seen unprecedented changes in the lifestyles of those who were better off. While Ba enjoyed visits from Taraben and Shantaben, she continued to be identified with her regional peers from Saurashtra.

As women arrived to join their husbands in the decade after the First World War, the South Asian population in East Africa doubled and the growing communities were consolidated from within. Various groups from the subcontinent settled into the patterns of stratified living which a colonial polity dictated, and very different futures for women within the South Asian communities accordingly emerged. Early marriages for some, resulting at times in adolescent widowhood, while others were equipped with the skills which would enable the provision of nursing, medical and educational services.[ii] The women who took up public roles, their faces bright and earnest as they took to their tasks, were looked upon with a mixture of admiration and envy by the housebound women. At times some of them fell prey to the lascivious advances of men who considered any working woman fair game.[iii]

The children played around Ba and their father when the latter returned from his work. The two would converse quietly: about their day, the books he had brought back from the library, the ones they had just completed reading. *Jayant, Shrikant, Saraswati Chandra, Patanni Prabhuta*. Ba was able to share her husband's taste for Gujarati novels and historical romances without breaching the confinement of her intellect to the domestic and vernacular sphere upon which the sisterhood around her insisted. She had studied two *chopdi* at a school in Kharagpur, each *chopdi* (book) marking a year of drilled recitations. She had learnt the basics of reading and writing; learnt too the intricate workings of privilege as she watched the Brahman teacher sprinkle a slate with some water before picking it up from the hands of a *dalit* child. She would read late into the night in the house on the road named after Lord Milner (who had approved the policy of racial segregation of residential and commercial properties in Kenya in 1920), shading the light with a cloth in order not to disturb the sleeping children.

The Simpson Report of 1913 had called for the segregation of living and commercial places, in order, it said, to prevent disease, and on the grounds that Africans, Asians and Europeans had different standards of health and sanitation. While this had led to angry rejoinders from those who were opposed to the prejudice which emanated from the settler quarters, separation of the three 'races' nonetheless became institutionalised. The African urban poor set up homes outside the city, where in time the areas of Majengo, Kabete, Kibera and Pumwani became large and sprawling. As English families enjoyed the views of lush vegetation across Ngong, Muthaiga and Parklands, those Indian indentured labourers who had remained behind set up small artisanal workshops in Eastleigh, Pangani, and Race Course Road. The most ostracised section of the Sikh community (referred to contemptuously as *rangrejias*) established two Ramgarhia temples, and attempted to enhance their status through the seclusion of women. As the colonial polity overturned established practices, the male elders became fierce in the retention of communal boundaries.[iv] The colonial regulation of each community's legal and civic space entrenched the internal laws of those communities, ensuring that the rule of the fathers was safeguarded within each. There was little sharing of lived experiences, no exchange of cultures or languages, which had earlier blossomed in the coastal Swahili areas; the result was a distinctive and impoverishing differentiation.

Ba laboured to establish her family in the communal compound on Milner Road. Unable to accompany her husband in more cosmopolitan company, having refused to wear the smart buttoned up shoes which he bought for her because it would draw undue attention, she visited the City Park with the other young mothers, and while bringing up nine children (Hasu, Madhu, Sharad and Tara followed Bena) she worked hard at retaining a large circle of relationships amongst neighbours and friends. She was not a solitary person. My grandfather, too, enjoyed hosting lavishly at home. If at times, worn out by the chores, Ba's face lost its welcome, he would sing a Saurashtrian couplet:

Mehmano ne maan dil bhari didha nathi
te ghar nathi masssan cche saacho Sorathio bhane.

'If you do not give abundantly to guests then your house is in truth a crematorium, so says the Sorathio.'

It was clear that he too held dear a philosophy that laid stress on the courtesies of hospitality, derived from the intricate princely–pastoral codes of Saurashtra. But unlike her he spoke out angrily against community depredations. When a male cousin died, and they did what they did to his widow, he was in a towering temper and made his views known loud and long. Ba says that when angry he would thump his fist on the table, calling out 'No, no, no' in English while pacing the floor.

We talk between us, in disturbed, agitated voices – Hasu, Madhu, Tara, Bena, Bindu and I. What must it have been like for her when Kaka died? Why does she never talk about it? And it was the very women and men we knew and could name who . . .? Unforgivable. Monstrous. And yet *she's* forgiven them. Or has she? She has never said anything. But she must have forgiven – that is the philosophical foundation of her existence.

The resounding silence, the uncommunicated part of her story points perhaps in a different direction. It signals a recognition of the moment which was a violation of her personhood. The silence is a retention of integrity, for to lay bare the wound to the light would be to admit to a terrible time when she had lost all claims to being treated with a semblance of sympathy by her fellow creatures. She was a widow who was left with nine children to care for. The eldest was at secondary school – he had not yet graduated to the position of a wage-earning son who could shield her from the whims of caste members. He was to be initiated quickly into the sordid workings of community power, when he was unable to stand out, young as he was, against 'that which had to be done'. The memory of that time lies heavy with him now – though then it was in part washed away by his blind entry into a room full of veiled women, when he put his head on his mother's lap, and sobbed in a harsh, racked voice. The assembly of women understood.

We, the daughters and granddaughters, have always been aware of her utter aloneness at that time. We have realised dimly that this is the context within which her silence has to be placed. And yet, frail creatures though we are, we seek to understand. To know. In order to be able to protect her better. (It is just beginning to dawn on me, though, that her complete isolation then cannot be compensated for by a lifetime of protectiveness thereafter.)

When we are together, Madhu and I, or Hasu and I, or Bindu and I: in the middle of a chore, in the midst of a different conversation – what it must have been like for her? Nine children: no one to support her. Has she forgotten completely? She's never shown ... It is not, however, the dispossession of everyday movable goods – chair, beds, a cupboard – which haunts us. It is the moment when male society (guarded by its female henchmen) wreaked its vengeance on her in a terrifyingly personal way, which stalks us always. We will remain confused about this all our lives, in the way children are, torn between anger for her and respect for her staunch selfhood that says that it is destructive to hold a vengeful grudge against another.

I thrash around, like a fish out of water. I grasp at conclusions which appear sound in the historical context, but which waft away like straws in the wind when I look in her face. What is it that enables her to have that serenity, that, yes, contentment? To dub a whole generation of these elders as 'reactionaries' as some have done, does not reach the core of their being. No, Ba's core is far from a conservative one, for it is imbued with a fine empathy for exiles in all walks of life. Watching groups of refugees trudging out of Kosovo on the TV screen, their faces lined with grief, she shakes her head slowly, does not speak throughout the evening.

Ba's spirituality, that transforming of faith into the web of human relationships; her ability to reach out to those who have acted on their darker side; the depth of grace which makes her insist that those individuals who brutalise others find themselves in a strange, warped world deprived of the truth of human connectedness – none of this contains a full answer. Her face is beginning uncannily to mirror that of Mohandas Karamchand Gandhi, (Plate VIII) a man whose teachings she had imbibed as a child from her parents and her older brother. Ba cannot be called a Gandhian, though, despite sharing a language and a remarkably similar homespun philosophy with the individual who was to overturn the colonial world through peaceful mass resistance. Her mother had espoused the spinning wheel, spending long hours at this, contributing through her efforts to the achievement of national self-sufficiency. When Gandhi visited Kharagpur on 21 September 1921, Ba had placed a garland that her mother had hand-spun round his neck, and he had smiled down at her. Throughout their lives, both her father and her eldest brother were to remain clad in khadi, the garb that marked them out as believers in Gandhian philosophy, and they were known by the street people of Kharagpur for their regular distribution of warm shawls as the winter cold set in. It is, however, difficult to equate Ba's vision of the world with that of Gandhi, who preached a fully conscious moral and political message about the transformative power of love to move the heart of the oppressor. 'A satyagrahi's path is the path of love, not one of enmity,' he wrote. 'It should be the ambition of a satyagrahi to win over even the most hard-hearted of enemies through love.'[v]

I do not remember Ba talking about love and winning over

the most hard-hearted enemies through love in the Gandhian sense. The most telling part of this story is that she has refused to name or utter a comment on those who wronged her. The staunch silence has encapsulated her in a space that no one has been able to enter.

In everyday conversations, what has enraged someone like her youngest daughter Tara is Ba's constant use of a colloquialism: hashe. This hashe can be and has been produced in tense situations to lower the temperature and remove the heat out of one's anger. The Gujarati–English dictionary defines hashe as 'maybe, perhaps; never mind', and hashedrashti (a hashe perspective) as a 'tolerant attitude'. Tara has traced, through her personal diaries, her own lack of public assertiveness to always being told, 'hashe'. This hashe reined in our personal wrath, offered comfort and told us that we should not allow the injustice to consume us. However, while Ba's injunction to rise above injuries and wrongs has helped to enable me to prevent corrosive anger, always, after I have flared up on a point of principle that I believe in deeply, I am left with a niggling sense of 'not having acted right'. Try as I do to shake this off, her words lie heavy in the air all around me: 'Kadva vaind paccha na khenchay'. (You can never pull back an arrow which has shot out angry, acrid words.)

If Ba had given us details about the moment of her violation after the death of my grandfather, we, her daughters and granddaughters, would have been able to make a clear pro- nouncement: 'unjust'. Instead, we observe the alchemical magic with which she has changed her pain into a rill of gold whose burnish draws those who have been scarred into her presence. We pay tribute to her efforts, for we know that this is the ground of her daily puja. We hover around her, like anxious butterflies over a precious flower. We are chary of drinking of her sweetness, fearful of depleting this, intent always to say: 'Oh, but you are beautiful.' And swift comes the reply: 'Your eyes have made me so.'

Encircling her in a protective embrace, we have (between ourselves) arrived at a fair approximation of the significant public events that took place after my grandfather died. An upper-caste widow, unsophisticated in financial affairs, had those possessions that were left in the house confiscated by those who claimed to be her husband's creditors. The move from a two-room rented property to a one-room dwelling accompanied the assumption of the mantle of widowhood. There were only two white *sadlas* to clothe her new persona: one she wore, the other hung on the washing line. If the scriptures enjoined a widow to eat frugally, and only once a day, then this well suited the circumstances of those times. 'She ate last, after everyone else had eaten,' say Madhu and Hasu. 'We know, we were with her.' 'She fasted a lot,' says Bena, 'she still does. Can't you see, it's a carry-over from that period.' 'No, no,' I protest, 'she now chooses to. You can't reduce her spiritual quest to that.'

Today, the deterioration in her health means that she is unable to travel to the place that she visits in song when she hums to herself: Sudamapuri, the magical city that was conjured up by Krishna for his childhood friend, known today as Porbander. Over half a century has elapsed since Ba left a marginalised region of British India to join her husband in Nairobi. It is over twenty-four years now since she journeyed from Nairobi to London, where she now lives in a terraced house. As Ba and my aunts grow old in the different cities to which they have migrated, and as those of us who were born in the second generation in East Africa circulate within comfortable professional jobs in the diaspora, Ba continues to eat a single meal a day. Someone always sits by her side to ensure that she does not serve herself too abstemiously. At times, to humour one of us, she will lick a choc ice on a summer's afternoon, or suck a Cadbury's milk chocolate on a cold December evening. We watch her, thrilled, as one watches a revolutionary, transgressive act performed by a *dosima* who has no teeth and who has never got used to her dentures. We pride ourselves on having struck a blow against an iniquitous system that says a widow cannot enjoy the small delectables available from every corner shop. 'But no,' she says, 'I feel much stronger in myself when I observe my vows.

Do not make me eat *kattane* outside the prescribed times.' And we wilt. How she has tamed us. No anger. No speaking of any hurts. No uttering of harsh truths. And yet none of us has succeeded in living within the confines of her moral code.

We have at times had terrible disagreements between ourselves, her daughters and granddaughters. And yet we are bound to one another through our joint assessment which can be summed up in a simple statement: she has been hurt enough. We must do nothing to add to this. Though we are constantly unsuccessful in this resolve, it still holds us together. Our emotional endeavours continue to be directed towards this.

Widows, and the unspoken, dimly articulated narratives of widowhood, remain as the unhealed wounds in the social memory of the history of migration, settlement, transformation, and very real gains achieved in the lives of many women in my family. There was another widow who migrated alone, from the town of Amreli in Saurashtra, to the small town of Moshi in Tanganyika Territory. This was my maternal great-grandmother. She left behind her a daughter (already married at a young age) and a son-in-law, to start a new life in Moshi where teachers were being recruited to the Aga Khan School. She could not have been more than twenty-six. She must have gone to the Political Agent in Rajkot, demanding a permit to work in another British territory. She must have had to travel to Bombay to acquire a passport which had 'British Indian' stamped on it, then made the sea voyage. She must surely have known someone sympathetic in Moshi who facilitated the first place of shelter. She was plainly disliked by the male elders, who venomously declared that God had destroyed a hundred men in order to be able to give form to her. A slight woman, she always wore a *sadlo* of ochre brown, the older insignia of widowhood. She then called over both her daughter and her son-in-law (also a teacher) to Moshi. His entry into employment was facilitated by her: he started teaching in the same school as his mother-in-law. My mother was the third child born to my maternal grandmother in Moshi.

My maternal great-grandmother (or Ma as she is known in the family) and my paternal grandmother (Ba) stand in a dual relationship with one another. The first came as an independent woman to a new world, and bore within her the fury of one capable of standing on her own feet, who was thwarted by the petty jealousies and injustices of men. The latter came as a dependant of her husband, and continued to live as a dependant of her son. She contained within herself the uncertainty of one who is not her own mistress, while Ma contained the intransigence of one who is. One evoked protectiveness, the other an awed fear and terror. Ma was unable to win the affection of those around her, reducing them to a state of abject dread. It is said that at the end, when she was laid on the floor, her body cold and lifeless, her daughter-in-law was fearful of approaching in case Ma sat up and berated her in a loud, angry voice.

Ma returned to Gujarat later in her life, and stamped her personality on those around her. And as an act of vengeance (upon whom – her close ones, herself, the world?) she continued to have her head shaved regularly in order to make her widowhood visible till the end of her life. What events made her impose this on herself – for it was self-imposed – one will never know. There were others, of course, who had not chosen this penultimate act of self-annihilation for themselves.

ARCHIVE ODYSSEY: DHANKOR'S STORY

My intellectual quest could have led me to reach for the skies and traverse the vast universe. It could also have seen me join the company of hip globetrotters for whom the earth is an oyster shell whose pearls they plunder at will. Even as my energies have been directed to understanding the contemporary world, to arguing fiercely against developmental projects which have been built on the sacrifice of the lives and livelihoods of the poor, I have still found myself, time and again, haunting the Gujarat archives, poring again and again over manuscripts describing the contestations that took place in the nineteenth century over the plight of widows. It is as if I am a thread on a loom shuttling back and forth, back and forth, on the same weave. My *chundaldi* has been woven on this experience and both my body and spirit bear the mark of this. There are three movements that have stamped this. One is a shard of memory handed down by Hasu and Madhu to me, the first daughter in the third generation, of the time when their father died and their mother was left defenceless. I was a child who looked up to them as my source of comfort, nurture and pleasure. When, in the midst of making papier mâché toys for me, their faces contorted with the memory of a day in 1948 when Hasu was six and Madhu four, the loom clacked sharply. Ba's holding on to a silence stilled the loom for an everlasting moment, leaving a gaping hole in the pattern. Then my father's closed countenance. The loom turned frenetically in its clickety-clack, clickety-clack, clickety-clack.

The odyssey has taken me to a place far-flung both in space and time. It has made me chart the rough seas of those who were similarly wounded, as well as those who were able to break out of the shackles of high-caste customs that held them in their life-extinguishing grip. At times my ship has struck a reef and has been grounded for long months, at others it has risen with the swell of breakers. I sit on the shore to watch the tide slowly ebb away, carrying with it the accumulated debris of history.

Ba had taken one small tentative step out into the world of the pleasures of the mind when she fed on the feast of books that had been brought into the house by my grandfather. The fictional landscape of Bengal had shown her that women had expressed desires of the mind and heart which were familiar to many. Ba did not know, however, that progressive reformers like Rammohun Roy had been forced, in the Bengal of the early nineteenth century, to defend the rights of widows to live on this earth (rather than be cremated together with their husbands' corpses) through a liberal reading of the ancient lawgiver Manu. And little did she know that interpretation of specific religious texts (an art form that she excels in) was to affect the life-chances of thousands of colonial female subjects throughout the British Empire.

Both in Kenya and India, as elsewhere, women in the pre-colonial period had had to fight battles with powerful members of the community over the issues of marriage, divorce and child custody. The nineteenth century and the early years of the twentieth saw the legal codification of diverse 'customary laws'. This meant that women had to go to colonial courts that adjudicated over both civil and criminal cases. In Kikuyu country in the first part of the twentieth century, as land became appropriated and privatised, women, as non-landowners, found themselves more and more reliant upon agricultural labour. The power of the *mbari*, particularly the elders of the sub-clan, was increased as they were granted legitimacy by the colonial government. Male control over land became fierce at a time of scarcity. The agrarian reforms that were introduced in the mid-1950s to muffle support for the Mau Mau movement in Kikuyu country saw women being caught between the authority of the male *mbari* and the colonial courts. A widow who wished to register her land in the names of her two unmarried daughters was thwarted in this by the claims of her deceased husband's brother to the land: the *mbari* too feared the loss of territory that would be suffered if a daughter married. Another widow divided the land that she held in a coffee zone between her two married daughters. Her daughters were forced off the land by their paternal uncle who claimed inheritance to it through 'customary practices'. The *mbari* supported him and the widow did not have the financial resources to go to court.[vi]

The reforming legislation concerning widowhood which had taken place in colonial India was to affect the lives of caste-women throughout the diaspora, as the codified laws were replicated in other British territories where separate and distinct laws governed different 'races'. By the start of the twentieth century, though, the earlier vibrant debate about the social position of widows had been hushed. Reform in nineteenth-century India had been concerned with controlling the sexuality of widows, for it was considered that once a woman had had knowledge of her husband, she would have a voracious sexual appetite. The movement for remarriage of widows sought to channel this along safe lines. But the desires and aspirations of women to spin variegated dreams, other than remarriage, remained unacknowledged. If the pain of widows acted as a call for the upper-caste society in India to rework itself, then narratives of widows occupied the minds of the male literati incessantly, as if to demonstrate that the psychic fears raised by the combined forces of imperialism and the repressed passions of women were enough to drive otherwise humane men back to their bunkers.[vii] The emphasis was on the right (or otherwise) of the widow, whether child or adult, to remarry, with concern being voiced about her vulnerable and exposed sexuality. It remained an age when a male custodian was deemed necessary for a woman – and intimate knowledge of a husband bound a woman to him even after his death. Even when widow remarriage became legally recognised in 1856, its practice remained limited to a small number of childless women.

However, widow remarriage, which had so exercised the consciousness of anguished social reformers,[viii] was not an issue in Ba's case: she had been taken up with providing for her children. Not for her the social drama of Dhankor, the first Gujarati widow to enter into a remarriage, whose story challenged the orthodoxy prevalent in upper-caste Gujarati society in the nineteenth century. Bindu and I read the narrative of Dhankor which I have photocopied and brought back from a musty archive in Ahmadabad. We compare the story of Dhankor with that of Ba. We give our hearts to the couple whose faces accompany the written story: Dhankor's, sturdy and solid, her head partially covered by her *sadlo*, the mouth set in a firm line; Madhavdas' thin cheeks and gentle demeanour, the Parsee-style hat sitting over-large on his head. Yes, Dhankor found a mature

24

love. 'Look at these letters she received from Madhavdas,' I exclaim, 'no one writes to me like that.' 'You are not a widow living in the nineteenth century,' Bindu replies witheringly.

The recorded remarriage between Dhankor, who came from the trading caste of the Kapod Baniya community, and Madhavdas Rughnathdas, a cloth merchant, took place on 2 May 1871 in the city of Bombay, in the presence of about 200 reformists. The remarriage vows were solemnised without the knowledge of Dhankor's family, and did not have the blessing of her mother or brother. Dhankor had left her natal home with only the clothes she was wearing, trusting her future to Madhavdas on the basis of two personal conversations with him and having read one newspaper article published under his name. The story, not of these two lives, but of the remarriage itself, has been narrated by Madhavdas in Ek Punarvivahni Kahani (A Story of a Remarriage) which was first published in 1882.

Over a century later, I attend to the narrative and delight in the first letters written by these two individuals who had decided to break with convention and establish a joint life together. Yes, it is the story of a widow whose inheritance had been snatched away by her in-laws and who lived what she saw as a wretched life with her brother and sister-in-law. She braved the wrath of her kin to come out of her brother's house, all alone, to make her way to the house of another man. The initiative was her own. It catapulted her into the politics of the time: Dhankor was received by the Governor of Bombay and she herself gave a party for Lady Manning, an educational reformer, in the Remarriage Hall on 24 November 1888. Seventeen years prior to this, when Dhankor had left her home to join Madhavdas, her mother and other women of her family had mourned, beaten their breasts at Dhankor's remarriage, and had declared her socially dead. She was never again to see them.[ix]

Dhankor's story is evocative less for its heroism than for the texture of its warp and weft. The images conjured up – of her wretched dependence on her brother and sister-in-law, her shy yet determined seeking of an alternative, the drama of a runaway marriage in which the colonial police offered protection to the horse and carriage – allow us an entry into the turbulence of the times. We can glimpse some of the servitude and impoverishment entailed in widowhood from the two letters Dhankor wrote, both of which are reproduced verbatim in *The Story of a Remarriage*.

One was to Madhavdas, in which she responded to his call in the edition of the newspaper *Rasgoftar* published on 2 April 1871 for a widow to come forward. After visiting his house accompanied by a twelve-year-old female relative, she sought out, with some trepidation, his views on the possibility of a remarriage. He assured her in turn that 'I will never do anything to make you grieve. As long as I live, there is no one who can harm a hair on your head, you must see the truth of this, but in the end you need to consult your own mind.'[x]

Dhankor smuggled a reply out to him a few days later to inform him of her decision. She addressed him here by name, as an equal who had the extraordinary power to tilt her world, as 'Paradukhbhanjan Madhavdas' (Madhavdas the Destroyer of Others' Sufferings). She told him that while her mother was alive, existence was bearable, but that a life under the insults of her brother and sister-in-law, 'eating *oshiada rotla*, does not appear proper to me. Whatever little wealth I possessed has been snatched by my relatives. If I ask them for it, I seem to them to be an enemy. This is why I have finally come to a decision to try out the path suggested by your good will.'[xi]

Nowhere does Madhavdas more merit the respect of feminists today than where he addressed Dhankor in his reply as 'Mara bhavishyana thanara pyara Dhankor' (My future loved one Dhankor), and signed off 'Maadhu Bhula'. In this one stroke, he distanced himself from the public language of the male social reformers of the time (including himself) in which they preached the necessity of widow remarriage for the 'uplift' of victimised women. In the private letter that he wrote to Dhankor, Madhavdas reached out to her in a fine statement that reassured her of his regard for her in the future, and which acknowledged the importance of her presence in his life.[xii] In this letter, and in the concern he showed for her needs prior to the wedding, Madhavdas emerges not as a social reformer bestowing patronage on an unhappy widow in order to insert himself into the history of a self-congratulatory modernity, but as an emotionally mature adult prepared to take on a lifelong responsibility for a person who he knew was prone to 'hysteria'.[xiii]

Dhankor chose a life with the reformist Madhavdas, who had carried through his resolve to marry a widow as a second wife, rather than eat rotla for which she was indebted to others. In the letter that she wrote to her mother prior to leaving the house for the last time, Dhankor told her that she could no longer continue living the cruel life of a widow, when for twelve months she had given up on food, taking nothing but 'dahi [yogurt] worth one paisa, even that in the hope that this would bring death nearer.'[xiv] She breaks out into bitter cries against privation and want: survival on a paisa worth of dahi had made her susceptible to a nervous mental condition with hideous physical manifestations. Dhankor's story bears a terrifyingly close resemblance to those of impoverished, pauperised, malnourished women who sit just where the equator tips down into the tropic of Capricorn, watching others consuming the foods denied to those in their condition.

Unlike Dhankor, Ba was surrounded by her children, who gave her their affections and enveloped her in their care. Ba's betrayal did not come from within the family but without. Herein lies the key to the collective endeavours of the daughters and granddaughters. There was (and continues to be) a struggle to keep her within the folds of family life, to ensure that she does not give up on the ties that bind her to this earth. While personal affection has undoubtedly had the power to cleave her to us (and hence to life) how it appeared at times fragile, requiring an immense labour of love. The emotional energies of the women and older men in the large extended family have been poured into ensuring that Ba feels valued, and we revolve around her constantly, ever watchful for blows that may fall on her from outside.

My childhood understanding of the marginalisation that is entailed in the life of an exile derived from being with my Ba. If 'belonging' to a community means participating in the public theatre of bonding, then Ba was not a part of this. She attended no wedding. She ate at no caste feast. New Year's day, after Diwali – when everyone was dressed in their finest clothes, and the round of visiting others to wish them *sal mubaarak* began at four o'clock in the morning – found her sitting at home, alone and composed. When the whole household was preparing to deck itself for a public showing, Ba remained at home. And I took to staying in with her. This tie to Ba made me draw apart from the caste community in a profound way. Absence from weddings as a child, in order to provide company to my grandmother, later turned into the shunning of wedding ceremonies altogether. The political rationale for this was the ostentatious giving and dowry-taking. The emotional root lay in a deep-founded sense of distancing and alienation from a community which had found no place within itself for Ba.

My close link to the marginal in the community has also, paradoxically, made me travel back in the direction of what she has left behind. I have utilised the educational skills that were not accessible to her to build up a picture, stage by stage, of the structures of power that so affect an individual's life that they leave jagged shards in the lives of the generations to come. In this particular narrative of daughters and granddaughters, rotating around the person of Ba, I am neither writing a story of roots nor am I able to embrace a playful perspective that seeks joy in the multiplicity of identities that I undoubtedly inhabit. No, this is a story which follows the pathway of pain, which connects with a myriad other lives similarly wounded, and which seeks threads in the historical record in order to disentangle these.

VOICES THAT RISE
FROM THE PAST

I encountered Chandrashankar Shukla in the second week of December 1994, down in the basement store of the Gandhian university in Ahmadabad, the Gujarat Vidyapith. This store houses nineteenth-century archives. Descending a flight of steps, one enters a large cavern, little frequented, lit only by one long tube light, hung askew. This is not adequate to read the frail manuscripts that often crumble at one's touch. Despite my asthma and shortness of breath, I love taking in the ambience of those times that the dusty, crumbling index cards and manuscripts convey. Chandrashankar Shukla came to me out of the shadowy depths during one such peregrination amongst the manuscripts. He was a Public Works Department engineer, and must thus have had a scientific turn of mind. Despite being untutored in the scriptures, he wrote a tract entitled *Vidhvavapan Nishedh, Etle Vidhvanu Mundan Shastrokt Nathi* (Prohibit the Tonsure of Widows: the Tonsure of Widows is not Sanctioned by the Shastras) which was published in 1892. The preface to the tract outlines the events that made a lasting imprint on Chandrashankar's mind, propelling him to enter into a debate with Brahman pundits. The first paragraph described how his job with the Public Works Department had caused him to live in a particular (unnamed) town, where the neighbourhood contained a large number of widows:

> Some were surrounded by family affection, some were alone. Some were young in age, others were elderly. But all were tonsured. It so happened that one poor ageing widow, who was on her own [*ek garib vraddha ekaki vidhva*] and who came to my house regularly to do the morning chores, did not appear for three days. On asking her the reason for this on her arrival

29

on the fourth day, she started a loud weeping.[xv]

This *garib, vraddha, ekaki vidhva* narrated how the barber had kept her waiting for three days, so that she had remained *bhukhi* (hungry) till late. When the barber did finally arrive, he abused her roundly, his stark actions conveyed to the listening Chandrashankar by a woman who wept bitterly.

'He beat this inauspicious *dochko* [head] as in mourning.' So saying, she hit her head with both her hands and began a loud weeping. In that state of fury, she abused her dead husband, caste [*nyat*] and those who made the law on tonsure a thousand times, uttered terrible curses against them, and uncovering her head showed three deep cuts on it ... That left a strong impression on my mind, and having studied the matter for a long time, I found that there were thousands of widows in this world who were no better off than she was.[xvi]

A sobbing, cursing widow. And later, the memory of a twelve-year-old who came and sat near Chandrashankar when he visited the region of Karnali, just as she had done at a previous time, but this time with her head shorn. The testimonies of a domestic servant who beat her *dochko* with her own hands and that of a child widow who wept with the women in the household not fully cognisant of her own fate, affected Chandrashankar so deeply that he was moved to take up pen to argue for the prohibition of this practice: 'It has left such a strong impression on me that it will not be wiped away to the end of my life,' he wrote in his preface.

The publication of this tract elicited a sharp response from a Harikrishna Lalshankar Dave, in *Vidhvavapannishedh Lakhnarne Javaaab* (A Reply to the Writer of *Vidhvavapan Nishedh*, 1892). Chandrashankar's pamphlet had dropped through his letterbox, sent by someone well aware of the impact this would have. One can imagine him, this haughty Brahman who takes pride in his caste status, who delights in cutting down an opponent through a demonstration of greater scriptural knowledge, and who is at pains to prove that what has been declared a cruel custom is actually motivated by pity. Dave's tract in reply to Chandrashankar shows the hardening of the conservative reaction in response to the reformist impulse. There is an implacable coldness in Dave's language, a terrible malignancy in his resolute upholding of the ancestral scriptures:

The tract was begun after a *dosi* had been hurt in two or three places by a barber's razor and the desire to write was strengthened after seeing a twelve-year-old's tonsured head ... At least that much has been established, that the writer's heart has been filled with compassion ... [This custom has been established] for at least five hundred years ... [That makes] for twenty-one generations between the practitioners of this custom and the writer. One must then assume that all these others were made of iron-hearts. For there must have been many old women in this period whose heads were shaven. There must have been those fated to be child-widows too. And not all barbers having the necessary dexterity, there must have been many who were hurt by the razor. Even then, no one felt compassion for them, no one took up the pen for them, and no one took up the work for the banning of tonsure. What could be the reason for this? If one reflects on this, one understands that they [those who did not] were the wise ones ... To continue to work within the sacred precepts even when these may appear pitiless is not to lack compassion, but is to be merciful.'[xvii]

While Chandrashankar's tract brings to us the mutilated face of an old woman who roundly cursed both her departed husband and those who sought to brand her for the sin of outliving him, as well as the image of a twelve-year-old and her weeping relatives, Harikrishna Lalshankar Dave moved to erase and efface those who for at least 'twenty-one generations' had experienced

31

pain. However, Chandrashankar could never win the intellectual argument using the armoury of a liberal reading of the scriptures. An engineer by training, who took from other people's writings in his zeal to build up a religious argument against the tonsure of widows, he was hampered, as were so many others before and after him, by the absence of a political discourse which stressed ethical considerations, and which would have displaced religious texts as the starting point of a debate about liberties and rights.

The nineteenth century is full of the experiences of reformist men such as Chandrashankar who looked at the wasted lives of widows around them (aunts, sisters, daughters, neighbours)[xviii] and who endeavoured to bring about a shift in public culture. When cogitating upon their efforts to bring about change, I can feel the sense of defeat and loss that they endured in their lives when these efforts crumbled under the conservative onslaught. The voices of the widows themselves rise up too: when these leap out of the records and speak to me words full of pain, and when these reverberate in the empty spaces of my mind, then I am filled both with a sense of awe and a strange feeling of fear, as if I am treading upon a dark, inner recess.

The women who lived in the Poona Widows and Orphans Home have described with great poignancy the terror that faced an upper-caste widow immediately following her husband's death. The women had been encouraged to write essays by the secretary of the Widows and Orphans Home. These essays were then translated and compiled into a petition by a certain B. A. Gupte on 27 April 1911, with a view to presenting them to the Government of India, in order to bring about a legislative banning of the practice of tonsure – the women writers insist that this was 'the greatest of all miseries' amidst all the other 'cruel customs'. In the twelve translated essays written by the 'widows and other girls' who lived in the Poona Home, the women gave full rein to their anguish, in language which bleaches the experience to its bones and strips it of all religious sanctity. Amidst vivid, at times lurid descriptions of tonsure, which are dominated by an overwhelming fear of the figure of the barber and their own subsequent entry into non-personhood, the widows also spoke of the mood of elation felt by those upholders of caste privilege who thought that they had 'achieved a victory as soon as she [the widow] is disfigured'. This 'demoniacal work', they said, neither protected the widow from 'moral temptations' (which the essayists declare that even the gods succumb to) nor from 'bad people who covet[ed] her'.

The writings break out into anguished bitterness against those who sought to 'protect' the chastity of women through this act of disfigurement. Ambu Bai Bapat argued bluntly that 'To protect young widows from worldly temptations, the best course would be to educate them. If they cannot be literary scholars, they may be trained to embroider caps or to weave woollen stuff.' Ambubai Gumaste related how a young girl of nine or ten had been driven to commit suicide after the imposition of tonsure. Another child-widow of eleven or twelve was said to have 'piteously begged to be excused from that horrid operation' – and since no one heeded her prayer, she stopped eating completely.[xix] This symbolic 'social death' is described by one son who was active in Gandhian politics in twentieth century Maharashtra as having driven his mother to insanity; she cried out in her madness, in words so terrible that they break one's heart, 'What is a head? It is only a vegetable marrow put on one's shoulder.'[xx]

The journey to locate the source of the pain has led me to become intimately familiar with the shapes and contours of the lives of cloistered women. The odyssey has tossed me into the turbulent waters and surging waves which surrounded many widows in their lives, impacting profoundly as well on the lives of those who were close to them. My eyes turn to the only photographs that have survived out of the period subsequent to my grandfather's death, of my father and Hasu (Plates III and IV), these show a look on their face which haunts, which tells of hurt, vulnerability and defensiveness: that look on a photograph

33

which makes me want to reach out to cup the face in my hand at the same time as covering it protectively with my own. Placed in front of a camera, the eyes say, 'You will not be able to fathom my depths.'

At times, in the quiet of a late summer evening, as I watch the limpid clouds float past in the sky, I think of the exceptional and gifted widow Pandita Ramabai, whom I hold close to my heart. I know that if I were ever to meet her in that firmament which lies way beyond the eye, I would be rendered speechless, but that she would understand nevertheless. As I pick up a book on her life and times,[xxi] my throat goes tight and my eyes widen, as if I have met a spirit who has actually acted in this world as I know I myself ought to. Pandita Ramabai's life shows that it *was* possible in the late nineteenth century to take the question of women's liberties seriously, simply by lending a respectful ear to the testimonies of widows themselves. While both the colonial authorities and the indigenous male elites attempted to formulate legislation based on what could be justified from the reading of scriptures, Ramabai disrupted this, both by her very presence and by the stands she took. A high-caste widow who converted to Christianity, Ramabai took to a public platform wearing white and with her hair cropped short. She set up Sharada Sadan (a home for widows) in 1889 and worked untiringly throughout her life for this, as well as for the Mukti Sadan refuge she set up to provide shelter for hundreds of young women who were made destitute by the terrible famine of 1897. She was extraordinary in the way that she was able to combine resistance to a narrowly defined vision of nationhood, to a Hindu religious revivalism which was unutterably anti-humanist, to a church hierarchy which trampled on her own spiritual quest, and to the high-handedness of the colonial state towards its subjects during times of plague. Ramabai utilised her formidable learning to expose the violation of women's dignity, in a climate in which men would shout her down in public meetings. In December 1889, during the third National Social Conference, which was set up to discuss the modification of cruel social customs, when the question of banning the tonsure of women was raised, Ramabai argued that a widow herself should decide on the way she wanted to live.[xxii]

Ba, and countless other caste widows across the diaspora, were not able so to decide, even in the twentieth century. As I write the story of the tight web of emotional interiority which has bound together the lives of Ba's daughters and granddaughters, I know that this story fits into neither the self-satisfied narrative of progress nor that of community virtue retained amidst upheavals. And I ask myself: can the weight of the history that I carry in my skin ever be sloughed off, or do I just have to live with this? Can the threads now be woven in a different pattern, or will they fray during the attempted imposition, then finally snap? As I long to have my sibling near me – for she is the one person who can provide the unspoken acknowledgement that my questings within the depths of the cultural tradition have substance and weight – I know that far away as she is, her soul too is dyed in Ba's colours.

JOURNEYING ON

Chewing on the actions of those who sought widowhood reform, and holding Dhankor and Ramabai close to me, I like to think that my grandfather would have taken an interest in Pandita Ramabai life's and that he would have had admiration for the stands she took. He certainly moved in very wide political and literary circles in Nairobi and forged friendships with a diverse set of companions. They say he knew the fiery Issher Dass (who had accompanied Kenyatta to London in 1929) as well as Chunilal Madan (a member of the Municipal and later the Legislative Council).[xxiii] He had been a drinking partner of journalists who went on to establish the *Daily Chronicle* as a rival to the more conservative *Colonial Times* in late 1947. Ba only heard whispers of the immense political contestations that were taking place, suffused with the politics of race: the issue of a common electoral roll, urban segregation, representation of Indians and Africans in municipal and central government, the enforced carrying of a *kipande* card. It is difficult to place my grandfather either in the 'radical' or the 'moderate' political camp of the period, for he had friends in both, just as it is impossible to say what course his life might have taken had he lived longer. He enjoyed meeting people from all walks of life. He visited acquaintances in their affluent homes, as well as the carpenters and artisans who lived on Race Course Road, and those inhabitants of the shanty town of Eastleigh who were considered disreputable by polite society. He freely exchanged ideas with women around him and took heed of their opinions. He was particularly fond of a self-willed young woman called Kunta who lived in the same compound, and whose independent spirit he nurtured. The last cup of tea that he drank was held to his lips by her just before he died. They say he wined and dined with the Governor, Philip Mitchell,[xxiv] in an age when there was a colour bar in hotels and restaurants, as well as a segregation of social and welfare services. Mitchell judged others according to his own personal predilections: he held that 'civilised men were anglicised men',[xxv] and he aimed to build a multiracial society while remaining limited by the entrenched interests of the settlers.

My grandfather, known to be a liberal man, with all the tensions that this included, had earned the ire of some of his kinsfolk by his mode of life and thought. 'He did as he pleased,' says his eldest son, 'he would not be stopped by anyone. Mind you, he had a lot of respect for the elder relatives who surrounded him. But he was independent in his mind. And it showed.'

These elders were to close ranks at the possibility of change in Ba's life – that possibility which comes in life in sudden shafts, as when raindrops splinter either into the eye of a storm or into the hues of a rainbow. If Ba had stepped outside the confines of domesticity and the community into the wider circle that had been inhabited by my grandfather's acquaintances; if she had built up alliances with those who lived beyond the closed communal courtyard, then voices may have been raised in her favour. But she remained close to the familiar world of her community, and she paid the price exacted upon all those who are unable to disentangle themselves from the tentacles of traditions – traditions whose dead foliage is not cut down, so that the over-nurtured vine creeps up around the neck, throttling, choking.

Did no one come to her aid? 'No,' says her eldest son Harshad. 'When you are down, everyone moves away.'

I examine, carefully, the history of philanthropic activities in East Africa. In my endeavour to arrive at a truth which I can live with, I know I must be scrupulous in attending to the nuances of power and patronage that were relevant to this time. I find that the remarkable efflorescence of welfare provision set up by Indian migrants from the late nineteenth century onwards is well documented.[xxvi] An immense effort was put into providing an infrastructure for the sick, the needy, the destitute: from raising funds for leprosy and polio patients, to providing famine relief, to the setting up of medical facilities – dispensaries, clinics, hospitals. The distribution of educational bursaries and scholarships cut across racial lines, but since the colonial government in Kenya had, by 1923, established a tripartite system of educational apartheid, much of the self-organisation went into the building of schools. Of the twelve assisted schools built through Indian voluntary effort, eight were for girls.[xvii] By 1948, it is recorded that there was a 'marked expansion of the efforts of voluntary organisations, especially those devoted to Asian general uplift and African primary education'.[xxviii]

A large portion of the burgeoning welfare services was open to everyone regardless of caste, religion or 'race'.[xxix] The historian of the 'African poor', John Iliffe, has paid tribute to these efforts, writing that 'No community was more generous than the Indians of East Africa, who not only provided for their own members by means of out-relief, widows' houses, children's homes, and medical institutions, but also extended charity to Africans.'[xxx]

However, the history of the steady accumulation of capital, upon which the network of charities was grown, is not a glorious one, despite the pride that is taken in it by the entrepreneurial group. Upper-caste affluent men who were keen to do 'social service' appear at the same time to have utilised their power in squalid ways. Ba's story adds a very different texture to the historical narrative of Asian charity. One of the philanthropists who has been much lauded in the story of benevolence in East Africa, and whose family name appears regularly in the list of the top twenty Asian millionaires in Britain, arrived as a central figure in Ba's tale on the day that he entered her home and stripped it of all its possessions.[xxxi] And, at the same time as men were performing good works and taking up the weapons of political nationalism in Kenya, within the inner recesses of the segregated communities, women's bodies were being marked to ensure distinct ethnic and community identities.[xxxii]

Speculation now appears superfluous. What if ...? What if she had shown more courage, stood up to the women and men around her, equipped herself with skills to earn an income for herself and her nine children through teaching in one of the schools? Would she then have been able to stand up against those who corralled her within a feudally inscribed widowhood? Or would she have turned against these newly acquired liberties herself and willed a life of discipline? What if she had tucked the *pallav* of her white *sadlo* (the one with the blue dots on it) round her waist with a self-assured air, marched to the house of the self-proclaimed creditors and demanded to see their books? Looked the world in the eye and said, 'I am more than the detritus of his ashes which the ocean has thrown up'? Stop, Pari. Stop this.

Time turned back for her. To the time of the ancient Dedo when men fought over cattle and the deaths of these braves were immortalised in hero-stones.[xxxiii] When women mourned, beat their breasts, and made lament into an art form. You talk to me of colonialism? Capitalism? My heart bears the marks of wounds inflicted by an epoch that is unnameable.

And Ba – having joined the ranks of expelled women, she turned to the dense yet luminous world of the extraterrestrial, where a dark magic wove a web within which neither time nor space had meaning, where childhood stories of *dosimas* muttering incantations rose up vividly in her solitary condition. She had no sister then to lean on, and her brother too was far away. Motherless since eight, she clung to the figure of Ambaji, the Goddess of Motherhood-made-Incarnate. She took to an enclosed life within the walls of the compound and became ascetical. It was only after her first daughter-in-law, Hansa, came into the family in January 1955 (Plate V) that she was able to transmute her experience into a publicly acknowledged aesthetics of discipline, whereby the body's desires were subjugated and the cultural realm was expanded to incorporate such a yearning for the Beloved that this had to break out into song. Ba's merging of her fine sense of both integrity and beauty into her passion for shared song allowed her to transform her pain.

Ba initiated one of the first women's devotional gatherings in Nairobi and presided over the congregational gathering of widows. The devotional movement which had swept northern India in the fifteenth and sixteenth centuries had repudiated the power of the priest as intermediary between the believer and the Believed-in; opened the gates of worship to *dalits*, women, the ostracised and the marginal; made the landscape echo with the songs of those searching for liberation, songs which reverberate to the present day. Ba gathered around her the women whose personal faith, marked by pathos, strife and a yearning for a better life, was removed by some distance from a high Hinduism. She gave them and herself a voice. Song is the medium for the alchemy through which Ba has turned suffering into an expressive art. She both creates and performs songs, her only possessions in the world being the handwritten books which bear their words.

ARRIVING

Ba's entry into the sphere outside the family took place at the same time as my arrival in this world. If the weft between us contains that impossible longing for the Beloved who is not visible to the eye, it also threads together a specific emotional structure which emphasises the quest rather than the reaching: Prembhakti, the Path of Love, with viraha, separation, the ground for the forward journey. Each Tuesday afternoon, I accompanied Ba to the house of Labhumasi, a Vaishnav widow who had trained to be a teacher and who taught in the Visa Oshwal Girls' School, and was surrounded by voices that emerged out of the figures clad in soft white cotton.

In my memory, the faces of the widows appear in solid proximity, and I am able to feel the touch of their bodies so close to mine, as well as absorb their desires which echoed out in the form of song. The afternoon devotional sessions were a realm of freedom and creativity for the widows, a space which was their own. Some brought garlands of flowers, marigolds, jasmine and roses stitched together; others bunches of bananas or a papaya fruit as an offering to the deities. In this setting, the laughter and buzz as the women greeted each other settled into a quiet and intense singing through which the restrictions of widowhood were transformed into dreams addressed to Krishna.[xxxiv] The women vied with each other to compose devotional songs which excelled over the rest in emotional expression and which would move the collective to tears. There was a critically receptive audience, a sophisticated cognoscenti which would announce its judgements: 'Muktaben, you must copy the words of the bhajan you've just sung in my book. I'd like to learn them. Labhuben, oh, ho, ho, your calls to Krishna brought a lump to my throat. These gatherings are never the same without your presence.' Children's school exercise books and smudged mathematics books with lined squares were passed around, in order that the newly received songs could be copied in a spidery handwriting, where one word merged into the other and punctuation marks were conspicuous by their absence.

The intensity of the singing was brought to a close by the quiet and frugal sharing of *prasad*, some nuts, raisins, fresh fruit – the remains would be tied up in old newspapers to be shared at home. I was at ease in this community of elderly women, felt a part of it. Through my grandmother, I was connected to the other women who wore white *sadlas*. The experience of seeing the women create their own songs, observing the transmutation of self-denial into verse and song, provided the ground for my later years of research on women's religious expression in the villages and towns of Rajasthan and Gujarat.[xxxv]

Besides the world of the women in the *bhajan* gatherings and their books carefully folded into home-sewn cotton bags; the world of *dosimas* conjured up by the passed down stories; and that of the four aunts (three of whom lingered over their carefully put together trousseaus – saris embroidered, painted, sequinned; petticoats bordered with lace; tablecloths where the needlepoint was exquisitely traced; pillow cases with a sampler of Sweet Dreams) – there was also the world of school. The tense negotiation between my own fraught reality and that represented by the school regime began aged four, and has not yet reached a successful conclusion. The distant world fascinated, drawing me within its seductive reach. The Trans-Siberian Railway was the longest railway construction in the world, and I saw myself, nose pressed to the window, whizzing through the snowy steppes. Slaves built pyramids for the Pharoahs. Shah Jahan had the Taj Mahal constructed for his Mumtaz. We chanted, '*je suis, tu es, il est, elle est, nous sommes, vous êtes,*' all together, twenty-two in the class, without being able to provide substantive content to the rhyme.

MIGRATORY BIRDS

While I accompanied Ba, from an early age, to the afternoon devotional gatherings, the young aunts remained at home. Bena had been my grandfather's special favourite, the first daughter to arrive after five sons. Hasu–Madhu grew into adulthood almost as conjoint twins, their names rarely uttered separately, so Hasu–Madhu it was, or Hasli–Madhli, the Laughing Face peeping out from within the Sweet-Scented Creeper.

Bena sang the songs for which she had received praise from her Gujarati teacher as she bustled about the house. Madhu tended the plants on the veranda and dreamt her dreams. Hasu embroidered her saris, her face soft as she thought of the life ahead of her. Tara clicked around on her high-heeled shoes, covetous of a *Sadhna* haircut, fretting at the lack of liberties. The four women were preparing themselves for a romance, some love in marriage, a little tenderness from a person yet unknown. Their yearnings seeped into some part of me.

The longings of the four aunts rise up before me today. The memory surfaces of Madhu singing a song from a Hindi film when she thought herself alone on the veranda; in the film, the song was put in the mouth of a lonely, misunderstood, alcohol-sodden Devanand, but it was feminised here by Madhu, made particular, emboldened by hope. '*Kabhina kabhi, kahin na kahin, koina koi to aayega, apna mujhe banaayega, dil mein mujhe chhupaayega*'. ('Sometimes, somewhere, someone will arrive; make me his own, enfold me in his heart'). Tara, overhearing, ragged her, and I watched as Madhu smiled sheepishly, enjoying her discomfort but fully conscious that she was not disavowing the feelings.

The four young aunts created a specific culture of romantic love and domesticity within which I was enveloped. While their imagining of love is indelibly imprinted with the soft focus contained in black-and-white films, they also ensured that the house was permeated by the richness of cooking experiments, by the smell of newspaper soaked in fenugreek glue ready for moulding papier mâché toys the next day; and filled with the dresses which flapped in the bedroom as the oil-paint designs dried on them. Some nights, they would put *mehndi* on my hand, simply for the pleasure of it, drawing green leaves and mango fruit on my palm while small circles dotted the three blocks on my fingers. I would wake up with the sock-covered hand stiff from being held in an upright position to prevent the bed covers being stained. One of them would wash the *mehndi* off my hand, rub oil on it, then exclamations of delight would follow: 'Pari's got the best colour of everyone!' They gave me an inordinate love, these aunts, petted and coddled me while also setting me arithmetic problems to solve on a black slate, for they knew how much grief was caused by my lagging behind in this subject. When their hands wiped off the chalk writing on the slate, as the reality of arithmetical sums vanished into a cloud of dust, then I knew that these problems were erasable and I could return to the secure world of my story books again. But when the aunts had all left the house and were not there to dispel the foreboding gloom of the classroom with their laughter and acceptance, with their eyes that said that the universe is moved by enchantment, then the nightmares began, long endless terrors which still haunt me, when numbers pursued and beat me as I lay flailing.

The aunts had internalised some of Ba's vision of love while imbuing it with their own dreams and imaginings. At its simplest and most profound, love, as defined and acted out by Ba, is a relationship of sympathy: to listen to someone with sympathy, to talk to that person in sympathy, to understand, accept, welcome, feed another with *sympathy* is the essence of her domestic religion. In the chaotic jumble of extended family living, when individual sensitivities were prone to be stepped upon, Hasu–Madhu covered hurts with a balm of sympathy, and brought into the house a vision of both romantic wifehood and motherhood.

All four aunts have a deep love for words, music, colour. Educated at the Arya Samaj Girls' School, in the 'Gujarati medium', they had excelled in poetry competitions and music contests, and had been much sought after during the Festival of Nine Nights for their songs. Their education was dominated by the exhortations of Dayanand Saraswati, founder of the vedic-centred Arya Samaj movement,[xxxvi] who had attempted to reform Hinduism of its rituals in the late nineteenth century and who had preached a muscular religious assertiveness in answer to the work of Christian missionaries. The words of the deified song, *'Gyanki jyot jagaii he, rishi Dayanadne . . .; sauti kaum jagaii he, rishi Dayanandne'*[xxxvii] rise unbidden to Bena's lips when she thinks back to her schooldays. It is not, however, the religious revivalism of the Arya Samaj movement which has stayed with my aunts, but the ethic of feminine nurture, one which they took to with zest. The Arya Samaj movement, the advocates of which had been running a primary school for girls in Nairobi since 1910, had carved out a particular niche for inculcating the moral, social and personal values of good wifehood and motherhood amongst caste-Hindus, while also bringing young women into the arena of a modern educational system. The curriculum stressed handicrafts, domestic science and hygiene. It also sought to train some young women as schoolmistresses, and Bena saw her best friend Jasu graduate to be a teacher in the very school within which she had studied, removing the saffron cotton *kurta* and white pyjama in order to stand in front of the blackboard in a nylon sari.

The four aunts were caught up in the contradictory tides of the era, whereby the nationalist fervour which swept through all the Indian-funded schools saw the teaching of a patriotic history of India, which had to jostle with Shakespearean sonnets for attention. They read the heroic stories of the land of Gujarat written by Kanaihyalal Munshi; became familiar with the structure of the stories of the Bengali writer, Sharatchandra Chattopadhyay; wrote a précis of the arguments of the nationalist Ishwar Petlikar on the reform of women's position in society;

sang the songs of the Saurashtrian folklorist Jhaverchand Meghani – '*Koina ladakvaiyani na koiye khabare pucchavi ...*' They made the home ring with devotional *bhajans*, film songs, popular tunes. To be able to write, however – and through this to give full expression to their great feel for the texture of the language and its usages – was denied them. In this milieu, a young woman who was versed in the art of letter writing would send one to a brother who was studying far from home, but she would not communicate in writing to a friend – and never, never must she be seen to be writing to the man she was betrothed to, for this would show an unseemly ease and freedom on her part.

Setting verses to music, knowing how right it was that Banquo's ghost should put in an appearance just when he did, apprehending well the import of 'not all the scents of Arabia ...' – the four lived in that period of transition when Indian nationalism had matured into a powerful force, and African nationalism was coming into its own. For the four young women growing up in this period, the languages acquired and the cultural effect internalised were varied and diverse. But it all remained in waiting, held in suspense for the one momentous event that was being anticipated.

Why do cultures place so much emphasis on marriage as well as on love absolute and transcendental, while shackling the hearts of women and men? At the time that my aunts were growing up, the affirmation of love was becoming more overt in the public realm. The radio blared out film songs, an instrument of cultural diffusion and democratic levelling, as women and men went about their daily chores. Dilip Kumar was admired as the king of tragedy on the big screen. Madhubala[xxxviii] etched lasting images on the mind as she danced, bells on her feet, flaunting her love while speaking the most pliant of feminine emotions. *Janak Jhanak Payal Baaje* provided songs to test the voice, together with an ideal model for a petticoat, which was sewn and decorated to the exact same specifications as the film, by one of the aunts for her trousseau. The songs in V. Shantaram's film

Rangoli found favour with all four, while Baiju Baawara furnished emotional material sufficient to last a lifetime and more, as the two lovers called out to each other across the banks of a river: 'hoji ho o o o o.' There was also the sound of doves cooing softly in less passionate songs. And the most delectable of filmic devices, where two parted lovers sing to each other across an expanse, each voice merging with and enlarging the other, the same soft wind caressing their faces. She:

Bairi banke yeh duniya khadi hai,
mere paun mein bedi padi hai.

This world stands as an enemy
tying manacles to my feet.

And he:

Kin ghadio main akhian ladi hai,
baaro mahine savanki zari hai;
ik pal mukhda dikhaja,
dilka dukhda mitaja,
tuj bin soona soona mera hai jahaan re.

Since your eyes met mine
the rains have fallen each month of the year;
show your face for a moment,
wipe away the pain of my heart,
my life is barren without you.

Bena, Hasu, Madhu: I saw them depart, each fluttering away bearing messages of goodwill, turning back again and again to look at what she was leaving behind. I watched Mradulakaki, Ushakaki and Kokilakaki welcomed as daughters-in-law in the family. I was initially shy of these incomers, but even as a child I grew fierce in my defence of them if they were slighted by someone from outside. My maternal aunts, Kantamasi, Vimlamasi, Prafullamasi left their paternal home, too, migrating to

Amreli, Arusha, Tabora. Two of my mother's sisters, Yashumasi and Shadamasi, were married into families who lived in Nairobi, so my mother was not completely severed from her siblings. Each of the women was a daughter who went to be a daughter-in-law. I often wonder about the pain embedded in this departure. But they had all been schooled to be expelled from the father's house. They knew there was no return. When the shy and seductive romancing of filmy tunes matured into the hard slog of nurturing the extended network of in-laws, the songs which the Gujarati primers had taught, and which the teachers had imparted, filled their heads:

Dada ho dikri,
dada ho dikri,
Vagad main na desho re sain,
Vagad ni vadhiyari sasu dohyali re
Dada ho dikri.

(Grandfather, do not give any daughter in the land of Vagad, where the mothers-in-law are harsh.)

And:

Sukhna vara Mata vahi gayaa ho ji,
dukhna ugiyaa re jina jad jo,
kapraa saasriyaa maain jivvu re lol.

(The days of happiness, mother, are in the past. A tree of misery has grown, oh, what it is to live in the house of cruel in-laws!)

Beautiful young women who poured all that they had into the shaping of an affective sphere, first as daughters and sisters, then as wives and mothers. Their creativity and giving was wrapped into relationships with family and neighbours. Dependent upon brothers, and later upon husbands and in-laws, they

47

had to embrace what the world granted to them. And they did, attempting to bring beauty and fragrance into their lives, while remaining bewildered by the petty jealousies heaped upon them within the circle of in-laws.

The first aunt to leave my family home, in May 1960, was Bena. The evening when the bus that carried the wedding party accompanying Bena to her marital home in Tanga left on its journey, they say that Bindu and I were nowhere to be found. A frantic search ensued and we were at last discovered hiding in a corner, clinging crying to each other. Bena enjoyed daily evening walks with her husband by the sea and surprised him by quoting *Macbeth* in its entirety. The second to leave was Hasu. She travelled to Dar es Salaam where she groomed herself to accompany her husband on his social rounds. There are black-and-white photographs of the young couple picnicking in beautiful locations. When Madhu and Tara left for India with Ba in 1965, I was desolate. Madhu was soon betrothed to Arvindkumar in Bhavnagar, where she trained her voice to sing classical *ragas* in the midst of the demands of husband, in-laws and later, two children, while Tara enrolled for a science degree at the Maharaja Sayajirao University in Baroda.

Torn apart from the web of these relationships, I was left to spin around myself, turning inward to the world of the imagination to seek sustenance. Sometimes I think that it was Hasu–Madhu, perhaps Bena the eldest, who inculcated a deep and lasting empathy for the iconic figure of the *dosima* in my heart. I wonder whether Ba's daughters passed down the burden of memory and the reel of responsibility to the child left behind, in order that she wind it round and round her finger, never breaking the cord. But then I upbraid myself for over-reading those *sukshma* influences, carried in enfolded messages and stories and rhymes, and I think: is this not all part of a large cultural tradition? And is the act of receiving not more important in propelling a life forward than that of giving? Ba's daughters may have left the paternal home but they have returned to her, as do homing pigeons released in the skies, which fly back with ragged feathers and tired wings, their work completed, to rest in a secure place.

The nights, just before sleep stole upon us, were filled with stories, as Ba, the aunts, Bindu and I shared both the same sleeping-and story-space. The four aunts, educated in the Gujarati tradition, as well as Ba, have bestowed a language which is achingly familiar, swept to one side by the discourses of the public world, but which, when stumbled upon in unguarded moments, touches chords that the Booker awards are unable to reach. This language, derived in the Kathiawar landscape (which elite Gujaratis educated in Ahmadabad call a dialect) can flash up images, traces of feeling and memories in such an uncanny way that these feel more solid than the table upon which I write. A single rhyme, a short jingle, an allusion to a story draws me ineluctably into a child-world. There was thus the appearance (in a nonsense rhyme) of a louse − no stranger, her − whose stomach burst, bloodying the torrents of a river (*junka pet phutia, nadi loi, loi*); a tiny little ant (*kidi bichari kidli re*) who struggled to keep up with the onward march of a marriage party, not knowing that she herself was to be the bride; a mouse with seven tails who learnt that he could never obliterate difference even when he mutilated himself by cutting off his tails. Bindu and I also learnt of the terrifying power of a guru-teacher when Drona asked Eklavya (a tribal disciple) for his index finger as a guru-gift because he did not wish to see a tribal surpass an aristocrat in archery. Epochs were recognised in spectacles of power and pageantry, both human and animal.

My sister and I listened to stories from the great epics and *vratta-katha* − the stock of folklore ranged from the most ribald to the most elegiac, morality tales derived from scriptural texts. The origins of the *dosima* rhymes and stories, however, are obscure, thickly enfolded in the dense texture of oral tradition which appears to have been passed down the generations − both in the interiority of the family, as well as in the rough-and-ready cruelties of street life and the daily colloquialisms exchanged in school playgrounds, workplaces, bus journeys and train stations. To attempt to trace their source is to reduce, for the stream flows from many mountain tops, and perhaps it is the Old Woman on the Moon who has sent them down, laughing, on a moonbeam. But if it is true that the imaginative landscape weaves the thread of our lives in subtle and unknowable ways, then this may to some extent explain the way I gaze at creation.

Which Saurashtrian and Gujarati-speaker is not familiar with the figure of the *dosima* who leads a peripatetic existence (*chhalak chhalanu*), not finding a home either with one son or the other, and who elicits the following couplet from passers-by: *Chhalak chhalanu, kona ghare bhanu?* Those who encounter her, a *dosima* whose face betrays that anxious-to-please smile on the street, ask '*Kona ghare bhanu?*' (Which house is your next meal coming from?) The *dosima* gives a timid half-smile in response to the titters which surround her, for she has lost the ability to stand up for herself – her food bowl reliant on eliciting the goodwill of others. There is also the enduring image of a foraging old *dosima* who found a rupee in a cowpat and who was followed by raucous laughter as she used it to buy some *gantthia* (savouries) for herself. The cultural tradition contains many rhymes and tales which provide evidence of the world standing sentinel over the *dosima's* dried-up body and over the juices in her mouth.

Through this empathy for the condition of the *dosima*, I am linked to all those who have leant an ear to her, extending a word, a nod, a hand to bestow recognition. My aunts, Bindu and I know that Ba is well protected in our family, and yet it has been the knowledge of what has been done to others that has bound us together. Something much larger than kinship ties and our personal make-up place us in the same imaginative sphere, one that has scored our beings with a language that has become an entire emotional world. If you were to ask me whether stories such as these are imaginative constructions of the world around me or whether they create their own world, I would simply say: a world without the story-world is not thinkable. The two permeate and inform the other. As the story-creations wafted into my everyday consciousness, like wisps of clouds which blew hither and thither to hover, for one illuminating second, above an old woman – a neighbour who sat in the communal veranda of my maternal grandparents' home in Moshi picking at her head – I knew that *dosimas* (despite being known to have magical powers to transmogrify themselves into an eagle, a deer, a speaking bird) were often defenceless in a universe filled with devouring forces. And from childhood onwards, my sister and I had learnt that it was the daughter who was close to the *dosima* who needed to demonstrate cunning, in order to provide her mother with protection from the malignant beasts of prey.

A *dosima* once packed her meagre belongings into a cloth bundle, and made her way to her daughter's house in a neighbouring village. She met many predatory animals who would have pounced on her and eaten her up in one mouthful, but the *dosima* averted this by saying each time, '*Dikrini ghare jaava de, taaji maaji thava de, pachhi mane khaaje*'. 'Let me go to my daughter's house, let me become hail and hearty there, and then you can eat me up,' she beseeched, first the wolf, then the lion, then the bear, all of whom announced, *dosi, dosi, tane khaun!* (*dosi, dosi,* I will eat you up!), as she travelled to her daughter's house. The fear inspired by the two syllables in *tane khaun* (words which are invariably accompanied in the telling with a raising of the voice and with hands which reach out to pounce on the young listener) remains vivid in memory today, and I have seen children shrink away both from the words and from the teller-become-bear-wolf-for-the-while when this story is told and retold. The animals let the old woman go to her daughter, in the hope of a more succulent meal to follow. The daughter fed her mother well, and then, devised a plan to outwit the wolf, the lion and the bear.[xxxix]

It requires daughterly cunning to protect a *dosima*. I am not sure whether any of us, Ba's daughters or granddaughters, have this, and perhaps that is the core of our anxiety, for surely if we were quick to plot and outwit, then we would not be inwardly entangled? My mother has felt both alarmed and excluded from this deep texture of lives kneaded together, her daughters snatched from her to spin in a different whirlpool. A mother, taken up with looking after the needs of a large extended family into which she had married, who lost her daughters to a mother- and sisters-in-law. This loss made her cling to my brother, born five years after Bindu, for she needed someone to call her very own who would provide her with the deep constancy which surpasses all else.

Of Ba's four migratory daughters, only Tara occupies a public space outside the fold of domesticity. She had returned to Nairobi with Ba in 1969, for Baroda was not a hospitable place for two trusting women who lacked cunning. I was in secondary school then, and I recognised that Tara's search for personal fulfilment had made her heart sore. Hasu and Bena were in Tanzania, and on the occasions that they visited the family home, a large part of their time was taken up with making calls on their network of in-laws in Nairobi. At night, though, they would snuggle beside Ba, and I would hear their voices continue into the early hours. There rises in my nostrils now the smell of damp cotton nappies being dried beside a coal stove on December afternoons, as Ba turned them over and over for Bena and Hasu's babies. I would pull the string of the cradle with my right hand even as my eyes followed the pages of the book held in my left, and try as I do to retrieve an image of the baby, it eludes me.

Madhu was far away in Bhavnagar, severed from her twin sibling as well as from her mother, and she had no one around with whom she could tie together the different seams of her life. The migration of family members to Britain absorbed all their emotional energies at that time, so that Madhu was bereft of close family nurturing for many years, and remained separated from the collective reworking of experience. She has told me of the vast loneliness that engulfed her, kithless as she was in a place where childhood memories rose up to haunt her. On my first independent trip to India, in the winter of 1980, I visited her at her home in Bhavnagar. We held each other and cried and laughed and talked, but when the time came for me to leave, she looked far away from me, into the distance, and said, 'Don't worry about me. I will forget that you have been here, just as I have forgotten about my previous life with all of you.' Every time I think of her face and her words, something inside me rips, and I sob, and wish that I could enfold Madhu close to me.

THE PASSAGE

The migrations that had dominated the lives of the women in my family had been those founded on the experience of marriage, and the welcome visits back to the natal home that accompanied that experience. When the time came to disentangle themselves from the place where they had built their lives, none of them (my mother, Ba, the aunts) had much say about whether and where to migrate. They witnessed expulsions carried out through the workings of racial politics, a phenomenon in which the women found themselves implicated, primarily through their domestic, emotional labour – for they had remained bound to the close nurturing of familial relationships, separated and enclosed from the wider world.

The women in the house emigrated together with the men and children as the tide turned against the *wahindi*, the *dukawallah*, and as hostility to the image of the short-changing trader became diffused to every member of the 'Asian' community, regardless of their particular individual or collective endeavours.[xl] Complex and variegated histories were eradicated as everyone became tarred with the same brush: bloodsuckers! The potent power of stereotypes and the forces that they are able to unleash has never ceased to amaze me.

The women took care to pack everyday objects that would be useful in setting up home in a new country, preserving fragments of their lives. They knew the history of the denial of personal choice in marriage, as a friend knows the locked pain in another's heart. They saw this question take a radically new turn in neighbouring post-revolutionary Zanzibar. They heard and heard again that President Karume had passed a decree making it illegal for a woman to reject an offer of marriage. Karume's proposals to right a historical wrong through other acts of violation was a clear example of the deformation of social and political processes within this region. 'In colonial times the Arabs took African concubines without bothering to marry them. Now that we are in power, the shoe is on the other foot,' he stated at a public rally in June 1970. Rumours circulated and spread: of women fleeing marriage proposals that had been put to them by Zanzibar state officials and army personnel, families crossing over to the mainland in dhows in the dead of night, small boats capsizing in the sea, siblings left behind who were driven wild with grief. These events, avidly followed in the international press, culminated in the forcible marriages of four teenage Irani women (the youngest of whom, Nazren Hussein, was 14) to senior army officers in September 1970. The subsequent escape in February 1973 of Fawzia Mussa, Badira Mussa and Wajiha Yussef first to the mainland, then on to Nairobi and Iran forms one of the most well-known stories of this era. Their reports of having suffered terror and assault are part of a situation in which women who are married to military men feel the intimate impact of their power.[xli]

The trickle of migration became a wave. The women in the family turned their back on the political wars of the times. They would have to wait another decade and more to see their daughters able to exercise a choice about their own life partner, unfettered by community or national considerations. They girded their saris round their waists and set their faces to the task of wrapping up their here-and-now, which was soon to become an unvisited past. The earthenware jars shattered on the journey, as did so many unspoken futures. The women left behind, on the doorstep of the house where they had cooked and sung and kept an eye on their children, an *ardoosi* plant: its leaves, when picked and crushed, had brought relief to the hacking cough of a baby slung on the back of a vegetable vendor.

The passage was not easy, the crossing was choppy. But then the lunar maria were known at close quarters, when the lava had gushed out to fill those 'seas' carrying astounding names: the Sea of Clouds, the Sea of Rains. We knew of the star-scars left by the collision of meteorites: and the ways in which fairy castles, meticulously built up, then showed themselves to be unsolid, empty space. In this particular story, which begins with Ba's expulsion to the moon, the crumbling into dust of lives which had been forged in innocent anticipation of continuity[xlii] remains as a founding allegory.

The women in my family do not discuss the expulsion from the country. It is as if, having arrived from across the skies, they are eager to touch land and look up at the moon from this vantage point. The early days of settlement in Britain, marked by the search for employment in small engineering factories, are over now. My mother had spent half a year in 1970–71 working in the General Electric Company, and I would watch her admire her reflection in the long mirror as she zipped up her trousers and pulled a warm Russian hat on her head, going out in her new attire as if preparing to brave Arctic conditions. She worked to assemble electric wires for bulbs, the thunder of machines from other sections beating at her eardrums, her arthritic fingers moving with an unbreakable rhythm. Ushakaki accompanied her, while Kokilakaki remained at home to tend to the domestic chores. Those endeavours which were expended in the first setting up of homes in the Wembley area are in the past now, the houses being given decidedly minimalist makeovers. As Ba's daughters become wrapped up in looking after their grand-children, and her daughters-in-law savour the dubious pleasures of living in a non-extended family household, her granddaughters remain busy in their professional lives.

Today, I see Ba safely ensconced in a terraced house in north-west London. Bena, Hasu, Madhu and Tara, scattered to the four comers of the earth, are ageing too and require cosseting. My mother is involved in carrying forward the teachings of the

Brahma Kumaris,[xliii] a predominantly female religious order that she joined when the walls echoed out their silence and loneliness came to eat her up. Every time I am with her now, I implore her not to leave the house at dawn to attend the early-morning meditation service: 'I'm here, Ma, *talk to me.*' On the days when I am able to keep her for myself I feel as if I am bigger than all the world religions put together, and I hug myself in glee.

Amidst the changes that have taken place in the lives of the women and the men in the family, as the earth rotates and the moon continues its orbital round (the first chasing the second, attempting to learn lessons from it and succeeding at times in crossing its face for a few hours), we are caught within that war of stars: between the close nurture of aunts, uncles and cousins, which requires such an enormous amount of emotional labour, and the fissile world that we inhabit.

Ba holds us in her eyes, orbs that of late have been filmed in milky white. Although they are now dim and her hearing is not as acute as it once was, every time I come in her presence, I am undone. I have spent my whole lifetime attempting to enter her world (no facile attempt, this). I have railed at her gods and carried a vast and irredeemable anger towards those forces that have cast their shadow over her. But in a crowded family gathering, I have been aware (in that electric way in which hands touch across the weight of other bodies) of a pair of eyes that have followed my every move, ears that have strained to hear me, a mind that has stored up every word I utter. Sometimes, walking on a Northumberland beach, chewing on the taste of polemical writings, I am assailed by a terrible fear. I rush to the phone: you are not going to leave me, are you? Not yet, comes the calm reply. I want to see Neera and Shyama on their feet. The self-serving question, what about *me*, hangs between us. Once, she answered it: '*Koi Harino Lal madi jaase*'. (You will find someone intoxicated with the love of Krishna.) Someone drunk on the Song of Love, maddened with longing for the Beloved – this is what she and I have sought for in the congregation of people around us.

As I go about my life, teaching and writing in a professional world where intellectual fashions come and go, I know that it is only Ba's fourth daughter-in-law, Kokila (Plate VI), who can provide the close caring that Ba continues to require. Rani Kokila we call her, the queen who rules over her domain with such transparent grace. It is only in the raj of Kokilarani (who is devoid of earthly cunning) that a meticulous attentiveness to the lunar calendar (which requires elaborate culinary and devotional preparations) has been maintained. Kokila, who has rejected book learning, and who wends her way through the complications of contemporary life with ease. Kokilakaki, the daughter-in-law with a generous laugh and dark rings under her eyes. Monghi, Pushkerkaka used to call her. The Precious One. The pendant that rests on the heart.

Tara and I were sitting with Ba yesterday, wrapped within her stories and sadlo. Old, worn-out white sadlas are carefully folded by her after being washed, and are presented to those who will make good use of them. They provide swaddling for babies, and for dolls, teddy bears, a friendly one-eyed lion. The best shrikhand is made with yogurt sieved through the fine cotton mesh of a sadlo. Bleeding fingers are tied with strips of a white sadlo, and heal well. Much is contained in the story of a white sadlo.

Part Two

HARSHAD

'Peel them [three pears] for you?' cried Geppeto, astonished.
'I would never have thought, my lad, that you were so refined
and fastidious. That's too bad! We should get used, from
childhood, to eating everything, and liking it; for one never
knows what might happen in this curious world.'

CARLO COLLODI, *The Adventures of Pinnochio*

Sukh dukh manmain na aandiye.
Ghat saathe re ghadiyaa
Taadiya te koina nav tade.
Raghunathna jadiyaa
Sukh dukh manmain na aandiye.

Happiness and sorrow, do not let your mind house either of
these. Given form at the same time as the body was, they
cannot be eradicated, endeavour as one might. Raghunath
experienced this truth himself. Happiness and sorrow, do not
let your mind house either of these.

NARSINHA MEHTA, fifteenth century

HUNGER STORIES

I spent a large part of the years from October 1984 to February 1989 doing research in India, where I sat in devotional gatherings and watched the dawn break over the gaunt faces of singers who raised their voices to the heavens all night long. I took time out of the research to walk along the Narmada valley, visiting the villages which were to be submerged by the building of a dam, and trekked in the magical Chamba valley of Himachal Pradesh – where women and men returned to the mountain villages at the melting of the snow, the former with cooking utensils slung round their bodies, the latter carrying lambs in their capacious pockets as they coaxed their flocks of goats along rickety wooden bridges over the torrential tributaries of the Ravi river.

I returned to Britain to find myself in a dazed state, in which my eyes appeared incapable of *seeing* what was in front of them, returning again and again to images with a sharper grain, more brilliant colour, greater depth. The railway station at Oxford on the drizzly summer morning of 3 June 1989 was a drab grey, and the college spires failed to inspire me. On my way to a conference organised by the *History Workshop Journal* in Ruskin College, I thought about *Jude the Obscure*, Harshad-who-had-wanted-to-be-a-barrister, the expression in his eyes on a photograph I hold close to me (Plate III), his pride in Pari-who-was-completing-her-Ph.D., the luminous communities she was writing about, the passions which could not be encompassed by the dull skies. The conference gathering consisted of teachers from primary and secondary schools, as well as lecturers from colleges and universities. In the registration lobby where people thronged to discuss the implications of the Conservative government's decision to introduce a standardised national curriculum in all schools, I was able to pick out some familiar faces and others that I did not yet know.

The introduction of a national curriculum was a worrying development for the teaching of history, for I knew that this intervention by the government was a clear directive to foreground the history of conquest and empire. The preceding years had been marked by a close alliance between Margaret Thatcher and Ronald Reagan, encapsulated by the disarmament campaign's poster which depicted Thatcher swooning in Reagan's arms, *Gone with the Wind* style: she promised to follow him to the end of the world, he promised to ensure that this happened. National pride had been tied to a peculiar British subordination to American military power which (so I read in the *Guardian Weekly*) some patriots such as Enoch Powell found extremely distasteful. Our conference debated the uses of history and the best ways of encouraging school and college students to develop an informed and enquiring attitude to the world around them. The teaching of the history of empire was clearly a controversial subject, as was the history of the diverse migrant communities who had been brought to these shores through the despoliation of the colonies. Stuart Hall, an eminent Caribbean intellectual and cultural historian, began to talk about the necessity of integrating the experience and legacies of empire into the school curriculum.[i] The room that sticky morning contained both those already convinced by the argument and experiencing déjà vu, and others displaying an unserious indolence. Ever quick to pick up the nuances of an audience, Stuart Hall leant forward, his eyes bright, hands held out in a large gesture. 'Please,' he said, 'I beg you not to think that you are doing this for *black* children. You have to do this for *all* children, so that they do not go out *and eat this world*.' My eyes pricked, the room receded and there, in that hazy space, was a moment of acute and intense recognition.

Do not go out and eat this world. How well I knew these sentiments, how familiar they were! It required a sojourner who had travelled a similar path in life to give voice to them in a public forum, and thus show clearly the profligate use of both human beings and material resources which has been such a central feature of history since the Columbian expansion. In a world that has been dominated for at least the past five hundred years by the appropriation of this earth for ever-increasing profits, the injunction – *do not go out and eat this world* – demands the forging of an ethical culture to counter this grasping, greedy self-assertion.

The three generations of family members that I am closely linked with in this story have not gone out to eat this world. My father has spent enormous energy instilling in us the moral belief that possessions do not count for very much: acquisitiveness is corrosive. That being caught in the spiral of wanting more and more and more leads ultimately to a state of dissatisfaction and envy. And that the world is peopled by those who are avaricious, as well as those who are not. 'Never suck the roots of a sweet tree for it will wither and die,' says Ba. 'There are so many wonderful individuals who have worked to make this world a better place for everyone,' says Harshad. '*That* is real achievement. To improve things only for yourself – anyone can do this.' His lips curl in disparagement.

The nurturing of this particular ethical idea within my family has been carried out through the everyday bearing of Ba, and has led to the braiding of a very specific culture. The public world – the world of professional and voluntary involvement in civic organisations, where the impulse to give of oneself to others is displayed – is permeated by the presence of my father, Harshad. The contrast between the pair who head the first and second generations (the first bound to the family, the second glued every day to the BBC news on a spluttering transistor radio) irradiated the household in different ways, just as the story of going hungry in the past was transmitted to children in different ways: by aunts to nieces, father to daughter. The history of hunger was also learnt through absorbing the words of those close to us, becoming familiar with the flickering emotions on their faces as a memory of humiliation was revived by the sight of a *puran-podi* or some other similar delectable. It has led to the evolution of a state of mind in which the hunger story is entwined with the related injunction – *do not go out and eat this world*. Amidst the conquering of stomach-hunger, and the attainment of considerable worldly gains in the move to the heart of the metropolis, the imparting of the philosophical and cultural wisdom of 'not eating the world' has remained constant within my family.

The story of family beginnings has transmitted a particular shard of memory that has continued to score the lives of three generations of family members. The story of hunger – of my father giving up his studies to support his mother and siblings immediately after my grandfather died, of the ten of them eating *bhakhri* and salt for a period of seven years – has created an emotional personality which feels, perceives and acts in ways that are specific to this particular story. The received memory carries a revelation of Ba at a time when that which she manifests most – mother-love – was both shattered and enthroned.

There is an image of a thirty-three-year-old mother, recently widowed, sitting on the floor of a kitchen by a coal-*chula* in the evening, baking *bhakhri*. Her nine children, the youngest aged six months, surround her. She regularly sings the devotional song with which this chapter begins. It is derived from the powerful spiritual movement that swept northern India in the fifteenth and sixteenth centuries, and is attributed to the *bhakta* Narsinha. The eight older children provide a chorus while they wait for the meal to begin. If at times tears course down her cheeks as she cooks and sings, she answers the younger children's anxious queries by saying that this is due to smoke from the *chula*. The eldest son thinks that it is her absorption in the devotional song which occasions these tears. The singing of these devotional songs, and the loyalty that arises from the sharing of a frugal meal which consisted simply of *bhakhri* flavoured with salt – these things provide the weave of life between the three generations, braiding the story of motherhood wounded, and a father lost, with the contours of differently constructed and complex futures.

This particular story emerged in a period during which the colonial bureaucracy was well established in the capital city of Kenya, manned by Indian scribes, clerks and lawyers who had a deeply fraught relationship with their British paymasters. The young women who had come as brides in order to join their working menfolk bore the impossible burden of creating a domain of emotions, affection and sentiment which would absorb the shocks, both petty and large, of social life in the new world. It was around the maternal figure, rather than the wife, that norms of etiquette crystallised. The social ideal did not revolve around a romantically linked couple, but around the Mother who forgave children their sins and cleansed their hearts of sorrows. If a birth mother turned vengeful (as was sometimes the way) then another Mother was ready to envelop the reprobate in her embrace. Pariah, orphan, castaway, each found solace in the folds of a *sadlo* or *duppata*. In an environment where the Mother reigned supreme, the point of identification in the story of family origins for all of us is the mother figure who first emigrated out, embodying as she does the lived hurts and bearing as she does the scars of those times.

The heritage transmitted by the shared story of a mother feeding her children solely on *bhakhri* and salt has been threefold. Within the generation of those nine children there is a fierce loyalty between those members who have actually partaken of this meal of scarcity. There is also a taut bond that links all those who are aware of this history without having experienced it: emotional life which is centred on a constant, nagging worry for anyone who has gone hungry in the past. Overarching this, the story has led to the creation of an emotional domain which is suffused with fraught attempts to tilt the universe away from a past memory of hunger, to seek restitution.

However, we must push the story back to the time and the place from whence that first father set off on a journey to build a new life. His voyage across the Indian Ocean to the shores of

East Africa was not undertaken as a result of impoverishment – a difference from those originary narratives which dog the actual and imagined histories of both global and internal migrants. Rather, it was set in motion by a turbulent set of circumstances which had changed the global balance of maritime power, upturning the lives of those living in the colonies. Saurashtra is cradled by the Indian Ocean on three sides: it abounds in creeks, it has a shoreline from which dolphins can be seen to frolic, and it has a long history of men setting out across the sea to return with a catch for the women and children left behind. It has a language rich in words to describe seagoing vessels: *baghala, batelo, kothia, fatemari, galbat, hodi, machhva*. Pilgrims used to set sail from Somnath Patan to Mecca and Medina. Large vessels with two masts and sails had crossed to Basra, Aden, Zanzibar. The merchant communities of Lohanas, Memons and Bhatias (inordinate ghee-eaters all) had flourished, as had the humbler weavers, carpenters, joiners, welders and caulkers who worked to craft the boats. The sailors who went to sea, as well as the fishermen in the small boats, knew that Dariya pir, the Saint of the Seas, had to be propitiated in order to stop him from sporting with them, for he, like the Great Storm-Cat, enjoyed playing with the men–mice, biding time till the boat was outside a safe haven before unleashing high winds and lashing waves. Three or four vessels disappeared in the middle of the ocean every year, or were dashed on the reefs of the Arabian Sea. There are stirring hymns sung to the goddess Ambaji, of merchants crying out when their vessel filled with water: *Kiddhi kamani shun kamni re, java betha jyan pran Bhid-bhanjni* ... (Of what use are these riches accumulated when one's very life is slipping away!) The fishing communities which dot the coastline today continue to sing to the Dariya pir, reliant as they are on the mercy and bounty of the ocean.

The port towns of Porbander, Veraval, Mandvi, Mahuva, Bhavnagar, Salaya, Talaja and Mangrol, became overshadowed by the newly created city of Bombay. By the early twentieth century, Saurashtra had become a peripheral region in the colonial economy. The advance of colonial capitalism witnessed a growth of quasi-feudal relationships in this part of the British Empire, rather than their disintegration – one of those ironies of history for which neither the English Utilitarians nor Karl Marx had been prepared. Governed by a group of landed gentry, under the supreme power of the British government, the princely states of Saurashtra saw a time of thwarted and deformed promises.

The terrible famine of 1899, known as the *cchapanio*, had entered into dark and fearful folklore. The moneylenders had grown fat from the people's distress – they had bought up everything of value, even cooking pots – while also living in fear of those who turned desperate in their starvation. People ate the bark of trees; no grass grew, and the corpses of cattle lay on the land. An estimated three million people died in Bombay Presidency. Two thirds of these deaths took place in the princely states where both my grandmother and grandfather's families lived. Throughout the famine, the Bombay government continued to extract revenue from a starving peasantry. While this period exists in popular consciousness as one when the world disintegrated – children were sold and women bartered their bodies – there was another, more lasting form of expropriation, which was to transform the nature of existence in this region. This was the imposition of a system of taxation, to be paid in cash rather than kind, which necessitated the growing of crops for sale. Food crops – the millets, *bajri* and *juvar* as well as *kodra* (*Pappalum scrobiculatum*), *bavto* (*Penicum frumentaceum*) and legumes – had to be partially replaced by cash crops of wheat, rice and groundnuts. The dramatic shift in cropping and food patterns (which continues adversely to affect the life chances of the poor worldwide) had begun, and was soon to accelerate.

The power of the moneylender increased. This figure personifies avarice, evil, fraud; he appropriated land, wealth from cattle dealing and the bodies of women. The dominant cash crop in this region became cotton. In the villages around the town of Lathi, where my grandmother's paternal family lived, the cotton grown was referred to as *dhankniu* or *dabliu*, since it was enclosed in a pod and did not burst forth in the wind. Women and children laboured to extract the crop from the sharp protection of its covering: the fingers of both their hands bled till lesions developed, so hard that even a caress on a child's cheek left a mark. Sometimes an iron pestle was necessary to break open the pod out of which white clouds would waft in the air. Nasal and lung passages became blocked. And still the pods had to be broken open, the cotton extracted, the seed stored. This seed was then resown, the dried pods provided kindling for a fire, while the cotton travelled first to the gins to be pressed into bales, and later to far-off destinations.

The cotton grown in Bhavnagar district, where my grandfather's family lived, was called *desan*. It was of a creamy white colour, fine in texture, with a yellow tinge, and it became a major export. The merchant moneylenders grew fat from their profits. On 3 January 1922, a year before my grandfather left for East Africa, about twelve *kheduts* (farmers) presented a petition to the Revenue Commissioner of Bhavnagar state, saying that the monstrous rates of interest levied by Panachand Jadavji Shah and Ramji Bechar Shah were causing them severe hardship. They asked for a judicial review to be undertaken: the Revenue Commissioner investigated the particular case and found that even where debts had been repaid, there was no record of this in the books of Panachand Shah. Increasing evidence of fraudulent practices and of debt among the peasantry prodded the progressive princely state of Bhavnagar to order an inquiry. The committee of inquiry began its work in 1924 and carried out a thorough search. It reported in 1931 that within the fourteen villages of Gadhda *mahal*, sixty-one per cent of the populace was in severe debt. It demonstrated that the small debts which had been accrued by the small farmers during the 1899 famine had been multiplying in the moneylenders' books.[iii]

Some members of my paternal family were permanent tenants, with occupancy rights over a *vadi* (orchard) and a small *khordu* (dwelling) in the village of Lakhanka, in the same Gadhda *mahal* of Bhavnagar state, on the banks of the Ghelo river. The river often lived up to its name, rising in mad fury in the monsoon periods. My great-grandfather lived on the land, and he and Santokma had three sons, Ratilal, Himmat and Labhu. My paternal family was closely linked to the ruling Gohil house in the village, with the men in the two families sharing a taste for enjoyment, adventure and bravado. However, the major transformation in their life did not initially come from the aspirations of the young men themselves. It came, rather, through the social connections of my great-grandmother, Santokma, and her brother, the pleader Venilal Upadhyay, who practised in Bhavnagar. Santokma's two older sons were drawn away from the village of Lakhanka and to the wider metropolitan centre of Bhavnagar through their maternal family. Both were educated in this thriving cultural and educational town, then the elder son began teaching in a Bhavnagar secondary school, where he also acted as personal tutor to Bahadursinh Raol, the successor to the Gohil house. The latter remembers both sons demonstrating a keen pleasure in the cultural and artistic activities of the town. The move represented a huge cognitive leap for my grandfather: a life that was centred on an agrarian base was left behind and wider intellectual horizons were embraced. It was this that was to lead him to the possibility of migrating out of a newly peripheralised region of the Indian Empire to travel to British East Africa.

The fairly recent peasant moorings of the family, on both my grandmother and grandfather's side, are crucial to the formation of the emotional core of three generations within this family. My grandmother retains recollections, now a little romanticised, of a girlhood spent in fetching water from a village well; she upholds a moral world view which emphasises the fullness of life as expressed through a communion forged by the sharing of food with strangers and guests who do not speak her language; she adheres to a politics of subsistence; and she is never happier than when she is poring over the pages of a *panchang*, planning her activities through the astrological reckoning of an almanac. She continues to describe her days and nights by the cusp of the moon, and the seasons according to the North Indian agricultural cycle, while she lives in a North London terraced house: *punam*, *amavas*, *bij*, *trij*, *chauth*, *shiado*, *unado*, *chaumasu*. (Full moon, no moon, second, third and fourth day of the lunar fortnight, winter, summer, rains.) The ageing women and men of the second generation who were born in the colonial capital of Kenya, and who are now scattered in cities around the globe (London, Miami, Toronto, Ahmadabad), display both a horrified fascination with the fast-moving roller-coaster of urban culture, and an adherence to the vision of a patriarchal peasant utopia, in which they dream of being enveloped in a harmonious village community, far removed from the stresses and conflicts of contemporary life. They yearn to live in a small mud house (cunningly contrived to have a flushing lavatory and a bathroom), shaded by mango groves where dancing peacocks announce the coming of the rains. For my sister and I, who head the third generation and who were first drawn to socialist activism in the Britain of the 1970s, the peasant milieu continues to be one which enchants and puzzles, riven as it is by a stubborn but finely crafted paternalism, which carries the seeds of its own destruction within itself, into the Europe of the third millennium.

My father has in his possession my grandfather's first passport which he had used when he travelled from Bombay to Mombasa early in the twentieth century. In a small bag he retains old passports, school leaving certificates, certificates of merit, astrological charts. He is a good keeper-of-history, my father, bestowing both a sympathetic and discerning gaze which traces shifts, large and small, that have taken place in the lives of all those around him. His warm interest in human foibles and achievements, his acute sense of the traces that historical transformations leave in the hearts and minds of people, and his fine empathy with their tribulations, enables him to connect with all. The photograph on my grandfather's passport shows a young man wearing a black cap, in an attempt to lend dignity and maturity to a childlike face. The passport is marked 'British Indian Passport: Indian Empire'. It was issued at Bombay on 7 May 1923. He must have set sail almost immediately, for the disembarkation date at the port of Mombasa is 7 June 1923. The year of birth is given as 1905, which would make him eighteen in 1923. The face, however, belies this. Eager to acquire the status of an independent adult worker, many young men shook off their juvenile status by claiming an earlier date of birth.

My grandfather arrived in East Africa at a time when European settlers, large numbers of whom had come from South Africa, had succeeded in achieving economic and political domination over the colony. The years 1890–1900 had been marked by famine, plague and smallpox: cattle herds of the Maasai, Kamba, Kikuyu had been reduced by the rinderpest. The displacement of African communities from the land, the setting up of Native Reserves and the control established over large tracts by white settlers had been completed. Coffee became the major crop, exported to nurture the tastes of metropolitan sophisticates. The numbers of women and children employed in picking coffee berries had risen substantially, so that they formed forty per cent of the workforce in the peak coffee-picking season. The small-scale peasant farmers who had harvested millet, maize, sweet potatoes, yams, bananas, peas and beans early in the twentieth century found that the cash taxes imposed on them forced them to hire out their labour for wages on European plantations. Women were not able to harvest the food crops (millet, kidney beans, lablab beans, green gram), for the months in which they could do this coincided with the time when the settlers required thousands of women to pick the coffee berries. Women and children returned to their homesteads worn out with the pain in their bodies, fingers stiff and swollen. The settlers, meanwhile, enjoyed an aristocratic lifestyle, full of grandeur and seigneurial pretensions unimaginable in the homes they had left behind. The war of attrition against pastoral communities continued. By the early 1920s the settler population was boasting of the advantage it had, since it could utilise labour that was 'probably the cheapest in the world'.[iv] In 1921 the Labour Bureau Commission warned the settlers and the British government of the effect of deleterious working conditions on the health of workers. In 1922 medical administrators estimated the infant mortality rate to be four hundred per thousand, an astoundingly grim figure. Loss of land, inadequate housing, low wages and the lack of public medical provision meant that these appalling conditions continued.[v] Territories which had been racked by the impact of slave trading became involved with producing cash crops which enhanced the quality of life for those who lived far away at the centre of the Empire.

My father knows that Indian Question was being fought out vociferously by European settlers during the year in which my grandfather arrived in Nairobi. The major demands of the Indian communities – a common electoral roll and representation on the legislative and municipal councils, an end to residential and commercial segregation, an end to the prohibition on settlement in the highlands, and the ending of restrictions on immigration – were met with violent opposition. The white settlers, looking to their counterparts in South Africa for support, launched a counter-movement and passed various resolutions in meetings held up and down the country in late 1922 and early 1923. These resolutions proclaimed that the settlers would enforce their race privilege with armed force if necessary. Refusing to be classed with the 'Asiatics, imported for pick-and-shovel work, a people alien in mind, colour, religion, morality', they declared that it was 'unthinkable' to 'live side by side with the Indians and under their rule'.[vi]

I do not know whether my grandfather, a young aspirant to a better life, was aware of the politics of racial hatred which would surround him, as they did the 4,405 other Indians who arrived in Kenya in the same year, and which would draw him in, regardless of his personal inclinations. The eyes that gaze out from his passport photograph are serious, though outward looking (Plate II). A month and sixteen days after his arrival in Kenya Colony, a White Paper on the status of Indians in Kenya advocated the adoption of a communal system of political representation.[vii] The deformation of political allegiances which were determined by racial category was thus institutionalised.

It is difficult to piece together the tribulations and achievements of a man whose face is glimpsed in a black-and-white photograph, and whose name has achieved a mythical status in family memory, unsubstantiated by any actual traces left by him. From the day he arrived in Mombasa on 7 June 1923 to the day he left this world on 11 March 1948, his travails have acquired a quixotic rise and fall through their epic telling – a tale in which children brought up in the lap of luxury had to rest content with eating *bhakhri* and salt once he had departed. My grandmother did not concern herself much with the outside world of work, so the children were unaware of how their daily comforts were acquired until they were taken away. A petrol pump in Nairobi has been mentioned but the enterprise did not last long. There are fabulous stories told, of great wealth accumulated, and largesse showered on all and sundry: necklaces, diamond rings, watches. They say my grandfather was always well dressed, in the smartest suits. He was driven around by a chauffeur. He had owned two houses in Nairobi. Why then the move to live in two rented rooms with his wife and nine children, rooms which were pared down to one after his death. And why were bangles pawned? Bad habits. Bad company. Lack of acumen and an over-generous heart. It may be that the depression years had affected him badly. Perhaps he was simply unlucky. The unearthing of a second passport provides another clue: here, under the category 'profession', he is listed as 'insurance clerk'.

The legendary tales have often appeared to me to be magical stories, necessary to the imagination of those suddenly starved of a father's solid, secure presence. Whatever the material reality of my grandfather's rise and fall, however, the passing down of the story of hunger has, curiously, not emphasised the fall from the heights of luxury, nor dwelt on reminiscences of riches lost. Memories of wealth have evaporated into the mists of the past, and have not been recaptured. The originary father-figure has joined the list of ancestors, being the first among the *pitru* who are propitiated every year with ritual offerings of food. A slight aura of disrepute has hung around my grandfather's portrait, and the family story has solidified and congealed around a mother brought to the brink of a condition that tested the limits of her faith.

Those of us who were born in Nairobi in the third generation lived in a large rented house on Roorkee (later Kipande) Road: grandmother, aunts and uncles, parents and cousins together. The first two generations were not able to tell us very much about the days before my grandfather died, and as a child I did not know which questions to ask. The burdensome memory of being marginalised in the community was a trauma that the aunts and uncles replayed over and over again, transmitting it through the story of hunger. Every morning before I left for school, I would sit on the floor with Hasu and Madhu and we would eat bhakhri and salt for breakfast out of the same tin plate. 'This is what we ate after Kaka died,' Madhu would say, turning to both the telling of the tale and the accepting of it, 'there was nothing else.' Hasu would nod, her eyes wide, and then she would begin to crack her finger joints to make me laugh. This pattern was ever the same: the three of us together in the morning, embarking on our day by acknowledging this weave in our lives. It bound us together, as does the sharing of a conspiratorial silence or a laugh.

To traverse this universe carrying a story of hunger as the origin of one's family beginnings is to hold a very specific set of relationships with the world around oneself. This originary hunger story inhabits my skin, it snuggles in my mouth, films my eyes, flavours my experiences. None of the aunts and uncles remembers a time preceding their life in the large communal compound on Milner Road, where they had two rented rooms. They have memories of the rough and tumble of playing in a crowded, congested neighbourhood, where girls and boys climbed up fruit trees trying to be the first to sink their teeth into a guava, a lukat, a mango. However, in the retelling of the family story, it is only my father who has retained a strong

74

sense of anything preceding the events of 11 March 1948. He remembers pocket money bestowed on him, which he hoarded, and which went towards buying a cheap gramophone player from an auction. My grandfather complemented this machine by bringing home a collection of records by the popular singer K. L. Saigal. The handle was turned and the strains of '*do naina matware tihare . . . hum par zullum kare*' came floating out. He was no philistine, this grandfather, but an avid reader who sent his son to the Desai Memorial Library on a daily basis to exchange the book just finished.

For all the others, apart from my father, nothing is remembered prior to the death of my grandfather. This was the moment when they were made conscious of a hostile world, not only brutal in its race and class privileges, but ruthless in the very fibre of the community. Their mother drew on her inner strength to sing the devotional song composed by Narsinha to her children, in order to impart her deeply held vision. In doing this she was turning material desire into an aestheticised one, transmuting pain felt in the skin to a space somewhere outside the body. When she regularly sang – '*Such dukh manmain na aandiye, ghat sathe reghadiya, taadiya te koina nav tade*', (Happiness and sorrow, do not let your mind house either of these. Given form at the same time as the body was, they cannot be eradicated) – she was not schooling her children to accept their condition fatalistically. Creditors had swooped upon them, like locusts, and stripped the rooms. She did not comment on the actions of those who did this. She held on fast to her eldest son, protected the minds of all nine, taught them, in songs which they continue to echo today, that each had the capacity to bear the vicissitudes of life. The elegiac singing of the *bhajan* articulated a condition of downfall in their lives and said that this had to be borne *without burdening the mind.*[viii] The profound and subtle injunction to keep the mind intact amidst the vagaries of life – to bear happiness and sorrow in equal measure – has been the greatest gift my grandmother has imparted.

The East African Railways and Harbour provided the family

with the means through which it was able to survive on bhakhri and salt. The eldest son, shaken from having performed his father's funeral rites (a cruel rite of passage, the lighted torch and the flames burning away the traces of a remembered childhood) was unable to complete the last year of secondary education and had to abandon his dream of becoming a barrister. Karamchand Handa, the landlord (or Bauji, as he is known in the family) was owed rent. He called Harshad over and asked him to get ready to accompany him to work the next day. Bauji lent Harshad a suit, over-large and ill-fitting, took him by the hand, and led him into the Railways Office. Here, Harshad was interviewed by Alexander Henry, a man who had done service in the Indian Empire and who spoke pidgin Hindustani. The image of Harshad sitting confused at a desk, hardly registering that this was the first day of what was to be a long working life, is as important as the fact that he found in Henry a paternal figure, who (seeing Harshad's youth) would send him with five shillings every Saturday to accompany his own young children, aged seven and eight, to the Empire cinema. Here, the three watched *Aladdin, The Thief of Baghdad, Ali Baba and the Forty Thieves*, and ate some chocolate together.

The young Harshad became the mainstay of a large family overnight. His starting salary of a hundred shillings a month had to suffice for eight siblings and a housebound mother. Here enters bhakhri and salt, lodged deep within the fabric of family ties, woven staunchly into the structure of emotional allegiance, and providing the root to the shared history of hunger and its assuagement.

Bhakhri is cooked in the family with wheat flour. A table-spoonful or so of ghee is mixed into the flour to ensure that the bhakhri does not become rubbery. Water is added. A ball of this dough is taken, rolled out and baked over a low heat. When ready, it has a thick, crumbly texture. One and a half bhakhri by itself will satisfy an adult's hunger. Cooked over a coal chula, each one can take up to ten minutes to bake. Salt is supplied on the side, and a cup of sugary masala tea accompanies the meal.

The *bhakhri* is broken, dipped in the tea, dipped again in the salt (which is soon stained in tannin), and eaten.

This meal was eaten on a daily basis for seven years. The variation was a garlic chutney which replaced salt, or – the height of luxury – yogurt with a garlic chutney and *bhakhri*. The counterpart of *bhakhri* and salt amongst those placed within a separate and racially differentiated price index in Kenya in colonial times was *ugali* – maize flour stirred in a pot with water and a pinch of salt till it is cooked to a thick consistency. *Ugali* was sometimes accompanied by beans, *posho* or *maragwe*. In India today, large sections of the poor continue to eat a meal which is very similar to *bhakhri* and salt throughout their lives. The difference is that wheat is replaced by what colonial classifications described as 'coarser grains': *juvaar*, *baajra*, *jaar*, millets which are ground, mixed, rolled out and baked. Dried, red chillies replace the salt.

The communal compound in which my family lived also housed four other families. In an open living space, there was nothing hidden, especially as there were five kitchens in a row, where the cooking took place with doors open: the meals were eaten with everyone sitting on the floor, in full view of each other. The other families were well aware of what ours ate every day. While family members acquired and have retained a *love* for *bhakhri* and salt, those outside the family saw the meal as a badge of stigma. 'Huh, what can you expect of those brought up on *bhakhri* and salt?' was a common put-down, or 'What do *you* know – you eat *bhakhri* and salt.' This culminated in my maternal grandfather from Moshi being told in June 1952: 'You must be mad to agree to give your daughter in marriage to that family ... they eat nothing but *bhakhri* and salt.' This schoolmaster shook his head at those who proffered this advice, returned home and pondered on the matter. Later, he called his daughters and sons together and then, Geppeto-like, enjoined them to eat only *bhakhri* and salt that whole month, for the world was a curious place, and who knew what might happen in it. At the end of the month, an engagement was agreed between the daughter of the schoolmaster and the railway worker. My mother had just turned fifteen.

It is said that we are what we eat. This philosophical system is set out by no less a person than the divine Krishna, who divided nature and humankind into three categories, with an aplomb that leaves me speechless: *sattva*, *rajas* and *tamas*.

> *Sattva*, *Rajas*, *Tamas* – light, fire and darkness – are the three constituents of nature [said Krishna to Arjuna on the battlefield of Kurukshetra]. They appear to limit in finite bodies the liberty of their infinite Spirit...
>
> Men of light worship the gods of light; men of fire worship the gods of power and wealth; men of darkness worship ghosts and spirits of night...
>
> Men who are pure like food which is pure: which gives health, mental power, strength and long life; which has taste, is soothing and nourishing, and which makes glad the heart of man.
>
> Men of *Rajas* like food of *Rajas*: acid and sharp, and salty and dry, and which brings heaviness and sickness and pain.
>
> Men of darkness eat food which is stale and tasteless, which is rotten and left overnight, impure, unfit for holy offerings.[ix]

Perhaps it is this self-righteous vision which makes Krishna unaware of the conditions of the people he reigns over as each morning I watched family members bow their heads to him after their ablutions). But if it is correct that the eating of cold food, left overnight as is *bhakhri*, demonstrates the *tamas* nature which 'darkens the soul of all men ... [binding] them to sleepy dullness, and then they do not watch and then they do not work'[x] – then perhaps one has found the measurable cause for the political apathy of that large body of humankind which experiences involuntary hunger. It is, however, difficult – not to say impossible – to reconcile this philosophical system with the

Plate 1: Studio photograph of my grandmother and grandfather, Nairobi, circa 1940.

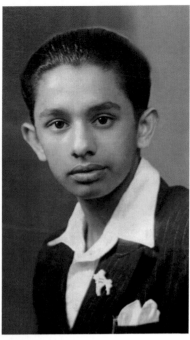

Above Plate II:
Passport photograph
of my grandfather,
1923, probably
taken in Bombay.

Above Plate III:
Photograph of
my father aged
sixteen, Nairobi.

Right Plate IV:
Photograph of
my aunt Hasu,
aged thirteen or
so, Nairobi.

Opposite Plate V:
Photograph of my
parents four days
after the wedding,
1955, Nairobi.

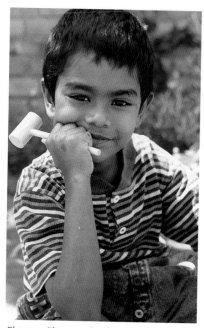

Plate XVI: Photograph of my sister, Bindu, 2000, Warwickshire.

Plate XVII: Photograph of Sonpari, 2000, Warwickshire.

Plate XV: Photograph of my nephew Moonie, 1998, Warwickshire.

Plate XVIII: Photograph of my niece, Suchi, 1998, Warwickshire.

Plate XIX: Reproduction of a painting by Khodisbhai Parmar, 1970.

Plate XX: Sculpture entitled 'A Woman Writing,' Khajuraho temples, North India, tenth/eleventh century.

political economy of food and hunger that I teach to my undergraduate students, for whom the intentional polemics of Susan George (rather than the sober prose of the Nobel prize-winner Amartya Sen) appear to be a favourite read.[xi]

That first generation born in Nairobi was defined within the community as eaters of bhakhri and salt. And yet Harshad the railway worker, having installed himself in the job, entered into vigorous political debates with his elders, relished the cut and thrust of debate, enjoyed scoring points and retained his dignity by being articulate about his views at all times. As my uncles left school, also to take up clerical jobs, the family's circumstances improved to the extent where they were able to move out of the communal compound into a roomier first-floor rented apartment, which offered some privacy. But it was a growing family, and the male earners were aware of the unmet needs of their sisters and sisters-in-law. After a lifetime of paring down his material needs to a minimum, my father is now unable to retain in his possession more than two warm sweaters and shirts. When he recently bought himself an extra cardigan, he lay awake all night considering a man's relationship to needs and desires. 'I had to return the cardigan the next day,' he says, 'it pricked me. I do not need more than I have.' Presents given to him disappear. They are redistributed elsewhere, and when I open the built-in cupboards in his room to fold away the spare duvet covers, the empty hanging space and shelves make me pause and muse.

The East African Railways are indelibly linked both to the story of colonial 'progress' and to the assuagement of hunger in our family. First built by Indian indentured labour, the East African Railways continued to be manned by 'free' immigrants who arrived after the end of what has been called a second system of slavery. In the initial period, the man-eating lions of Tsavo had found the 'coolie' who resided in the labour camp a tasty morsel, and having acquired a liking for human flesh, they had the temerity to drag off a British official too. While the last incident has been illustrated in children's primers and taught in history lessons, there is a more lasting memorial to a railway worker on the Mackinnon Road, between Nairobi and Mombasa. The story of the railway *pir* is that a labourer worn out by pick-and-shovel work cried out to the Almighty to relieve him of his burden. His fellow workers watched in silence as his call was answered, and from then on this labourer went about his duties, his heavy load balanced in the air just two inches above his head. He expended his last breath on the railway line, and became a *pir*, often returning in extraterrestrial form to lighten the load of his former workmates. The *dargah* was a central focus of pilgrimage in the family when I was young: on those rare and memorable occasions when we went to see the waves come crashing onto the coast of Mombasa, we would stop, heads covered with scarves or handkerchiefs, to pay homage to *pir* Syed Baghali Shah, He-who-protected-Railway-workers.[xii]

The higher echelons of the East African Railways and Harbours were staffed by Europeans, as were the supervisory roles in each department. The claim that 'unskilled and semi-skilled labour is provided by the Africans; skilled labour, retail trading and clerical duties are the most important Asian occupations; whilst Europeans provide management and supervision and highly skilled labour'[xiii] remained true throughout the colonial period. The disparity in income levels was great. While the majority of European men earned between £600 and £1,200 per annum, Asian men were said to earn between £150 and £600. This led to an irreconcilable gulf; so too did the fact acknowledged in the colonial records, that 'the proportion in the working age was lower, and the percentage of children was a great deal higher ... this meant that the Indian community as a whole was supported by a smaller number of workers whose output had to be shared over a large number of dependants.[xiv] The African communities were considered to be beyond the pale, demonstrated by the fact that separate retail price indices were kept by the colonial government, as 'it would not be possible in a multi-racial [sic] Colony such as Kenya to maintain only one cost of living index, for the standard of living of the three principal races all differ.'[xv]

By the time Harshad joined the East African Railways and Harbours, there was already in place a stratum of older men who were established workers – Sikhs in the engineering department, Patels as stationmasters, Goans as railway cooks and Punjabi–Gujarati caste members in office work. Harshad and his friends occupied subordinate positions in public services, and they were able to observe the minutiae of social etiquette and comportment that took place around them. Literate in English, and having access to the world of letters, they were also able to interpret the ways in which the administration ran its affairs, as memoranda, bills and ledgers passed through their hands. Answerable to English superiors, sitting enclosed within an Asian space, and dealing regularly with African staff who occupied the lowest rungs, Harshad took a lively interest in the political implications of the way the system ran.

In 1948, the year Harshad started working, clerical workers formed twenty per cent of the population of Asian men employed in Kenya. By 1962, they formed thirty-two per cent and numbered 11,836 men. While Goans and Parsees had initially been the first recruits to this type of job, the sector quickly expanded to include all those with the necessary academic skills.[xvi] This group continued to have a curious faith in British fairness and British justice, even when evidence to the contrary was everywhere visible. The imperial regime harnessed its energies, and it found its moorings in the emergence from highly stratified caste-communities (which were predicated on patronage, privilege and the exercise of unpredictable favours) into a more bureaucratically ordered world centred on work. Harshad put a tremendous stress on the value of education, and eagerly debated the tumultuous changes taking place in the world around him. Newspapers were scoured and strong positions were taken on each editorial. BBC radio was the hub around which he congregated with his peers. This clerical section enjoyed the world of communications that their jobs opened up for them, and they mapped the earth from this vantage point. The *National Geographic* remains a favourite read amongst many of them today.

Having become the family *bhakhri* earner, Harshad quickly attached himself to his job in the East African Railways Office, a dun-coloured building adjoining the railway station. The second son, Ramesh, volunteered within a year to forego further education, and took up a post in the East African Postal and Telegraphic Service: counting the words of a telegraph, looking up the country charges, sending them off; a sense of urgency pervaded the routine of his work. Meanwhile, Harshad became aware, sitting at his desk, of the bustle and activity of each of the stations. Checking up on the railway systems accounts, counting the numbers of tickets issued from the returns, tallying the charges, examining the excess fares invoiced, keeping an eye on the income and expenditure of every junction in Kenya, Uganda and Tanganyika, he got to know the stations intimately. Both brothers were active union members, and their sense of ownership of their job remains profound even in retirement. This pride in a job done well has been transmitted in their bearing, in their everyday language, and is very much a part of their real identity. So much so that my sister and I grew up aware that we were *real* railway children, far superior to those created by the writer who (as later I discovered) had moved within the Fabian socialist circle – *they* only lived by the railway. We had a railway pass which allowed us to travel on the trains any time we liked, long distance, from Nairobi to Mombasa to Dar es Salaam, free of charge, for our father was a railway worker. The smells of a railway station, the sight of a train gearing itself for a journey – shunting, wheezing, drawing in water, tooting – evokes and reconstitutes the memory of standing on the platform with a metal trunk, secure in the childlike knowledge that the railway system belonged to us.

Today, having reached an age when memories of the distant past are closer than the events that took place the day before yesterday, Harshad can recite in his dreams the code numbers given to each railway station: Simba Station, number 29; Tsavo Station, number 19; Kilindini, number 2; Changamwe, 3; Miritini, Mariakani, Morendat. Meanwhile, my own self-identity as a child of the railways has shifted as I have learnt that railways have actively contributed to the making of famines, that trains do not simply constitute a world of enchantment (as I believed, when, in the early morning light, rocked by the rhythm of the train, I watched gazelles run past, swift in their grace) and that they have carried human cargo to annihilation (Auschwitz and Birkenau in the Nazi era, the Amritsar–Lahore line in 1947). This knowledge sits sharply within me, as do all forms of knowledge which shatter, irrevocably, a childlike view based on the magic of the world.

Harshad and Ramesh took to their jobs with zest working within the imperial labour regime with methodical meticulousness. However, I am well aware of the fate of those who were resistant to the disciplining of body, mind and spirit which characterised the same imperial work regime. The floggings recorded by those who have written the history of the Maji Maji rebellion in German East Africa (1905–7) are just one of many examples of the brutal punishment of those not wedded to producing ever greater surpluses. The tale of the Maji Maji rebels is one of blood-curdling courage, as people rose up against enforced labour when the conscription of male workers for the harvesting of the cotton crop under the supervision of the hated *akidas* (agents) became unbearable. The rebels met the imperial bullets with faith in the *maji* (water) that was rubbed on their bodies after being blessed by the prophet Kinjikitele. In an age when the power of a millenarian faith could be mown down by a simple and cruel use of military might, the believers in the *maji* perished. Women and children were made to sit at the front to watch the public executions of the rebels. The German government then instituted a scorched earth policy to destroy the remarkable support the rebels commanded in the countryside. Nearly a million people died of the famine which accompanied the food shortages: men were reported to have denied their children and wives, and some men who had deserted their wives during the famine had to pay a second dowry to the parents when they were later reunited.[xvii] At the severest point, there had been no one to bury the corpses. The tale of the vengefully inflicted famine which was known as the Fugufugu – 'In my view only hunger and want can bring about a final submission,' declared a military commander in October 1905[xviii] – is one of diabolical evil, in which starvation was consciously utilised as a weapon against those who had dared revolt against an inhumane system.

My family has never experienced the levels of starvation found in times of famine. May no one *ever* experience this. The spectacles of the plundering of despair by the powerful and of the breakdown in personal, intimate relationships are the hallmarks of periods of starvation in history. And the final irony – which makes me sit for a moment in which the very breath that I take is stilled – is that those starved over a long period are claimed by death at the very time when food becomes available, for their bodies, shrunken and emaciated, are no longer able to tolerate nourishment.

What members of my family did experience was a form of endemic hunger during a particular period of their life. In large, extended families, where all resources are shared, the experience of everyday hunger is not an uncommon one. I know that my father, aunts and uncles have masked the seven years of hunger, and that they allude to the emptiness which must have been present in their stomachs by describing the way in which they were filled. 'We ate,' they say, 'we ate bhakhri and salt and we love it even now.' They have clung on to this with pride, imbuing this experience with a strongly held dignity which has stripped away the shame and humiliation of the external put-downs. Underneath this, though, lurks an understanding of that dark space in which needs are held in check and eyes are averted from that-which-cannot-be-had.

In October 1955 Harshad and Hansa became parents. A just man, Harshad has retained a clear notion that children have an absolute right to eat what they desire, that their tastes should not be subjugated, indeed that they ought not to be placed in the position of the juvenile poor. Harshad remembers with a wry smile how as a young man he had craved for bread, butter and jam, but these shop-bought foods, newly available in the market place and quintessentially, if rather simplistically associated with the colonial table, were not available to his family. The year Harshad became a father, the price of a loaf of white bread was ninety-five cents. A pound of butter cost three shillings and eighty-five cents. This compared with potatoes which cost twenty-four cents a pound and cabbage twenty-five cents a pound.[xix] The Lidbury Commission of 1954 had justified higher pay to Europeans within the civil service in order to encourage their recruitment,[xx] and although Harshad's salary between 1955 and 1963 was modest, my memory centres on the Saturday outings. He would take Bindu and me, hair gleaming and in identical clothes, to the market place, and from there on to the bakery near the Macmillan Library, where we had *madan-mus-chaamp* and *madan-mus-jarsis*,[xxi] nonsense phrases which he had made up for us to describe our treats. What are we going to have today? *Madan-mus-chaamp!* *Madan-mus-chaamp* conveys a taste not found in any delicacy today. On returning home, the whole family would feast on bread, butter and jam, freshly ripened fruit, sugar cane succulent with juice. Chewed cane piled in a tthali on the floor soon became a mound. As the rest of the family then took an afternoon nap, I would curl up with the book that had been borrowed from the Macmillan Library. My father's treats to himself were a copy of the American *Time* magazine, a Gujarati political weekly, and for my grandmother, *Jan Kalyaan*, bought from Gudka Stores.

Harshad became *Motabhai* (Elder Brother) to many at a young age, and he greyed early too. From my teenage years I was accustomed to hearing him being addressed as '*mzee*' (an honorific for 'elder') by those around him. I knew that in some ways the young man who operated the office lift, the messenger boy, the office cleaner, all had a close personal tie with him. He was not able to soar nor roam very far,[xxii] tied as he was to the nurturing of siblings, as well as kin-cousins in Kathiawar, to whom he regularly sent financial support, and with whose lives he came into daily contact. He did not seek to aggrandise himself, but tended with care and concern to those with whom he established quick ties. There is a fineness of understanding here, a largeness of heart, a ready reaching out to personal circumstances. And yet, my uncles and aunts maintained a distance from him, beheld him with an awe that I did not quite understand. But then I was his intellectual companion, a soulmate, so that when Tara or Bindu hurriedly tucked a thirty-two page novelette under the pillow at his entry, and he said with a look of injured pain, 'Beta, *don't read bad literature,*' I would grin to myself – for indeed stories which ended predictably and tediously in a first long kiss couldn't *possibly* be good literature!

I learnt a great deal from observing my father's responses to the plights of individuals he related to, and continue to be surprised at the generosity of his judgements. Now in the lull that follows lecture and seminars, I watch Gauri, my graduate student, sit in front of me, discussing her forthcoming research field trip and the seemingly impossible prospect of being able to find words to narrate the cruelties of deprivation embedded in the lives of migrant cane-cutters. We discuss the representation of hunger in literature, art, music, and I nod and nod again as Gauri speaks of how the very act of putting the pain of suffering into words distances and often objectifies. It is incredibly difficult to write good literature on hunger. In a world sated with material goods and desires, where the reigning intellectual paradigm has made the fashioning of the sleek, able body into an overriding aesthetic, my father and I talk about the steady corrosion of public culture, of the professional space being occupied by commercial considerations, of a globalised intelligentsia that is not much interested in writing about bodies that labour to feed metropolitan tastes, without being able adequately to replenish themselves.

WITNESSING HUNGER

The emotional lives and political loyalties of my unexceptional family are worth giving witness to, simply because they have formed a large part of the universe of some forty-five odd subjects – and also because they illuminate those shifts and transitions in feeling and thought, social identity and political allegiance, language and communication, which have marked the lives of those who have seen the coexistence of a peasant world view with one dominated by an unbridled system of international finance. While I seem to have ingested the story of hunger origins at the same time as being weaned on to solid food, the constant repetition of the story had dulled my sensitivity to the dark domain of the scission of needs, the cauterising of tastes, the lobotomising of desires. For of course, the deeply internalised norm of rejecting what is not necessary requires a harsh punishing of the self.

My grandmother has practised self-denial from the moment of her widowhood, and has turned it into an exquisite art: exquisite because her fine discernment of taste, texture, and fragrance allows her to determine the quality of a dish from the touch, smell, the colour, without ever putting it to her tongue. Her definition of sukh (happiness) and dukh (sorrow) is as follows. The first exists when life is lived eating in peace and contentment. It is neither the quality nor the adequacy of food that is at stake here, but the state of mind in which it is eaten. Dukh (sorrow) is not having enough to eat. If Ba's world view is encapsulated in a politics of subsistence, there is also present in her a strong moral indignation against those who grow large on the suffering of others.

Although born into a family who ran a Gujarati hotel serving the needs of railway workers in Kharagpur, Ba had nevertheless had her emotions schooled in a village where there had been no

87

shops. She had had to walk to the town of Lathi, eight miles away from the village of Virpur, to find a market place. The daily food had been *rotlo* made of millet flour with milk curds, sometimes accompanied by vegetables. This routine was periodically broken by cyclical feasting. When hard times struck, Ba transmitted her ideas of what constituted happiness and sorrow to her daughters and sons. The daughters-in-law who came into the family had mothers, grandmothers and aunts who shared very similar perspectives. It was a hallmark of extended family living that any resources that were available were shared out. The post-war period in Kenya was marked by the Mau Mau rising, which led to bitter divisions: between those who participated in the oathing and those who did not, between the town and the country, between an overbearing state and a ruptured society. The gaining of *uhuru* (freedom) in 1963 was ushered in with much dancing in the streets and public euphoria. This was soon snuffed out, as the political elite was seen to utilise public office to benefit itself. There arose the distinct perception soon after independence that some people had already 'started looking after their stomachs' – they *ate others*.[xxiii] The imagery of the powerful devouring all others was pervasive.

In the midst of dashed hopes, high prices and the endemic struggle in extended families where there were large numbers of dependants to feed, each married daughter who returned to her natal home to rest her tired limbs was sent back to her marital home with words which encouraged her to do her best to fit into that family – *not* to split it into a nuclear unit. Our extended family life on Roorkee Road (from early 1956 onwards) was centred on the growing into adulthood of the young aunts, and the arrival of children as Harshad married Hansa, and Ramesh was wedded to Mradula. The close sharing of resources – whereby the salaries of all the male earners were pooled, the wedding trousseaus of Hansa and Mradula were worn by their sisters-in-law, and domestic harmony was predicated upon the women sharing household chores between themselves – closely recalls the workings not only of a rural peasant household, but also of those large urban families who share both a close living space and a dense emotional life. The necessity for collective renewal of family life on limited material resources meant that the personal desires of the individual women and men were necessarily trampled upon. Perhaps closer to the grain is that this particular subsistence ethic prevented the leap up into the air, the reaching for the stars. My father, mother, aunts and uncles all became adept at crushing the expansion of their needs, stamping down on novel ideas and tastes.

As children, we were familiar with the person of the *maskini* – the elderly beggar who roamed the environs of the city mosque in the hope of a few coins from those who considered almsgiving a religious duty. As poverty in the post-independence era bit deep, with the country becoming more enmeshed in an export economy, and rural migrants joining the large and sprawling informal sector in the city, children as young as seven and eight haunted the main post office area, running away in fear at the sight of an oncoming policeman. The prose and poetry of the post-independence era gave expression to this.[xxiv]

My father, aunts and uncles, who grew to adulthood in the Kenya of the 1950s, continue to reach out in quick personal acts of support to those around them. They would send me running (the child who did not need to be thanked) to hand over a newspaper parcel containing food, sometimes warm clothing, to the vendor, the bicycle repairer, the wife of the man who ran the small kiosk who had left her *shamba* for a few days to visit the city. I would do so unselfconsciously. But now, having arrived at an understanding of the humiliation that is entailed in the acceptance of charity, I have lost this spontaneity.

Within that second generation who grew up in Nairobi and who now live across the globe, there is a discordance between past experiences and present realities, a dissonance between the world left behind and the new life created, a confusion about the advantages achieved by the lack of an articulated social history, the absence of a swaggering climb up the ladder which declares:

'We are here through our own efforts, we've made it despite the odds.' The flaunting of hunger origins with the sole purpose of declaring a distance, and preaching to those further down on the social ladder – 'Look, you can be here too, if you try harder' – is not a mark of this particular family, yet. Despite comfortable living standards, there remains a puzzling lack of assertiveness within this second generation of family members, born in Nairobi and now living in England, the US, Canada, or India.

Tara, the youngest of the nine who grew up loving the food that outsiders regarded as a badge of shame, is today chided by other members of the family for her wasteful expenditure and shopaholic tendencies. She admits:

Now there is plenty of food, and I have a habit of cooking more than is necessary. I always feel it will not be enough, though. I buy a lot of food and I am always going on shopping sprees. You know, when I am in a restaurant, I always order more than I can really eat, thinking I am so hungry that I will be able to eat it all, even though I have a small appetite. I also spend a lot on clothes – but I don't really believe that it's happening, that it's true, that I have all this money to spend.

The spendthrift with a delicate face and small appetite is a successful pharmacologist in Miami, where she lives in a house complete with swimming pool and jaccuzi, built with the income she has earned. She writes short stories in Gujarati which are finely etched, drawing upon mythology, epic, and personal history to craft small cameos. However, the disjuncture between the plenty found in the present and the memory of hunger lingers on, for the hunger story told within the confines of family life does not find a counterpart in the public narrations about worldwide hunger. There is no mirror against which the personal script of eating *bhakhri* and salt can be held up, deciphered, decoded. Unable to view themselves in the social universe, my father, aunts and uncles have imploded, the fissures leaving deep grooves on their faces.

There exists therefore the publicly recited and well-known story of days of hunger bravely endured, amongst an entrepreneurial class who became the representative voice of the national elite during the period of decolonisation. This newly risen elite then utilised patronage, both to consolidate its power, and more importantly, to preach a politics of austerity to others, much as an *éminence grise* would advocate the discipline of hardship to the nation while belching from a full stomach. There were innumerable public meetings, where Jomo Kenyatta waved a fly whisk in the exhortation: '*Harambee*'. The tales of leaders who wielded autocratic personal authority while those around them went hungry were legion, and Emperor Haile Selassie must surely hold pride of place among these. The exception remains M. K. Gandhi, whose legacy of living a politics of penance remains haunting.

The quiet, undramatic hunger story that my family continues to carry within its heart also stands in contrast to the grim spectacle of famine – in the Biafra war, Sudan, Somalia, Ethiopia, Kosovo – where war and genocide have worked together to create what have euphemistically been termed 'complex emergencies'. Don McCullin, the well-known photographer, found his understanding of his craft transformed when he went to Nigeria to document the war in Biafra between 1967 and 1970. Whereas he had entered with zest into the dangerous task of capturing scenes of warfare in Cyprus, the Congo and Vietnam, he admitted that in Biafra he was 'devastated by the sight of 900 children living in one camp ... at the point of death. It completely changed my attitude to warfare. Here was no adventure or stage for heroism.'[xxv]

His grim depiction of the starvation camps of Biafra made the western world take note of the shocking tragedy taking place there, and also raised questions about the role of the British government. There is one particular photograph by McCullin which remains etched in the minds of those who have seen it, never to be forgotten. This photograph, captured in 1969 in a refugee camp, shows a woman gazing straight at the camera, her face stern and closed, ribcage showing plainly through her paper-thin skin, her shrivelled dangling breasts bare to the eye as a naked, emaciated child attempted to suck at the left one.[xxvi] Mark Haworth-Booth[xxvii] has said of McCullin's photographs of Biafra that whenever they have appeared, they have borne the invisible captions which the Spanish painter Goya inscribed under his *The Disasters of War*: 'No se puede mirar,' (You cannot look at this) and 'Yo lo vi,' (I have seen this).[xxviii]

Photographs of starving civilians *are* difficult to look at, for they demand a response. You cannot *just look*. The act of witnessing is fraught with difficult tensions, and at times trauma. There are shocking nightmares,[xxix] sometimes death by suicide.

The story of the South African photographer, Kevin Carter, is instructive here, because it shows that implosion that takes place in the space between the act of witnessing and the act of taking responsibility for what has been witnessed. Kevin Carter took his own life two months after winning the 1994 Pulitzer prize, for the photograph that he had taken of a starving girl-child in the Sudan. The story tells how Carter heard a whimpering when he was seeking respite in the bush. On investigating this, he saw a small child curled up on the ground, who was being watched over by a vulture, eager for pickings. A brutal image, of a starving child bereft of protection, left to the pitiless attention of a bird of prey. One's instinct when one sees this photograph is to rush into it, pick the child up, and run with her, away from the beady eye and beak of the vulture. It is not clear that Carter did take any action to aid the small, human form whose image he captured on camera. He himself said that he waited twenty minutes for the vulture to spread its wings, since that would have framed the photograph with more visual drama. He then lit a cigarette and cried.[xxx]

Famine and hunger raise immense ethical questions about the responsibility of everyone who lives on this earth: photographers, writers, historians, scientists, consumers all who buy and buy and buy and thus deplete resources as well as creating exponentially increased desires; governments which hold back aid in times of starvation to penalise regimes to which they are politically opposed – as the US and Europe did during the terrible famine of 1983 and 1984 in Ethiopia, when 900,000 civilians starved. This famine sticks in the memory as the time when the world became accustomed to human suffering on a colossal scale, as the television screen flashed pictures of skeletal bodies lying contorted on the ground. These reached each living room in the West with 'almost pornographic vividness'.[xxxi] Band Aid was formed – rock against famine -and later there was Red Nose Day. Wear a red nose. Comic Relief. Children lie in the streets of South Africa, infected with HIV. They have lost their mothers to this. There is no money for them to have access to drugs. Wear red...

I do not mean to denigrate the efforts of individuals who endeavour to fulfil their responsibility to the hungry of this world. But when this takes the channel of fun, as if to make a chilling experience into a safely entertaining one, then my stomach curdles, for through this, the spectacle of suffering and want has been securely barricaded away from the lives of all of us who are privileged enough to have our thoughts filled with a plethora of pleasures and anxieties. Pain, hunger and starvation are not beautiful sights: they are the cruellest spectres haunting the world, and I find the vision of well-meaning, well-fed people turning this into a means of communication based on comicality distinctly ugly.

Despite my huge scepticism about nationalist rhetoric, I was brought up in an era when I had cultivated this so assiduously myself, through following the stories of freedom fighters, that it continues to occupy a subterranean part of me. The day Nelson Mandela visited Brixton after the end of apartheid and said to the huge crowds assembled in front of him 'I love you all,' my hands reached out in quick surprise at the wet on my cheeks even as my mind registered the obvious populism of this piece of public theatre. But Nelson had been my political idol since I was seven years old, and I am able to hear the smile in his voice even when I cannot see it. Here he was, free now and bestowing that large heart on all . . .

However, it is not against the narrative of the freedom movement but against the hunger story that I continue to judge the world. Listen carefully to the words of Fantaye whose husband died of starvation and disease in the 1984 Ethiopian famine, and you will see nationalism acquire a very different meaning: 'After the burial I went round the mountain and left, without telling anyone, without so much as a glance backwards. I did not say to the spirit of my country, "Follow me." I said, "Take me to a place where there is bread, so that I can work to make dough to eat and live. Do not return me to my country, send me away!" I turned round and left with my child.'[xxxii]

Food remains a political weapon in this world, not only in the war-torn zones such as Somalia, Afghanistan, Sarajevo and Rwanda,[xxxiii] but within an international economy in which the power to *consume* over and above one's minimum requirements is the means of admission into the human community. The hijacking of food supplies during conflicts, the differential distribution of food amongst civilians, the ethical basis of global governance, the terrible potential that science has to manufacture a 'terminator seed', and the need to build up structures that can ensure that no one remains hungry on this earth – these are profound questions that challenge us all. Above all, there is the need to evolve what that wonderful activist E. P. Thompson, who fought against the growing strength of militarism and who gave a large amount of his passion to the Campaign for Nuclear Disarmament, has called a 'customary consciousness', in which 'material satisfactions remain stable (if more equally distributed) and only cultural satisfactions enlarge.'[xxxiv]

EVERY DAY A DIWALI

Having seen his younger brother Rajni leave for England in 1963 to fulfil his ambition for further study, Harshad noted the political events around him and decided that his aspirations for his sister Tara as well as his daughter to occupy public roles would be better served by sending them, too, to England. The movement towards England was a response to the methods of intimidation through which the everyday living space was becoming criminalised in Nairobi. I do not remember much of that period between leaving Nairobi and arriving in Britain: it all happened too quickly, too unexpectedly. I am not able to grasp the fraught moment at which it was decided, nor my acceptance of a move which I had not planned. But then we all experience times when we walk along a road that winds along predictably, only to find ourselves, suddenly and irreversibly, on a cutting which leads to a different clearing.

The brutal silencing of voices in the public space – murders of political opponents, imprisonment of dissidents and repression of students – has remained one of the most perturbing features of Kenyan society. Harshad and Hansa were the last to leave the country, the former waiting till he had retired in 1992 before reluctantly joining his children who had settled in Britain. It was as if he wanted to enable the departure to other shores of everyone for whom he felt responsible, while he himself remained at his desk to mull over the course they were charting. In the late 1970s, as I took to the streets with Grunwick workers, students and anti-fascists, my father remained inordinately proud of my political activities. The demonstrations, pickets and meetings that caused disquiet to my mother brought a bright glow to his eyes. He had nurtured many young people in various professions, but it was the rebel who stood in the public realm, unaware of her body as she held a megaphone in her hand, who held his attention. The years of subordination and servicing a callous bureaucracy then fell away.

Politically, belligerent iconoclasm is anathema to the sensibilities of most members of my family, unlike those of some other families. No, the older members have not taken part in the often strident communal movements of diasporan politics, nor have they aligned themselves to the smart assertions of New Labour. My grandmother, however, has remained a staunch supporter of the Labour Party since she first voted in national elections in 1979, striding to the polling booth without the aid of a walking stick to cast her vote for the ideal imaginary (rather than the flesh-and-blood) candidate, having signed her name on the electoral registration form in a carefully practised hand.

My aunts and uncles, meanwhile, are uncomfortable with the increasing importance of big business in the Labour Party, as well as with the steady but insidious privatisation of public services. My father is awed and startled by the way in which the mantra of globalisation has been embraced by all political leaders. He shakes his head as the TV screen shows national sovereignty crumbling under pressure from the World Trade Organisation. He has retained some of the idealism that was to be found in the earlier nationalist impulse, that energy that had galvanised young men and women into saying 'We will make this land bloom for all.' The elders continue to attempt to grapple with the real and experienced traces of the past, and have not yet found a future within which this can be shaken off. They remain quiet supporters of trade unionism, the welfare state, and in particular the National Health Service, which draws gratitude from them even as it struggles to serve their needs. This generation is remarkably understanding and tolerant of the pressures on the NHS, quick to appreciate the endeavours of the medical staff with whom they come in contact, and chary of lodging complaints against them.

There has been no linear pattern of material gain and social ascent for those who had experienced the hunger story, so there has been no means whereby the hunger could be demoted, assimilated through erasure, transcended, sublimated. Economic insecurity and the threat of redundancy in lower-level clerical jobs dogged the lives of the first-generation migrants to Britain. Bereavement, ill health and the steady erosion of social power within the domestic milieu forms the backdrop of their experience, as they watch the generation born in the land of plenty seemingly disregard and dismiss the telltale signs of embodied hurt. The perceived obsession of the earlier generation with food, which makes them pile the plate high with home-cooked food the moment it is only half full, is at odds with the culture of eating small, ready-to-heat, shop-bought meals. The most telling part of this narrative is that the elders remain bewildered by the surfacing of *anorexia nervosa* within the corpus familia.

In the process of migration and resettlement, the story of *bhakhri* and salt occupies a sustained and sustaining place in the lives of family members. The stigma, transformed into a talisman, has been held through the years, from 1955, when the status of 'bhakhri-and-salt eaters' was shed in Nairobi, as more male members joined the labour market and pooled their incomes, right down to the arrival of some family members in the city of London in 1971, when Tara was dazzled by the motley array of packaged foodstuffs available in the supermarkets. It continued as other members arrived throughout the late 1970s, and Ealing Road in Wembley became an epicurean Mecca, where imported fruit and vegetables from all over the world were displayed – boxes of alphonso mangoes, melons of impossibly huge dimensions, the glorious fruit colours competing with the garish clothes and jewellery displayed in the windows of *Variety Silk House* and *Zhaveri*. The arrival of mothers, sisters and wives was accompanied by the displacement of canned produce, for who would eat tinned *patter-velia* when there were aunts to put in the labour of love? Fresh produce reigned, catering for the sight, taste and smell of those well versed in the art of food gathering. Watch the older women in their white *sadlas*, and the men who look so cold despite their well-muffled heads, as they pick and touch each aubergine, tomato, *valod* (black-seeded dolichos), sniff at a mango or a papaya, selecting each stalk or tuber before placing them carefully in a basket, sweet potatoes at the bottom, coriander at the top.

'In this country,' said Chandrakantaben, a neighbour from Nairobi who visited Ba one October morning, 'every day is Diwali.' And the women nodded their heads together. 'Yes. Yes. Every day is Diwali. For are not almonds and savouries and sweetmeats eaten every day?'

My earliest memories − sitting on the floor with Madhu and Hasu in Nairobi, eating the family meal from the same tin plate, swallowing gulps of watery, sugary tea − rise up vividly in a different context. The sharing of this meal from the same plate is an emotional habit lodged deep within us, and when one of them visits me in the different homes I have set up, we fall into this pattern with ease, without thinking, and then − 'Do you remember ... ?' We become silent, apprehending the dining table around which we sit, the fridge groaning with food, the cupboards full of nuts and grain and beans.

The arrival in England of different family members throughout the 1970s was accompanied by the reconstitution of the togetherness of the family in a radically different form: rather than sharing the same shelter and resources under one roof, four households began to live within a radius of a quarter of a mile from each other. This ensured a regular exchange of dishes, as every delicacy made in one household was sent over to the other three. That initial period of settlement in the Wembley area stands out in my memory as one long extended meal in the garden of the house at Holland Road, in which the pea shelling and *mula* grating merged into tales woven and biographies reworked, as the children ate first and the women last. Evening clouds peered down to watch the older women singing folk songs, while the teenagers kept a supercilious distance, and the nursery-going children staunchly refused to recite Gujarati rhymes, preferring 'Row, row, row the boat'. The lengthy summer days were spent in picnics for which Haba drove us all to Richmond Park, Epping Forest, Southend-on-Sea. These gave way to the chill of winter, which made the *bhajias* and *parathas* fried in hot oil taste all the better. As the flavour of roasted chestnuts was discovered on Oxford Street during the Christmas rush, and novel recipes were concocted to enliven the dreaded Brussels sprout, the story of *bhakhri* and salt snuggled on the tongue alongside the newly acquired tastes.

The family story of hunger, linked with the story of a mother who felt the pain of meting out a meagre meal to her nine children, has left an imprint on the culture of the family food table. An inordinate importance is placed on ensuring that the next generation is well fed. It is almost as if a spectacle of historical restitution is being enacted on a daily basis, in which mothers in particular are locked in a battle to tilt the scales away from the memory of a wounded maternal love. The public ethos deeply inculcated by Harshad, of not eating the world is linked with rectifying the past through an undesired over-compensation in the present within the home. We are not, however, dealing with issues concerned with the legal system, but with deep-seated intimate formations in the mind and heart, where the memory of children who remained hungry from between 1948 and 1955 is wreaked upon others around us. And here, I know that it is not simply a question of tilting the world away from the hunger story, but also of reminding those who are far removed from it of its palpable force.

I find myself narrating a tale that parallels the *bhakhri*-and-salt story to my sister's children, Suchi and Moonie, as they leave a late breakfast table with their plates full of uneaten toast. 'Did you know that bread and butter was craved by Dada when he was young?' I say. Suchi interrupts with a question which shows her fine sense of time: 'Parimasi, is that because it was *new*?' 'Yes, it was associated with British rule, and our family could not have afforded it then. But you know, when your Mum and I were little, he used to take us every Saturday to a bakery, and

each of us would choose a tiny cupcake. We knew not to take
the big ones...'

THE MAGICAL CONJURING OF FOOD

While the hunger story retains its sharpness of meaning, my
own memory does not encompass the experience of a child
craving for unattainable foods. Growing up in a period of family
history when material circumstances had improved enough for
us to be able to savour bowls full of fresh mango juice, bhajias
from Maru takeaway, ice cream bought at the entrance to the
drive-in cinema, I cannot remember going hungry. And yet –
the stories that have kept on surfacing since I began writing this
book revolve around the relationship of a little girl deprived of
food with a dosima who conjured up the choicest dishes for her.
The stories narrated to me in my childhood, derived from an
oral tradition, often concerned a hungry little girl, forced to
wash cooking utensils which contained the remnants of morsels
denied to her by a wicked stepmother. These stories remain as
significant markers in the landscape of memory. They continue
to evoke the magic of food being conjured up by a dosima who
cared that the little girl should not go hungry.

There was once a little girl in a village in Saurashtra who had
a stepmother and stepsister who were cruel to her. Once the
household had enjoyed eating dishes from which she was
excluded, her daily task was to take the pots and dishes to the
river to clean them. She would sit down, carefully scrape the
leavings from the pots, place these to one side, wash the pots
and pans, and then partake of her meal. One day, tired and
hungry, she ate the remains that were left, and tears streamed
down her face as the pangs in her stomach remained unappeased.
Putting her head on her knee, she wept, for her mother, for her
life, for food. Sensing someone standing by her she looked up,
and saw a dosima, bent over a walking stick, watching her. The

dosima gave the little girl a little casket, saying that any time she was hungry, all she had to do was open the *dabli*, imagine the dishes she wished to eat, and she would find them ready for her. Disbelieving, she reached for the *dabli* then and there, wished for *shrikhand* and *puri* – and seeing these appear before her, ate in a rush. The *dosima* advised her to bury the *dabli* under a tree by the river, so that it would be safe from the envy of her stepsister. The little girl now had some hope in her life: she would look forward to going to the river to wish for choice delectables, and her face grew round and it glowed.[xxxv]

The magic of *dosimas* has never left me. Appearing as suddenly as they were to depart, arriving alone in humble garb with only a walking stick for company, they were always ready to aid little girls in need of comfort and food. *Dosimas* who appeared as *daakins* and sorceresses to the well-fed members of society, came to hungry little girls and young women as protectors and conjurors of magical food.

I think I must have consoled myself as a child that if *dosimas* could magic up food for other children, then my grandmother must have been able to do the same for her children and for herself when this was necessary. Despite having been brought up on the staple narrative of hunger, and spending a lifetime watching its impact on the family faces around me, there is a dark area of fear in my mind that refuses to countenance the *reality* of hunger in their lives. I know that this is the shard of memory that makes my sister and me watch over the ailments of our elders with such a fierce intensity. Perhaps as a child these handed down folktales came to our aid by keeping us from a full confrontation with the truth. And is this not then what Ba has always striven for? Mediating through the magic of songs and stories the harshness of the social world, so that one emerged relatively unscathed from the scars of this memory? The stories act as a safe harbour against which memories dash in waves. They also stand as a lighthouse against the complete obliteration of memory.

There is another well-known story found in the women's

religious tradition. This story contains for me the most enchanting of relationships, between an orphaned young woman and a snake who became her adoptive mother. It also epitomises the generosity with which the poor share their food, taking me back to a time far away in history when gods in human form had not yet been created, and when snakes came as family to one who was hungry and kithless.

There was once a young woman who was the seventh daughter-in-law in a large and avaricious family, in which the status of each daughter-in-law was measured by the dowry and wealth she brought in. The orphaned daughter-in-law had no one who could secure her standing in the family by bestowing rich ornaments on the in-laws. She became the household drudge, cleaning the pots by the river, scraping the remains of what was left and swallowing these. One day, at a stage of pregnancy when she craved sweet foods, she collected some burnt khir from the pots and left it by a tree to enjoy after she had completed her chores by the river bank. There was a snake-hole by the tree, whose inhabitant also craved the burnt but sweet khir, as she herself was shortly to deliver a nest of snakes. The expectant snake lapped up the khir. When the young woman returned and found that it had gone, she lamented her bad fortune, but exclaimed at the same time 'Whoever's eaten the khir, *tenu pet tthare*' (may she feel the fullness of a satisfied stomach). The she-snake, appreciating the generosity of a heart which could hunger for the khir but not begrudge it to her, assumed human form, took the young woman to her heart, and went with bullocks, fine jewellery and resplendent clothes to celebrate the coming birth of her adoptive grandchild.

The young woman likewise attended her adoptive mother's labour. She was given clear not instructions not to stop the snake–mother from eating up her young – for such was the way of snakes. However, unable to witness the reptilian carnage, she dropped the lamp, and two snakelings escaped – but not before their tails had been bitten off and eaten. When they had grown older, they decided to visit the sister who had allowed them life, convinced that she would disclaim them. On nearing her house, they hid in a dark corner, and heard her exclaim, as she tripped her leg against the threshold, '*Khamain mara khandia, bandiya virne,*' (Bless my tailless brothers who are my brave ones).[xxxvi] The snake brothers looked after their human sister throughout her long life. She would say only that she was glad that they had not perished on the day of their birth.

THE HUES OF THE SKY

For all of us who have walked around in life carrying a story of stomach hunger, the past, present and future appear like a tangled skein that is difficult to unravel. The hunger story has also made us measure all other hungers and thirsts against the originary source, in complex and often contradictory ways. It is impossible to understand the variegated needs and desires of individual family members without referring, comparing, and measuring them against the memory of that first gnawing pain. The family hunger story has been transmitted both orally and symbolically, when get-togethers see the table laden with Mexican tacos, Gujaratified pizzas replete with garam masala, as well as *gulab-jamun* and assorted trifles. *Bhakhri* occupies a small but significant place at the side. It reminds us of who we are and where we came from. It enjoins us to repay our debt in life. Embedded within us at the same time is the terrible pull between remaining loyal to the family script, and breaking with it – distinctively, irrefutably. But can memories be obliterated so easily, and can stories be refuted so peremptorily, even over a lifetime?

Each of us who has a strong bond with the family members who experienced the pain of humiliation has made this hunger story our own, in unique and individual ways. The story has held us and we have streaked this universe with its colours. We have dyed the sky with its hues. We have constructed spaces within which we endeavour to ensure that humankind around us is not demeaned through the experience of humiliation. I look around me at a family gathering and am struck at how those of us who were born in the third generation in East Africa now occupy professional positions which involve striving to work with those who are disempowered and disenfranchised. In the move across the continents, and the opening up of vistas which have led to tangible gains, the treasuring of the story of hunger has led to a distinctive professional culture. However, in the gap that exists between those we work 'for' and one's own inner self, I know that there is often a marked absence of distancing, so that the hunger story shatters inside, breaking the poise and equilibrium which we hold with relative ease in public. I look and look again at the faces around me, and I think, 'Do they see what I do? Have we all made the link individually, in the private space of our heads, as we lie awake at night, between the hunger story and the world of work, which centres on the mouth and the palate, speech and powerlessness, writing and lecturing about hunger, the degradation embodied in the laws of tyrannical governments? And if we have, then why is it still difficult to give words to the sorrow which inhabits and impassions our life?'

Vipool, the railway worker's son, is today a legal advocate. As a little boy with long legs he used to come jumping home like a frisky deer from Parklands Primary School. He then went to Jamhuri High School in Nairobi, and later to Alperton High School in Middlesex and Liverpool University. He now spends long weekends preparing evidence to back the cases of those he is representing. From his North London office, he offers legal advice to asylum seekers who are worn out with battling with a Home Office that treats each case with suspicion. As refugees from Somalia, Eastern Europe, Kurdistan and Afghanistan arrive at his office door, Vipool is disgusted with the system of food vouchers through which they have to sustain themselves. They are marked out as 'scroungers' and forced to bear the abuse of the settled populace as they offer their vouchers at supermarket tills. These food vouchers act as stigmata, punishment and control, for they say that British cash handouts are the lure for the refugees – take this away and they will stop streaming in. The Labour Party has refused to listen to the protests that have taken place over this issue, and has indeed been taken to task for this by the Council of Europe. As Conservative politicians try to stir up feelings of English patriotism, Sainsbury's supermarket spoke out against the Asylum Act, which made it illegal to give change from food vouchers, declaring that it did not want to 'profit at the expense of asylum seekers'.[xxxvii] Vipool works to compile petitions backing the cases of the asylum seekers who arrive in his office, for without the regularisation of their political status, they will be forced to return to conditions of repression.

My brother is busy with his work. When we meet across the dining table at my parents' house, the talk revolves around the abuse of human rights found in different political regimes. Vipool is well versed not just in immigration and asylum law, but in that thin web of life that holds the asylum communities together in London, as those who have been sent north by the government's heavy-handed dispersal policy return to the tenuous security of London life. He has recently won the cases of two refugees from Kenya, in a climate where political activists (both women and men) who have faced torture, abuse and rape have often had their appeals rejected by the British government.[xxxviii] I know that the position of migrants such as myself and members of my family is incredibly stable now compared to that of the refugees in Britain, who live a perilously insecure existence. And at the end of the hottest summer day of 2000, we watched with set faces as the TV screen flashed pictures of fifty-eight bodies being taken out of the back of a lorry in Dover. The Chinese migrants had all suffocated to death, and the truck driver who had driven his cargo of refugees into Britain has been convicted of profiting from 'human trafficking'.

Harshad's second daughter, Bindu, is a schoolteacher in Yaoundé, the capital city of Cameroon, where she is also active in many civic organisations. Bindu (Plate XVI) has that wonderful capacity for harnessing energies and building human worth which acts as a buffer against isolated endeavours. Bindu *needs* to work collectively. Children turn to her, entrust their hurts and pains to her. My daughter talks about helping her Bindumasi set up a home for street children just outside Addis Ababa, when she is older.^{xxxix}

Ramesh's eldest son is a housing officer for Brent Council, while the second is an engineer. His third son, Chetan – or Chiku, the youngest born in the extended paternal family in Nairobi – was lavished with the most affection. He is a medical researcher at King's College Hospital, London, where he specialises in mouth cancer. Chiku (as he continues to be known in the family) has already made a mark in helping to bring about an understanding of this terrible illness, which can affect the ability to chew, swallow, eat and drink, as well as to speak. It can eat away at the cheeks, palate, gums, lips and tongue. The chewing of tobacco is one of the main causal factors. Chiku is not only involved in researching the clinical workings of mouth cancer, but has also set up an educational charity that disseminates information on the effects of the trade in tobacco within the various South Asian communities. The transmission of the originary hunger story has had some spectacular effects in diverse fields. Chiku retains the expectation that family members will retain the density of relationships that had existed in the Kipande Road household. But individuals have moved on, as they must, to make their own distinctive mark in this world.

Other family members are engaged in providing public services to various communities. Bena's family moved from Tanga to England in June 1973, after she lost her husband. She too had relayed the story of bhakhri and salt to her three children who were born in Tanga. Ketan, her eldest, is an educational worker for the Commission for Racial Equality in Camden, where he strives to enhance the educational and career prospects of young black people in the area. Challenging the minute workings of racial discrimination is his life.

Bena herself finds it difficult to integrate the different shards of history in her life, preferring to seek solace in the futures promised by New Age religious movements. Ketan once made a special trip to Stonehenge with her. Bena has become knowledgeable about the impact of stars, lucky stones and healing oils on individual actions. She also looks after her eldest daughter's twins three days a week, for Bhavna is keen not to lose her professional skills: she works with children in a Speech and Language Therapy Department of an NHS trust. She has become skilled at circumnavigating both parents' and teachers' perceptions in order to understand the individual child's capabilities of comprehension, expression, range of vocabulary and verbal skills. She deals with speech impairments with sensitivity, knowing just how important it is not to occupy the speech-space of the other. The use of the lips, tongue and palate become all-important in articulating a consonant or an aspirate.

Bena's second daughter, Deepa, is employed in a regeneration programme in Brent, where as project manager of a voluntary organisation, she witnessed the demolition of flats on the housing estate of Church End where she had once lived as a child. She says she has fond memories of a childhood spent around an estate that became stigmatised for its violence, drug dealing and black-on-black assault. The flat in which Deepa was brought up has made way for a different kind of social housing. She lives out in Middlesex now, but she commutes each working day into Kilburn to involve disenfranchised people in schemes that might build up their capacity to affect the built environment. She is keen to make further use of the skills she has acquired in a housing development project abroad, and is exploring the possibility of spending a few years in voluntary work, either in earthquake-torn Kutch or in West Africa.

Neera was the first female child to be born in Britain. Arriving seven years into the marriage, she was a much-wanted baby. The story of her conception is that Sheikhkaka, owner of a grocery store on St John's Road, Wembley, brought back a *taawiz* from a trip back home to Pakistan for his friend Pushkar to wear. This *taawiz* had special properties, and within nine months, a female baby with a soft black down on her head was born. The magic of this birth centres on a mother and father who hungered for a child, a visit to a pir in Pakistan, and a charm that travelled from Lahore to Wembley. Neera is a programme officer for the New Life organisation in Paddington, where she looks after the running of many community programmes: London Print Studio, Paddington Arts Programme, Queen's Park Bangladeshi Association, etc. She is thinking of joining her partner in Berlin, and hopes to become involved in the organisational work of the Médecins Sans Frontières there.

For a child born in Britain or the US, where snake worship appears a dim and distant phenomenon, and where society is said to have lost the rich texture of magical beliefs, the stories of both enchantment and hunger have been received within a very different visual and aural landscape. Those of us who came to this country bearing a vast universe of wondrous thaumaturgy, and those who enter this spellbinding world in a crowded semi-detached house near One-Tree Hill in Wembley, are bound by the stories which have outlasted the flux of migration, within which much has been lost: longstanding friendships, for example, and the ability to walk under the shade of a tree and say, 'We always enjoyed the guavas of this tree. I fell down from up there when I was seven and see – this cut on my forehead, that's how I received it.' Or to say, 'That small room in that compound – that's where Hasu, Madhu and Tara were born,' or 'That vendor who came every day: she has not been seen for a whole week. I wonder how her baby is faring?' Or 'That's the classroom where Flavian Tavares taught us black spirituals – that's where I learnt to love the songs he sang.' Memories float in the mind, inhabiting a body living in an environment where the smells, colours, textures and landscapes weave a very different story.

Neera says that her father and Ba, who left Nairobi to come to England in 1977, told her pretty much the same stories: of gods and demons, of the dosima who went to her daughter's and met a wolf, a bear and a lion on the way, of the young woman and her snake brothers. She recalls:

These stories were like Indian Disney to me. They have colour, I can see people dancing and singing in them, you know, to rhymes where the *dosima* says *dikrini ghare jaawa de*. They are like cartoon characters – and meaningful. I loved listening to those stories, loved the colour and song in them – it reminds me of being stroked on the head at night while the stories were told, held close, comforted, put to sleep.

The other story, the family story, of being poor and eating *bhahkri* and salt, of Ba having only two *sadlas*, that story is like it happened in a black-and-white movie. There was such hardship there, it's terrible to think of, but it's romantic as well. It's a different time, a different world – it feels like they wore black-and-white clothes, there's no colour – just splashes of emotion.

At the beginning, when I first heard the story, I didn't understand it, what it could have been like. But I remember I must have been aged nine, that's when Binduben was around, I started experimenting, tried to live on just *bhakhri* and salt like they had done. It was easy to do, Mum was always cooking it, it fitted in. Binduben and I just lapped it up – she always had extra ghee with her *bhakhri*. That's when I first started hearing proper information.

I remember aged twelve or so, walking down Wembley High Street with my Dad. I've always been brattish, always wanted something then and there – or never. I wanted something from Argos, and I was saying to my Dad, 'Why can't I have it now?' You know, between him and Rajnidada, we always got what we wanted. So this time why didn't he get it for me? We came back home and I wasn't talking to him. He sat me down and said, Look, it's possible to have everything one day, and nothing the other. Sometimes everything gets taken away from you, like it was from us – but you can still be happy. Don't you ever forget that.

That particular story has made me non-materialist. Now, it's not possessions, but I want all of us to have good times together. That's how Dad used to feel, you know that. He used to try to keep everyone together and happy, he used to go around all the houses in Wembley with great big carrier bags full of all kinds of food. That's how he was. And now I know why.

Now there doesn't have to be a reason for anyone to tell me that story. Now I want to know – not the story, but the details...

It had been Haba (Rajnidada) and Pushkerkaka, the two primary male migrants to Britain, who nourished the extended family in its period of first settlement. I, the eldest of the third generation, was a teenager, while the youngest to migrate was Deepa, no more than three years old. It was a large and growing extended family. Pushkerkaka returned from his clerical job in South London to work evenings as well as weekends at Sheikh and Sheikh, the grocery and vegetable shop on St John's Road in Wembley. The family 'ration' came from there. He ensured that we all ate well, and Haba was there to make sense of the wider world for us. He took pleasure in the leisure activities, which were family-centred in the main: picnics, song gatherings, amateur theatrical performances, cricket games, the occasional visit to the cinema on Ealing Road.

Haba did not say much about the bullying that his young son Bijal, who had a pretty face and long braids, faced from white kids at Barham Park Primary School. It was to be some years before Haba could afford to send Ushakaki and Bijal to Harsaddh Mata in Saurashtra, for the latter to have his head cut at the shrine of the family deity. Throughout his life, Bijal has had to struggle more with the weight of 'whiteness' around him than with the story of hunger. He works for an east London borough, surveying buildings on council estates, where he takes flak from tenants who are in urgent need of house repairs. His sister Sejal is a nursery nurse in one of the most deprived estates in Brent – family members have clubbed together to send toys and books there. Both Bijal and Sejal have inherited Haba's uncompetitive nature, and his smile which lights up their faces.

Now that a measure of security has been achieved in the family,

Ba and the first generation born in Nairobi are experiencing the insecurities of ageing, together with ill health and a sense of loneliness. High blood pressure, diabetes, kidney problems and myasthenia gravis, are areas in which expertise has been acquired. Tempers are often frayed, and tolerance in short supply. In the context of failing health, and with children who are now grown up with independent lives, remembering the past is no longer an *active* part of the present: not communally, at least. The thoughts of each individual raise fears, about the past as well as the future, particularly when one of them feels that there is no longer a willingness to listen to the stories that they, as elders, have to tell.

I look at the photographs of Hasu and Madhu that stand on my desk: Hasu's face young, soft, closed; Madhu singing for me at her home in Bhavnagar (Plate IX). Neither is now in good health. Hasu is struggling to keep diabetes under control, and she regularly walks around Hamilton in Ontario for an hour a day, even when the snow is many inches deep. Her daughter, Seema, is an IT support executive for a London firm, while her son, Sundeep, is an aeronautical engineer in Toronto.

Madhu's family moved to Ahmadabad in the mid-1980s to provide Sanjay, her eldest son, with better job opportunities, and the family was affected by the terrifying earthquake that shook the whole of Gujarat on India's Republic Day in January 2001. Over 50,000 lives were lost. Madhu was at home in her high-rise apartment in Ahmadabad with her family: 'The whole earth shook,' she said, 'it was as if I was swung around in it.' The apartments in which she lived collapsed, and there were many casualties. Thankfully no one from Madhu's family was injured, for this would have been a cruel blow. Madhu and her husband, however, experienced life in a relief camp for the first time. While most younger members of the diasporic family find the prospect of life in a camp unimaginable, Madhu knows that they were the fortunate survivors. 'We had food,' she says, 'though water became a problem. We wrapped a blanket around ourselves and listened to each other's stories.' This branch of the family is attempting to rebuild its base in the city of Ahmadabad, though Madhu still dreams of living in Junagadh, where the air is fresher and the mountains of Girnar beckon.

The women of the second generation (Hasu, Madhu, Bena, Tara) have thirsted for love, beauty, knowledge and artistic abilities, articulating distinctively feminine dreams that have borne very little relationship to the stolid world of money-making. My father continues to want to give his energies to building up the economic base of peripheral regions so that they are able to cast off their chains of dependency to the metropolis. He chafes at his ill health which prevents him from doing more, and delights in the achievements of all those who take a principled stand against power and tyranny. Within the third generation working in the professions today, those with memories of the social life in Nairobi are able to frame the story of hunger within the complicated ambience of lived experience, social history and personal biography. Those who have spent their lives in Britain, from childhood onwards, are eager to shake off the weight of this tale. It is, however, not a simple linear move from subsistence politics to clerical work to jobs in the professions. No, within the last category, while some are surrounded by peers who play games of status[xl] in order to demonstrate their grasp of travel, leisure and pleasure, my father's presence and his commitment to the public world, has kept those who are close to him stubbornly serious in the task of improving the conditions of those around them.

There are other variations of hunger and thirst which exist side by side within the extended family and which are not always in accord. There is the need for security in old age, the desire to win a groundbreaking legal case, the striving for a cure for mouth cancer, the dream of writing stories admired by Rohinton Mistry, the ambition to design a computer pack which will win fame and fortune. There is also the compulsion to hold the eyes of the beloved through all time, to have the other mirror one's beauty, to sing of one's life in a pure voice with no note breaking. There is the yearning to take in children whom war has deprived of home and safety, to feed them on choice morsels so that their bodies glow, to grow a family made truly universal by its statelessness. There is also the quest, in the era of Star Wars, for global peace, which can only be approached through a determined fight against bigotry. The story of family beginnings intersects with all these differing desires, and informs them in protean, even capricious, ways.

At times, some of those receiving the hunger story in Britain become impatient with the retelling. 'Yes, we know all this, you've told us many times – but what about now? We can't always live in the past.' Or, at a different time, 'Why are you always so miserable? Why these *dukhiari* stories of suffering? Look around you – it's different now.'

Underneath the surface of the rejection of this tale, behind the bravado of creating new times, those born in this country recognise the durability of memories that linger deep in those who arrived from across the seas. They know also that however many luxuries are heaped on them now, this will not efface that particular period from their minds. And they hover around the ageing elders with a watchful intensity, as I and Bindu do over my father, constantly asking, 'Are you all right?' The answer, 'Fine', contains both the tense consciousness of the past and the ephemeral solidity of the present.

Part Three
RAJ

You must know that in Dupeland there is a sacred field called the Field of Miracles. You dig a little hole in this field, and you put in it, let's say, a gold piece. Then you cover it with earth, water it from the spring with two buckets of water, sprinkle two pinches of salt over it, and go quietly to bed. During the night the gold pieces will grow and blossom; and the next morning, when you get up and go back to the field, what do you find? You find a marvellous tree, laden with as many gold pieces as an ear of corn has grains at harvest time.

CARLO COLLODI, *The Adventures of Pinnochio*

RAJ

He wasn't much to look at. Not much hair on his head, you know. Big Dot fancied him. When we attended the parties held at the Nursing College, and she called him over to dance with her – you could hardly see the size of him, he was that small. He sang lovely. Ee, everyone loved Raj. They did. Our Raj, Mam used to say. He was always kind. Courteous. Never a bad word for anyone. Unambitious for hisself.[i]

I found a faded clipping from a Gujarati newspaper in a folder in his old briefcase. This contained a black-and-white photograph of a young man dressed in a suit and tie. The two-and-a-half-inch by five-inch column carried the heading 'To UK for Further Studies'. It announced that Chiranjiv Rajnikant (son of the late Himmatlal Trivedy), who had passed his senior Cambridge examinations aged sixteen and his Higher School Certificates examinations (London) aged eighteen, was leaving for London by air (*havaai raste*) on 1 September 1957 to pursue further studies. He would remain there for four years.

There was also a letter dated 3 May 1954 which was signed by the Principal of the Duke of Gloucester School, (approved as the Government Asian High School, Nairobi). In this, Mr G. S. Amar stated that Rajnikant had been a student of that school from 7 May 1941 to 28 November 1953, and recommended him as 'a very well behaved boy with pleasant manners and good address'. A letter signed by the director of a pharmaceutical firm, Grayson and Company, which had its office on Government Road in Nairobi, testified that Rajnikant had been employed in their service since 1 March 1954. This particular letter, dated 31 August 1957, testified that he was 'a most intelligent, honest and industrious young man with a delightful personality [who] leaves us to take up Pharmacy as a career'. The director sent good wishes 'for his future success'. Another letter lying near this one signed off 'Yours obediently'. It was addressed to The Manager, Grayson and Company, and read:

> During my three and a half years' service with the company I have had good opportunity to learn something new which I did not in my school career. In the medicine line, I had a liking and it is from the nature of work the company carries in the pharmaceutical side, that has inspired me to take up pharmacy as a career ... I will be sorry to leave you all but my ambition demands this separation to arise. I would wish very much to join you again after I have completed my studies.

There was a careful filing of certificates of merit and work achievements which spanned the years 1941–70, all kept together in a pocket folder. A British Red Cross certificate for passing the first aid examination in Nairobi on 26 October 1951; also a certificate from the St John Ambulance Association in December 1952 for having 'attended a course of Instruction in First Aid to the Injured'. An Overseas School Certificate obtained in December 1951 for attaining a Pass level in the English Language test, in Elementary Mathematics and in Hygiene and Physiology, as well as a Credit level in Geography, Gujarati and General Science. Another certificate showed that he had then gone on to attain the principal standard pass for Physics and Chemistry, together with a subsidiary pass in Biology in December 1953. The letter of work achievement from Grayson and Company filled in the gap between the years 1954–7. Then the years of struggle in Britain, as he juggled to attain academic credential at the same time as seeking work to supplement the monthly instalments that were sent to him by his family back home. He was registered as an external student for the B.Pharm. degree in the Faculty of Medicine of the University of London, from 1 September 1953; he sat a mathematics exam at the Rutherford College of Technology, Newcastle-upon-Tyne, in January 1959, obtaining an ordinary pass standard; his index number for an examination taken in Biology at General Certificate of Education Advanced Level, while he was studying at the School of Pharmacy in Sunderland, was 480/81. He passed this in 'midsummer 1959'. He also obtained a General Certificate of Education in English Language at the Ordinary Level from the University of Durham in winter 1961, where his index number had been F8292.

A letter of recommendation from the Chief Pharmacist at Ryhope General Hospital, Co. Durham, stated that Rajnikant had worked as an assistant pharmacist at the hospital from 1 October 1961 to 28 February 1962. It ended with the words, 'He will, I am sure, prove most valuable in whatever field of the pharmaceutical world he cares to enter.' A letter dated 22 June 1970 from a D. S. Lawson, of Boots Pure Drug Company, certified that Mr R. H. Trivedy was currently employed as a postgraduate pharmacy student at the branch at 6, Front Street, Chester-le-Street, Co. Durham. It concluded that he would continue to be employed at this branch after he was admitted to the Register of Pharmaceutical Chemists, which he was expected to do on or around 20 July 1970.

Amidst the meticulous charting of academic efforts and work experience, just one personally written, handcrafted letter had been preserved. This was signed by someone named Betty, with an address in Coventry. She thanked him for attending Pratap's funeral and wrote that she was sorry he had not been able to come back to the house after that, as there was much she would have liked to have discussed with him.

Those who shared in his life in Sunderland speak of him with great affection:

Heather Thakkar
He'd just sing, wherever he was – in the college, on the bus,

Ashwin's flat, in the pub. The Star would be crowded, there would be a lot of noise – and then, when he began singing, there would be this hush. He would start off very gentle, very soft, and everyone around would go quiet. None of us understood the words, but there was magic in his voice. It would hold you. One day, when Ashwin had flown home to talk to his family about us, Raj and I went to the Seaburn funfair. He started singing on the merry-go-round and some kids came up and said, 'Are you a film star, maan?' He laughed and said yes and gave them his autograph to keep. They went away so happy. Whenever I think of Raj I smile: he was that sort of person.[ii] (Plate X)

Ashwin Thakkar

Raj was not pretentious in any way. There were no airs and graces with him. We'd both had a hard life, we knew what it was like to be poor. When I left Nairobi to study in England, my father said to me that I could do whatever I liked as long as it did not cost money! That limited me rather. I had been brought up in a vegetarian Jain household, but I was willing to try meat, and I liked it. But life was hard. Raj and I both worked in the lock-up wards at Cherry Knowle Hospital as auxiliary nurses to supplement our income, scrubbing floors and everything else. He was very thoughtful and kind. When I was working in Gateshead, he had a job at a pharmacy on Elswick Road. It was a very run-down area, and all kinds of people came in to ask for advice on ailments that they would not be able to take to another pharmacist: old people, young mothers, a number of prostitutes would come into the pharmacy where he was working. He treated everyone well.[iii]

John Macbeth

Raj, Ashwin and I were always together. I used to love talking to Raj. He taught me some Swahili words, and some Gujarati. He'd tell me about the social structures there. He talked about the monetary system – how it was all in one pot, how the family security rested on the eldest son and then the next and then the next – isn't that how it was? My uncle Ernie and my Aunt used to have Raj and Ashwin over, and they'd talk a lot. My father had been an engineering officer in the navy, and my uncle Jack had been a captain. They'd both been to India. My first career had been in the navy. I left the navy at the age of twenty-one, and came to Sunderland to the School of Pharmacy to study Chemistry. It was the leading School of Pharmacy then. It was a badge of honour to graduate from there. It's gone downhill now. There were a lot of Norwegian and Greek students who came then to escape conscription. With the richer students, money was no obstacle, especially with the School of Pharmacy having such a high reputation.

Well, the scene was like this: there were socials in Galen Building where we were, at other times over at the Teachers' Training College at Langham Towers, or the Nursing College. There were big bands that played there: the Notting Hillbillies who became famous later as Dire Straits, the Animals, Kenny Ball. In the summer we'd go to Seaburn with a group of nurses, and we would play cricket on the sands. On a Friday or a Saturday evening, we'd be at The Star, which was both a warm and a friendly place. The Norwegians would be sitting in one corner, the Greeks at the other, and the three of us here. Sometimes, the Norwegians would sing a drinking song and raise a toast. Then the Greeks would sing something else. And Raj – he was always singing. He used to love singing Geordie ballads, he ended up speaking like a Geordie himself. I still remember one of the songs he sang regularly – it was lovely, we'd all sing along with him, and he would use his hands for drumming.

Ho gore gore
O baanke cchore
Kabhi meri gali aaya karo.

Ho gori gori
O baanki chhori
Chahe roz bulaaya karo.

Oh fair ones
Dressed up all fine
Do visit my precincts sometime.

Oh fair lasses
Dressed up all fine
Do call us each day.

Long ago, in the days before indie pop and Asian dub, a young man went to the north-east to study, and he won the hearts of many people with his songs and his smile. He'd strike up a popular song from a Hindi film in which young women enticed young men to their precincts, the whirl of skirts and the tapping of shoes swimming in his eyes. The women danced and twirled, swirling away in the sure-footed knowledge that a small separation would add to the delight of moonlit meetings, while the men knelt in their suits on bended knees, arms flung wide – *chhodo, cchodo, jiya na todo, kisi aurko sataya karo.* (Stop breaking our hearts, save your tormenting for others.) Raj gained an added pleasure from the consciousness that those joining in the chorus of the song were fair ones from the north who, unbeknownst to them, were drawn by the seductiveness of his singing. The song, charged with the gentle aura of a playful come-on, has endured in the memories of those who knew Raj intimately during one of the most formative periods of his life. He stayed in that circle thirteen years, attracting those who opened themselves up to him with his sunny temperament. The waves dashed less cruelly when Raj was around, and the clouds scudded in merriment to the sound of his tunes.

He made two close friends, Ashwin Thakkar and John Macbeth. He also acquired a family, a mother and father who loved him to bits: they waited for him at night when he came home late, and they would have a cup of tea together before retiring upstairs to the bedrooms of a red-brick house on Westheath Avenue in Grangetown. Mr and Mrs Halcrow took Raj in as a tenant. The large family he had left behind knew of them as Pop and Mom. They sent Christmas greetings every year, and cards congratulating various family members on significant occasions: wedding bells with glitter edgings, a picture of a stork carrying a little bundle in its beak. Eddie and Vi Halcrow lived in a post-war council house and they gave affection and warmth to the young Raj. This was to draw him to that area throughout his life. An engine driver and his wife – Pop and Mom. There are stories here that need commemorating, of working people providing shelter from the cold, harsh winds which cut into the body, and from the torrents of rain which lashed the spirit. Raj became part of a community in a street which was full of families who knew death as the miner's illness. The coal allowance was swopped for horse manure, and vegetables from allotments were exchanged for eggs.

Raj grew to enjoy Mom's lavish helpings, the Sunday roast and the all-pervasive reek of boiled cabbage. He'd whistle and play the latest tunes from musicals on the piano that occupied a large space in the living room. He accompanied Pop to work sometimes, where he met all his mates. He assisted Mom in cleaning out the slop. He was not fussy and snuggled quietly into the warm glow of human companionship. Pop's brother was a miner in Easington Colliery. Raj became part of the family visits, whereby Uncle Hughey and Auntie Bessie would come to tea at Westheath Avenue one Saturday, and the next Saturday would expect the others in return. There was warmth, familiarity, a quiet rhythm to daily life. Pop addressed Raj as 'son', and the latter basked in the older man's presence. Mom opened a post-office savings account in his name, putting aside twenty-five pence from the rent she received from him to tide him over. His new family did not exact anything from him save his fond attachment.

Back home, the upper-caste communities were permeated by a stern morality. The guardians of this kept a watchful eye on those who had left for further shores. Distance provided no security, as rumours flew swiftly across the seas, exaggerating the extent of the new patterns in social living, magnifying transgressions. Smoking was seen to be a cardinal offence, and alcohol consumption was a sign of the drinker's impending doom as well as a moral blot on the upper-caste universe. Failing an exam was a heinous sin which called for swift and lasting retribution. These were all ominous portents of a family member sinking into the quicksands of life, from which there would be no return. The emotional value that was invested in this individual meant that he required careful monitoring. In the absence of actual knowledge about his quotidian existence, fears and anxieties filled the gap. Besides, everyone knew that England was full of tantalising young women who lured innocent young men into their snare, entrapped them and made them *push a pram* in public streets.

For centuries, genteel women and men had promenaded along the harbour quayside of the port of Sunderland to watch the activity of the water trade. In 1717, the River Wear Commissioners had sought to transform a decaying harbour and a lower river to meet the challenge of the developing coal trade. Many marriage and business contracts were cemented along that promenade, as merchants, bankers and shipyard owners (Protestant non-conformists and Quakers) struck up deals to enhance their prosperity. The Meeting House adjoined its school and burial grounds, while to its north stood a Methodist Chapel that had been opened by John Wesley in 1759. The town bustled with shipyards, cinder kilns, coke ovens, glass foundries and breweries which had their own wells. There were fine Georgian houses belonging to the coal-owning Mowbray family, as well as dwellings for artisans and labourers, and the Maritime Almshouses which took in the widows and unmarried daughters of master mariners. The Asylum, built in 1862, was home to orphans whose seafaring fathers had not returned home, and who would take the stormy sea themselves as young adults.[iv]

Raj enjoyed walking along the promenade on the north side, watching the docks looming to the south at the mouth of the river. He traipsed everywhere, noting the centres of activity, soaking up the foibles and follies of the townspeople. He paid weekly visits to the football stadium at Roker Park, and occasional days out on the river at Durham were exhilarating.

The seascape dominated everyone's lives. The areas around the Tyne had seen the presence of black seamen increase during the First World War, as the merchant navy sought recruits. 1919 witnessed the first major riots against black seamen in all the major ports of England – South Shields (five miles north of Sunderland), Cardiff, Liverpool, London – in which questions about the exclusionary practices of trade unions, racist violence by white workers and the demand for repatriation of black workers were raised.[v] Despite their endemic exclusion from employment and their execrable poverty, Somali and Arab seamen had settled in places near Sunderland, and significant communities had been forged, with men forming domestic units with local women. The Second World War had again witnessed the mobilisation of men and women in the war effort, and Sunderland shipyards had built three hundred vessels. The end of the Second World War saw military demobilisation and the inauguration of the National Health Service, when a group of Indian doctors settled in the town of Sunderland to give their medical skills to communities that doctors from the south of England did not wish to serve. Raj was often invited to the houses of two of these, Dr Mukherjee and Dr Banerjee, for an evening of song. He'd quietly accept the invitation to sing, chuckle, square his lungs and pour forth:

Bhookh hamein cchooo na saki,
bhookh garibonki sakhi.

Hunger could not touch us,
hunger is the friend of the poor.

He drew people to him like a magnet; his voice was soft and mellow. Oh, he sang beautifully. When he sang ... there would be a pin-drop silence. He would just sing, wherever he was. Sometimes, Raj went with his friends to eat at the Taj in South Shields. While it made a change from the daily fare of meat pies, cold potatoes and cabbage, he retained throughout his life a fondness and liking for plain English fare.

Post-war reconstruction had also brought about a boom in council housing. Raj spent twelve years in one of these council homes in the port town of Sunderland, where every household with a working man knew the maritime, coal and related industries at close quarters. It was a period during which the optimism of the 1950s continued to cast a soft glow over the political landscape, and when the shadow of closures that was to blight the area in the 1970s was only a small cloud peeping over the horizon. Raj lived on a large council estate, created by the municipal expansion of the times, during which avenues replaced the terraced streets of yore and gardens took the place of the back yard. There was, however, a chamber pot under the bed, a reminder of an epoch recently left behind.

The residents of the council estate in Grangetown complained to each other about the young kids who mucked about in the Hollow, smoking cigarettes and generally being a nuisance, because there was nowhere else for them to go. These young people would grow up to face the insecurity ushered in by the crumbling of the industrial base of the area, and when the time came for them to be parents, their own children would stare at a future of permanent unemployment. From the beginning of the welfare era, north-eastern towns had had a lower quality of life than the rest of the country, with an above-average incidence of perinatal mortality, low birth weights and higher numbers of families living under the poverty line. These trends were to continue as a national disgrace into the twenty-first century.

Raj whistled and waved at the children playing in the Hollow as he walked by. He wrote home only cursorily. He never described new scenes, nor novel experiences. He simply said that he was well and hoped everyone there was too. Between the friendship of college students and the companionship of Mom and Pop, he was content.

Raj's warm idyll around the coal fire and the piano, however, was broken by the inert body of Jimmy Shah, a second tenant who also lodged with Mom and Pop. The universe of working-class family comfort and student camaraderie was shattered by Jimmy taking his own life. Raj knew that the perishing cold and the piercing loneliness had been held at bay for Jimmy by a woman's soft, embracing, yielding arms. Without these the darkness came closing in to enfold Jimmy in its grip.

Winter's shadowy fingers pursued him down the streets, the wind sang strangely, blowing music through his head, the creeping cold fingers caressed without remission, and winter came hooowling in. Did anyone spare a thought for summer whose passage was complete ... when winter came hooowling in?[vi]

There are two ways of narrating this part of the tale. One is that Jimmy's family in Nairobi heard whispers which blew across the seas, and they wrote to him to forbid him from seeing his girl. Jimmy, unable to bear the bitter loneliness, took cyanide. Raj sat with Jimmy's body throughout that day and all night long while he waited for the parents to arrive. He read aloud the verses from the *Bhagavadgītā* to bring peace to Jimmy's tortured soul. We do not know what went on in Raj's heart during these hours as Jimmy's voice called out:

Bury my body, Lord I don't care where's at, bury my body, Lord I don't care where's at, bury my body 'cos my soul is going to live – with God. Bury my body, Lord I don't care where's at – my soul – my soul – gonna live with God – my soul – my soul – gonna live. I said all right – do you know it's alright – it's alright ... my soul – gonna live ...[vii]

127

Young men who had been sent out to study were priceless possessions: jewels in the crown who lived to bring lustre to the family name. They could not be given up, for to do so would tarnish the raj. The collective body lived to glory in the brightness of the diamonds, and paid little heed when they suppurated from the torment of cruel expectations. When these highly priced jewels found comfort in the company of working women, then the battalions of a curious Orientalised Sanskritism were brought in. '*Hai hai. No culture. Family of Labourers.* And you know these *dhodkis* (white women). They are fickle, unreliable creatures – they can be with one man one day, and with another the next. And then the poor children – where will they go? Neither this nor that. *Varnasankara.* Doesn't bear thinking of.'

The women got it from all sides, the popular songs of the time too ringing out the message that they had to be kept in their place, that the girl who had accompanied her man down south and become lippy would be sent straight back north to the dreary streets of Walker.[viii] Raj – when he sang and danced to this particular tune – had a smile on his face. Teasing. Tender. His hand reassuring. He had a way of shaking his head if he did not like something. Never said anything. 'If someone slips a whisper that it's a simple sister then slap them down and ... the fog on the Tyne is all mine oh mine, the fog on the Tyne is all mine. The fog on the Tyne is all mine oh mine, the fog on the Tyne ...'[ix]

The women there say that Jimmy was an insecure lad who'd threatened suicide before, to keep his hold on Jessie. He had sat in The Star looking forlorn that evening, and then went home to take the lethal dose. Perhaps it was done to scare. Not really meant ... just a form of emotional blackmail. And perhaps Jessie had lost interest in him because she knew that there was no chance of making a go of it with Jimmy, what with his family so set against it.

Jimmy. And then Pratap. The only personal letter found in Raj's briefcase was one from Betty thanking him for coming to Pratap's funeral. Pratap: a relative of Raj.

My father

Pratap was a quiet young man who had not had many friends in Nairobi. He had played cricket with Rajni in the communal compound. After Rajni went to study in England, Pratap followed a year later. He visited Sunderland and then enrolled in a college in Leeds. He met Betty there and married her. He did not announce his marriage to his family for a whole year. Rajni knew of course. He used to visit them. Pratap then asked Rajni to write home with the news. He did. Pratap's family cut him off. Kabisa. No letters. No contact. When he had left to study abroad, it had been 'Pratap, Pratap, Pratap'. After news of his marriage, his name was never uttered. He wrote to say that he would like to come home and see all of them. The father replied asking him never to show his face – ever. They did not even inform him of his mother's death. The man died early himself, his face lined with grief. A young man who had had wavy hair and shy manners. Rajni attended the funeral in Coventry.

Jimmy and Pratap: one lived in close proximity to Raj, the other grew up with him, a partner in childhood games. The only personal letter found in Raj's briefcase was one from Betty, thanking him for coming to Pratap's funeral and saying that she was sorry he had not been able to come back to the house after that, as there was much that she would have liked to have discussed with him. A letter buried under the certificates of achievement. Remnants of wounds that he had kept hidden inside.

Betty, Jessie, Heather, Hilda. They warmed the men who were in a far-off land, where there was no sister to smile at them, no mother to trace the hurts. One of these, lacking the companionship in which Raj had been enveloped, had been so lonely that he had taken to wandering the grounds of a cemetery, reading aloud the verses on tombstones, before Hilda came into his life.

POPAT BHUKHIYO NATTHI,
POPAT TARSIO NATTHI

Once upon a time there was a green *popat*, a parrot bright of eyes with shimmering feathers that he preened. He would sit on the branch of a tree and sing – bringing a smile to the ageing neighbours' eyes, teasing his sisters-in-law, squawking at the group of boys twirling their cricket bats.

One day, he decided he wanted to travel to far-off places and see the world. He left, assuring his mother that he would send his news often. He flew up and up, ever higher, and his mother and sisters flapped their wings at him till he was no more than a green fleck on the horizon. He crossed the seas and listened to stories of stormy passages from guillemots, black-backed gulls and cormorants, of days of hardship and of the young who tumbled into the crashing waves of the sea when the cliffs crumbled. He learnt to whistle with the oyster-catchers when they gave their piping performance, and he heard the dejected grey plovers emit their three-bar 'tee–oo–ee' notes in winter. Once, he heard the liquid song of a golden plover in the moorland, and its mournful sound made him hold his face between his wings. He visited a puffinry where he enjoyed the close network of living and noisy games that he encountered in the colony. He traversed across the rivers and watched the camouflaged pintail guarding her nest from predators. His mother came to his mind, but he pushed the thought away and sang his songs to those around him. He wanted to send a message back, but how was he to describe the new languages he had learnt, the new foods that he had tasted and the new song-mates that he had found? Would they understand or would they think he had left them far behind when they were often in his eyes, blurring his vision? He continued on his journey.

He met black-throated divers, waders, herons and warblers.

He encountered a shag who had fallen on hard times. He sympathised, for he knew what it was like to survive on meagre fare. But how could he tell that to those back on the home branch? He eyed the snow-white doves, cosy in their dovecote, and then slowly turned away and flew in the other direction. He gave a start and cocked his head to listen intently. There was a sound that reminded him of home and it came from the direction of the south-easterly winds. It was the sound of cowbells, and quick as a flash he darted over and sang:

Gaiyona govad, gaiyona govad,
Maari mane keje,
maara bapne keje,
Popat bhukhio nathi, popat tarsio nathi,
Popat ambani daad,
Popat sarovarni paad,
Popat kachi keri khai,
Popat paaki keri khai,
Popat majaa kare.

Cowherd oh cowherd,
Inform my mother,
my father tell,
The Parrot is neither hungry nor thirsty,
The Parrot on the branch of a mango tree,
The Parrot who is across the sea
enjoys eating green mangoes
and ripe ones,
The Parrot is making merry.[x]

Rajni was a beautiful little boy. He was his father's favourite. He learnt to crawl on all fours and his father took him to the studio to have him photographed. Rajni never liked conflict. He would not want to get involved. He would stand in front of the mirror and sing to himself. Everyone laughed at him and said he was *chaskel*, mad. All he wanted was a quiet life. Whenever an argument developed, he would stand in front of the mirror and sing...

When the green parrot with the red beak returned home, he circled round the place that had appeared vast and verdant to him when he last perched on that branch there. It now seemed small and stubbly. He circled again, gave a low call, and his wings rained down pieces of gold. He caught sight of his mother. Her eyes were dim from watching the skies for him, and she was oblivious to the dancing flecks of gold. With a wrench, he saw that she looked old and fragile. He flew down and touched her feet.

CATHERINE COOKSON COUNTRY

Five miles north of Sunderland lies the town of South Shields; a few miles west of Shields, along the Tyne, are Jarrow, Hebburn, and further upriver, Gateshead. The towns of Wallsend, Willington Quay and Newcastle are to be found on the other bank of the Tyne. All along the roads are signs that announce that this is Catherine Cookson country. This is the area that Raj left in 1971 to settle in London. His younger brother Sharad, who joined him in 1964 to live with Pop and Mom, has continued to live in Sunderland. Sharad married a nurse, Hilda Crompton, and they have two children, Sarita and Sumir. Both are now grown up and doing well: Sarita has a job as a medical rep in Edinburgh, and Sumir is preparing to go to university. Sharad is a Justice of the Peace in Sunderland, where he presides over a youth court. Recently, he had a case brought before him of a thirteen-year-old who had found himself locked in a rubbish skip outside a Macdonald's restaurant, while he had been rummaging for food inside it. A policeman testified in court that the young lad had been found in the skip, 'intoxicated on solvents'.

When the food gatherer was asked by the JP to give his birth date, he replied 'The seventeenth of July.' When this was followed up by a question as to which year, he looked the same JP straight in the face and said 'Every year.'

In order to make sense of Raj's life in the north-east, which retained its symbolic power well after he had left it, one must understand the thick density of the encounter between a student who came from outside, and the cultural milieu into which he entered. While Raj showed a ready willingness to be enfolded within this, and more significantly, found real relationships which made this possible, the weight of historical tensions was nevertheless palpable in the very air that he breathed: that subtle but unmistakable stress which was embodied in the meeting that took place between a student from the south and a woman from the north. While the two looked at each other with quick, curious glances, there was also present around them an external and subterranean world within which lay the ghost of what was known to the upper castes as *varnasankara* and to established white society as miscegenation. One of the novels of the popular writer, Catherine Cookson, is particularly useful in exploring the workings of this fearful and hate-filled view of this particular milieu. The novel in question lays bare the inner psyche of the north-eastern working class in the way it conceptualises not the inter-racial relationship itself, but its social consequences.

Catherine Cookson's books, both autobiographical and fictional, are important because they delineate those issues unspoken in labour and socialist history: the prejudices permeating working-class communities, and the endemic abuse of the most powerless members of these communities. Catherine Cookson wrote of her mother in *Our Kate* that 'the life she was made to endure because of me would have driven anyone less strong not only to drink but into the madhouse. The cruelty of the bigoted poor has to be witnessed to be believed. It has to be lived to be understood.'[xi]

Cookson's fictional writing has the universe of north-eastern communities at its core, and the remarkable outpouring of books even in the midst of deteriorating health is stamped by one central tenet. This is her abiding faith in the ability of working-class girls and boys, who grow up in querulous, squalid conditions, to escape their moorings by attaining the heterosexual love of a loyal and rugged life-partner. There is a tension in the fiction between the fantasy, sometimes realised, of obtaining a refined and wealthy love, and the longing for what is conceived as a raw and passionate attachment to a working-class man, as in *The Rag Nymph* and *The Girl*. One should be wary of categorising Cookson's work within the domain of schmaltzy melodrama which speaks specifically to the imagination of young working women and ageing, drained housewives. There is an ineluctable texture in the writing that brings one to a familiarity with the smell, space, look and gesture of both the brutalised and the escapee within the landscape of working-class life in the north-east of England.

Catherine Cookson's third book was entitled *Colour Blind*: it was written after *Kate Hannigan* and before *Maggie Rowan*, and it was published in 1953, four years before Raj arrived in England. Cookson's popular novel, which was subsequently made into a major film, explored the 'colour question' in the north-east, where the black citizenry continues to be called 'foreigners' in everyday communication, and where metropolitan discourses on race and rights are far away. In a popular genre in which marriage is both the ultimate quest and the final redemption, *Colour Blind* (beneath the fast-moving storyline and romance) conveys a bleak and pessimistic view of a relationship between a black man and a white woman, and of the future of their 'half-caste' daughter. Indeed, the preface carries the warning that 'In this story I make no effort to solve a problem. The solution, if there is one, for the living conflicts, the half-castes, would seem to lie in the far, far future' (italics mine).

The book begins with the narrative of a young woman, Bridget, who runs away from the attention of an incestuous brother: when she returns to the fifteen streets of her home town, she is encircled in the arms of a black man. She is carrying his bairn. The prose lingers on the physical prowess of the black man who protects Bridget from her fear of her brother Matt. When James returns to sea, however, Matt drags Bridget into the depths of his incestuous attentions, and violence erupts between Matt and James when the latter returns home after a sea voyage.

Cookson's story then has James run away, to escape being hanged, pursued as he is by a vengeful crowd. James is thus both an absent husband and an absent father. His daughter Rose Angela grows up to experience the gross violation of her personhood that racism inflicts upon her in the mean streets, with her 'ma' poverty-stricken and her 'da' in exile. The story details the young woman's fragile position: she awakens both the affection and the concern of her grandfather and mother, for she becomes the object of lustful envy in the places where she is employed.

Colour Blind is emblematic of a specific period of inter-racial relationships. It charts the period from the First World War through to the slump and into the years of the Depression.[xii] Cookson is acutely aware of the 1919 and 1930 riots that took place in protest against Arab seamen, the latter fomented by the National Union of Seamen. Rose Angela's prospect of finding a job off Holborn, the Arab quarter by Mill Dam bank, are discussed, and her grandfather Cavan responds angrily to his daughter Bridget's statement that the trouble had been started by the Arabs. He placed the responsibility on 'our blokes agitating them not to sign the PC5 form ... together with those bloody Arab boarding-house masters who bleed them dry ... It was the white agitators and the black masters who caused that shipping trouble, I'm telling you.'[xiii]

It is the non-militant, non-confrontational working-class voice that the Cookson novels propound,[xiv] and she has at the same time an uncanny ability to reach the underbelly of working-class existence. The 1919 and 1930 riots in South Shields (leading, in 1931, to the deportation of forty-eight Arab seamen) were accompanied by a sustained attack in the local press against the 'mongrelisation' of society: relationships between Arab seamen and local women were said to lead to the 'problem of the half-castes'.[xv] The widespread fear and abhorrence of inter-racial relationships, of seeing local women marry those who came from without, and of miscegenation requires more serious attention than has hitherto been granted it in the discussions of these race riots. The fictional account in *Colour Blind* fills in some of the tensions and dissonances that were widespread throughout this period.

The book is thus specific to a particular moment of north-eastern history. Moving on from the fictional writing of Catherine Cookson, an article by Sydney F. Collins published in 1951, entitled 'The Social Position of White and "Half-Caste" Women in Colored Groupings in Britain', gives a more layered interpretation of the broad contours of these relationships. This article shows that while many women who married out of their own race suffered ostracism, English parents considered the overseas students who lived in the town of Sunderland to be a more desirable match for their daughters than the Arab seamen from South Shields. Thus, while Collins conceded that white women were seen to be the 'colored men's best friends in Britain', he also found that most of these came from the 'lower class of English society';[xvi] and he noted that those women who came from the 'lower middle class' found that their forging of a relationship with a Somali technician, a Yemeni stowaway or a Pakistani seaman resulted in estrangement from their parents. He provided a graphic picture of a woman who, driven to anger because her husband found it impossible to find employment after their marriage, marched into the office of the Shipping Federation, and spoke to the clerk in a language which he recognised: 'Why don't you give my husband a ship? Hasn't he a wife and children like yourself? Must we starve? Even if you don't care for him, surely you must have some feelings for me with flesh and blood as your own.'

Her appeal to his sense of kinship was successful, and her husband was never without a job after this. The same study found that large numbers of women were employed in domestic services or light industries, and a few 'half-caste' girls were trained as nurses or typists – the one significant shift that had taken place after Rose Angela's time. Mothers discouraged daughters who had obtained such professional skills from associating with seamen, but urged them to seek companions 'among the student body of a neighbouring town'.[xvii]

Raj could not have been unfamiliar with these varied and contradictory pressures to build life anew, surrounded as he was by them. There were many diverse cultural channels through which he expressed his desires. His choice of a life partner would determine not just the direction of his own life, but would also impact on that fine and invisible thread of social relationships back home. The rock and roll he listened to borrowed heavily from black America in order to rend apart the fustiness of established western culture; the songs of Saigal, Pankaj Mullick and Hemantkumar, meanwhile, held a depth which the camaraderie of The Star elicited rather than erased. While he enjoyed a life that revolved round the student buildings, Grangetown, Seaburn and South Shields, his friend Ashwin says that Raj always felt 'very responsible towards his family. It went much deeper with him than it did with me. He felt that because he was not qualifying as quickly as he could have, he was letting the family down. His obligation to the family was foremost in his mind.' John Macbeth, too, says that Raj's life 'was cut and dry for him. His responsibilities were to his family back home. We break up and go to the far corners of the world, whereas you – you are very family-conscious, aren't you? I was young then and wicked: most of Ashwin's and Raj's drinking was due to my persuasion. No, I didn't think he would return to Nairobi. I thought he'd stay. He'd become a Geordie by then. But he was *deep* in family.'[xviii]

It must have been difficult for Raj to 'be a Geordie' while being '*deep* in family' which was both far away and locking in an awareness of his life within these communities. They say he was often disturbed, unhappy even. He hid this underneath a jokey exterior; he laughed and sang. But the weight of that hunger story, of eating *bhakhri* and salt: it haunted him. As he sang *bhookh hamein cchoo na saki, bhookh garibonki sakhi*, he must have felt not just the weight of the family story, but the imperative to remedy this through his actions as soon as he could.

Young men who were sent abroad to study carried tremendous emotional baggage. They were expected to shine in academic terms, with a respectable job at the end as the ultimate manifestation of this, *and* remain within the limits of upper-caste discipline. The 1950s migration of students from East Africa was stamped with the pressures of family life that were both internalised and acted out by the young men. Mukund Jasani, who had been Raj's childhood friend, was responsible for reassuring him that things would work out well for him in England. Mukund, now a specialist in osteoporosis in a teaching hospital, had himself arrived in London in August 1954 on a community scholarship, and he says that there was 'no question' about why the two of them pursued studies in England:

> Our plans to study were connected to the wish to win a better life for the family. Both Rajni and I were in very similar positions. He had lost his father when he was young. I had lost my mother. We both had younger brothers and sisters whom we felt responsible for. That is why I never went out with young women here. We appreciated each other's company, yes there was attraction – but I had to pass my examinations and return home. All other goals were subsidiary to this. At that time in Nairobi, both for Rajni's family and mine, it was quite a struggle to make ends meet. We were acutely aware of this. To have left them behind was hard – there was always this urge in us to make a better life for them.

The carrying of that original hunger story had become enmeshed with the life that Raj led with Mom and Pop. Auntie

Bessy and Uncle Hughey: Uncle Hughey who died early from going down the mine at a young age, his lungs clogged with coal dust. The buying of a cream cake every other Saturday on the way to tea at Uncle Hughey's was a ritual that Raj fully appreciated. He meticulously lived out his obligations to his family in Sunderland while determining to make life comfortable for those back home. His dream welded with those of many other students around him.

In England, the iconic myth of the man earning a 'family wage' was not incommensurate with women labouring in service or drudgery. In Catherine Cookson's popular fiction, the grinding, numbing work of both men and women could be made radiant only through the power of a sublime love. Herein is crystallised the problematic that lies at the heart of the Cookson solution to all that is profoundly political. While stating that there may not be a 'solution' to the 'problem' of the 'living conflicts', the 'half-castes', her writings are at all times suffused with the belief that the future for a woman is inextricably linked to 'being a lady'.[xix] Rose Angela, crushed between the knowledge of the hatred that Matt bore towards her, and her affection for the consumptive father in hiding, was in the end rescued by the love and patronage of an artist for whom she had worked as a domestic servant. The exaltation of the world of domestic service, and the virtue embedded within this, is a hallmark of the morality that Cookson propounded in large measure in her writings, in an outpouring of work that has retained its popularity within the English-reading public on both sides of the Atlantic. Its close mooring within north-eastern communities rendered the world of labour simultaneously as beatific and as the escape route to leisured respectability.

Cookson ultimately wrote an overarching historical drama which was intrinsically eugenic, and which carried within it both the errors of the past and the legacy of persecution into the future. The anguished personal dilemma in Colour Blind is articulated in terms of the visibility of blackness, both inside and out, which is made manifest in the child born of an inter-racial relationship – and in the paradigm within which *that which is sought to be erased will out*.[xx] This is the reason why in a book entitled *Colour Blind* (God was 'colour blind', a well-meaning priest had said to a bruised Rose Angela) the frontispiece doubted whether there was a 'solution' to the question of 'half-castes'. They were born with a mark, they lived with a stigma, and the tragedy would be carried into future generations.

In a region where the murderous activities of Combat 18 and the violence perpetrated in school playgrounds are put down (at best) to a mere ignorance, and at worst to the visible display of a genetic inheritance, the tragedy lies buried not in the 'blackness', but in the denial of the impact of whiteness on human relationships. The Rose Angelas who live in the north-east have to confront this, often without the mediation of sophisticated political discourses, and very often without their parents being able to provide the cultural wherewithal to sustain the integrity of self.[xxi]

In the summer of 1991, thirty years after Raj had left the north-east, where he had administered drugs in a pharmacy on Elswick Road to rheumatic old women, asthma-racked children and young women worn out by the demands on their bodies, Tyneside erupted. In areas that had witnessed over a decade of economic deprivation and political attrition, the homes of Asian shopkeepers who lived in flats above the shop premises were set alight. Women and men of the neighbourhood, protected by the mark of whiteness, saved lives as they rushed into the flames, screaming, 'There's bairns in there!' The arson spread to the derelict Dodds Arms pub in Elswick and then on to Scotswood.

Tyneside was not the only area that witnessed rioting by white male youths, intent on destroying the network of small trading and mutual aid services that had been patiently built up through community effort. Community centres, pensioners' clubs, co-operative societies were torched. Cardiff, Oxford, and later Coventry, were places which bore the brunt of the involuted anger. This has been unequivocally called 'lawless masculinity', as young men grabbed at the icon of a hip postmodern society –

the car – and whizzed around their localities doing handbrake turns in a spectacle of speed wizardry and death-defying élan.

The argument that 'there is an economic emergency in many neighbourhoods where the difference between what women and men do with their troubles and with their anger shapes their strategies of survival and solidarity on the one hand, danger and destruction on the other', is a sobering one for an area in which the flight of capital has been accompanied by the flight of young men into a 'lawless masculinity', ever further removed from the nurturing of life in the domestic and community space.[xxii]

Raj did not pay much attention to these events when they took place, for he was by then the mainstay of the large, extended family living in London. His brother Pushkar was lying critically ill in hospital during this summer of rioting, and Raj spent his time away from work visiting the hospital, after which he would return home, where Pushkar's daughters, Neera and Shyama, would rush into his arms. He had, in a rare moment of introspection, wondered what shape his life might have taken had he continued living in Sunderland. But then he had shaken his head, for he did not hold much with a 'what-if' mindset, and the growing children surrounded him with their calls. When he talked of Mom and Pop, though, a laugh would light up his eyes.

He had visited India in January 1967, where he had been called to give his younger sister Madhu in marriage to Arvindkumar. He had met Usha then, a young woman with a gentle voice and soft smile (Plate VII). They were married in Baroda on 1 February 1967. The two had travelled to Mount Abu together, where they had been rowed out on the lake, and had sat quietly, holding hands at the point of sunset as they watched the golden ball dip down into the valley below. Usha joined him in Sunderland in 1968, and they set up home in a large and draughty house on Roker Avenue which overlooked the river on one side and the sea on the other. The two were well known in the social gatherings which took place in Raj's college for their singing of tender duets.

Usha had learnt to light a coal fire, and to listen to the words spoken to her in the streets in an unfamiliar accent. She would walk around the department store, Binns, waiting for Raj to join her in between her studies. She attended the antenatal clinic at Fulwell, and Bijal was born in 1970. They would place Bijal in the Beetle, pick Mom and Pop up and go on Sunday outings – Finchale Priory, St Mary's Lighthouse, Seaburn, North Shields. Mom and Pop had cried when the three moved south to London in 1971, holding Bijal close on the last day of their stay in Sunderland. Raj, Usha and Bijal shared rented accommodation in St John's Avenue, Wembley with Pushkar and Kokila, Raj's brother and sister-in-law. Pushkar's salary was low, and other family members who would require a place of refuge were expected to arrive at his home. Sunderland was not deemed to be a hospitable place for a large family: outer London held growing and familiar communities, while inner London offered better job prospects. The weather was more clement, too. From then on, Raj's life was wrapped up in providing for his family. He loved going back to Sunderland, though, and his first port of call there was always Mom and Pop. To those family members who settled in London and who knew the north-east solely from the outside, Raj's past contained an aura of otherness, of having lived closely in a different space.

HABA

Everywhere he went in Sunderland, he was called Raj. My name for him when I was a baby, however, had been Haba, and it had stuck in the family. He was thought to be a bit of a simpleton. *Chaskel. Bhaan vagarno.* Mad. Lacked acumen. Couldn't say boo to a goose. No thrust in him. I knew that his childhood friends had dubbed him *ringanio*, a nonsense name that could be plucked up and thrown like a dart. Anyone could walk all over him and he wouldn't say a word. It was interpreted as weakness, as a lack of manliness. He didn't need to sing 'Baby, I'm gonna treat you right' because everyone knew that he could not do otherwise. He was laughed at. What purpose does manhood serve if it is not able to spark forth in anger? He would just sing, wherever he was.

Pancchi re,
Pancchi, kahe haut udaas,
Pancchi, kahe haut udaas.
Tu cchodna manka aas, pancchi
Cchod na ... manki aas
Pancchi kahe hot udaas.

Winged bird,
winged bird, why keep to sadness?
Winged bird, why keep to sadness?
Don't you give up on hope in your mind.
Don't give up on hope in your mind,
Winged bird, why keep to sadness?

A deep song, which had first been heard on a record, but which Haba sang constantly, losing himself in the texture of the words and the music. Haba's being is inextricably interwoven with a particular voice and personality, that of a singer/actor who became the cultural icon of his life. A voice, a larger-than-life figure on the big screen, a feeling that inhabited his core from his childhood to the last day of his life. This was Kundan Lal Saigal, who was born in 1904, a year before Raj's own father, and who died from cirrhosis of the liver in 1947, the year before Raj's father's death. Kundal Lal Saigal was personally associated with the major cultural figures of his age: P. C. Barua of New Theatres, the classical singer Faiyaz Khan, the musician Pahari Sanyal, the painter Jamini Roy, actress Kanan Devi, and Sarat Chandra Chattopadhyay, the creator and writer of *Devdas*.[xxii] Saigal's transformation from being a salesman for the Remington Typewriter Company to becoming the idol of millions throughout India and within the communities settled abroad, was emblematic of a very specific yearning that characterised the dreams of young men growing up in the colonial milieu in the early and the middle part of the century. The journey Saigal made, and which others sought to emulate, was one from making a living within the lower echelons of clerical, retailing and professional jobs, to entering the cultural stratosphere occupied by the cultural elite.

The figure of the babu, as popularly understood arose in the area of Bengal, where Calcutta remained the imperial capital till 1911. The term babu referred to the typically languorous middle-class Bengali Hindu male in colonial categorisation. The decline of the landholding rentier class in the late nineteenth century ensured that this group became defined more and more through administrative and professional employment. English satirists mocked the babu for having acquired English manners as well as the English language, and held up the world of the clerks, petty traders and shopkeepers to ridicule. This was not, however, the simple laughter of the dominant towards the newly emergent groups which they themselves had spawned, and who were essential to the running of the lower levels of government and the economy. The babu term mocked those men of the disenfranchised middle class who were challenging the racial exclusions of the British colonial administration.

The province of Bengal was also in many ways the linchpin of colonial administration, as well as the heartland of artistic trends. Quintessentially associated with 'culture', the educated Bengali male (and his female counterpart, the bhadramahila) was a model of social, cultural and personal comportment. Haba's mother was born in Bengal, and was well versed in the language. His father had been steeped in Bengali literature, which he read in Hindi and Gujarati translations, and was before hard times hit him, the very epitome of a particular kind of babu – earning money with easy grace and dispensing with it as easily. If Saigal was drawn to Calcutta as a moth is to the light, so were many young men to the cultural outpouring that emanated from this milieu. The gramophone and the collection of Saigal records had diffused the voice throughout the house on Milner Road. Saigal became a pan-Indian, indeed diasporic icon.[xxiii]

Saigal shot to fame through singing and acting in the film *Devdas*. The writer of this classic novel gave the go-ahead himself for Saigal to sing in the Bengali film. The Hindi version, with Saigal in the lead role, was released in 1935, the same year that Haba was born, and remade in 1955, two years before he set off for England. The second version was directed by Bimal Roy and had Dilip Kumar in the role of the tragic young man. *Devdas* became a classic, reworked in the popular psyche through the two films and the songs: a testament to a young man's inability to withstand the pressures of an upper-caste landed family, which led to his subsequent decline into drink and personal tragedy. *Devdas* became a symbol of those times when men of the emergent middle classes did not revolt against social conventions, nor stand up for their convictions. They were doomed by their lack of courage: they became a Devdas. It is said that Sarat Chandra publicly regretted having given birth to such a character.[xxiv] But by that time, the cult of *Devdas* had been established.

There was one distinctive difference between Haba and Devdas, though. The Devdas figure, who was weak and unable to take responsibility for shifting the contours of fixed relationships, also had inherited wealth. Devdas had enough funds to help the singer Chandramukhi set up a house in the village of Ashatjuri. The Devdas types were sensitive men who spent time on the arts, literature, poetry and music: cultured men whose finesse was founded on the legacy of landed wealth, on *zamindari*. But wealth could not by itself define this particular personality. Chandramukhi herself had been drawn to Devdas because of his inability to take advantage of her position as a singer. She had spoken of him having an 'inner beauty [which] cannot be seen by the eyes'.[xxv]

When Haba left Nairobi to come to England, my mother says that she felt as if a shimmery light had departed from the house, that the beauty of the home was dimmed. Haba had seen this sister-in-law shrink from the looks she received when she went about her chores in the communal compound on Milner Road. One of his first actions, made possible by his salary from Grayson's, had been to remove her from that compound and find accommodation for the extended family that afforded it better space and privacy. He had his fine senses always attuned to the needs of women around him.

The house on Holland Road in Wembley was bought by Haba in 1972, with my mother and Ushakaki embarking with zest on making it a home. It provided each of us with a welcoming shelter. When we say Holland Road, we mean the home that was permeated by Haba's gentle presence and his songs. Pushkarkaka and Kolilakaki's daughters grew up with Haba's children, Bijal and Sejal, in the same house, and lived there till October 1990. His sister Bena and her three children were in Holland Road till they were accommodated in Church End. Ramesh's family was housed there too before they moved to a terraced house three streets away. Ours was the first dwelling on Holland Road to be home to an Asian family; ten years later, there was only one family, living in the end house, which was English. Was this a flight of older residents out of the area, or a growing consolidation of families who spoke Gujarati and who were soon able to buy their hair oils and dental applications from the well-stocked shops? Monkey Brand tooth powder, Vajradanti, Shikakai shampoo, and, most importantly, Chyavanprash which opened up a child's hunger and provided vitamin supplements not found elsewhere. The years from 1972 to 1982 were marked by mothers taking their infants to the playgroup established in a church hall on Ealing Road and to Barham Park Primary; children learning to bicycle within the cul-de-sac; cricket matches in One-Tree Hill park; funfairs in Sudbury; and, marring the close and intense living, the name-calling and abuse by white kids from a nearby estate, when Manish pugnaciously took on the aggressors, as others cheered him from the sidelines. Manish stoically bore the scars inflicted on him.

For my sister Bindu and me, Holland Road remained as the home to which we returned with regularity: my summer vacations during the first two years of university life, Easter holidays and Christmas breaks were spent in the warmth of familial company and good food. Later, when friendships broke apart and the independent living space that Bindu and I had set up was threatened, Holland Road beckoned with the magic of Haba, and the densely familiar world of aunts and uncles and cousins. I would often enter to find Haba sitting on a red, sagging settee, singing a song in a voice that had lost one of its allure:

Aaa ... ek bangla bane nyyara,
soneka bangla,
chandanka jangla,
Vishwakarmaake dwara,
ati-sundar pyara pyara,
ek bangla bane nyaara.

Let there be built a rare mansion,
a mansion made of gold,
within a sandalwood forest,
created by the architect of this world,
so beautiful and dear,
let there be built a rare mansion.

I had always imagined that he held close to a known script and that the mansion conjured up in this song was simply a well-worn migrant's dream. I know now that as the architect of this house, he worked hard to contain the tensions which spilled out into the small living space, and that it was only the scent of the sandalwood emanating from his own generous scaffolding that made this small universe beautiful. Haba was that rare being – he created a world in which reaching the stars appeared possible, rainbows arched the sky, and there was security born of laughter. None of us was aware of the power he held within the core of our lives, unassuming as he was, till he vanished, in a flash, leaving us to look around and say, aghast: 'Why was I not aware of his presence till he was gone?'

I returned to England from a trip to Bombay in 1997 carrying poor-quality video cassettes of the major Saigal films in my hand luggage, for more than anything else I wished to understand the expressions from which Haba had derived beauty. Seeing the 1937 film *President* made by New Theatres Productions, in which Saigal sings the *ek bangla bane nyyara* song, made me sit on the edge of the sofa, fist balled against my mouth. Here, Saigal plays the part of a humble but charming machine operator–designer called Prakash who works in a textile mill. Dismissed from this job by a stern woman president for deviating from the set designs on the machine, Prakash keeps this blow from his widowed sister and her son Gopal whom he is supporting, for he knows that she would give up on the sole meal per day that she allows herself, should she know the truth. However, the woman president comes to appreciate Prakash's skills in the workplace and takes him back on. The day he is promoted to a managerial post in the mill, Prakash swans into the house playing an accordion, places presents in front of his sister and nephew and then: *ek bangla bane nyaara* . . .

Haba built a home where the brightness of his smile lit up the interior, and the sound of his voice singing enveloped our spirit. It is a simple truth that those of us who came to Britain from East Africa would not be where we are if it had not been for Haba. It is not necessary to embellish this. Bena's daughter Bhavna has described her arrival to this country in this way:

We got off the plane tired, bedraggled and very lost. Rajni-mama was there to collect us and take us 'home'. From that day on he was my substitute father . . . he made my childhood such a happy one. It was full of weekend outings to the zoo, seaside, Sunderland, Leicester. He'd wake up in the morning and say 'Come on kids, let's go to Woburn.' My mum and the aunts would pack bags full of food, we'd all cram into the orange Beetle and off he would drive. He took us all into his heart and home, and never complained about lack of space or privacy. Surely he must have wanted to have time with just his wife and children, but he always included us.

When we moved to Mayo Road on Church End he came with us for a few months to settle us in – I don't know of anyone else who would do that. When my mum went into hospital for several months he kept our world secure. I often wonder what would have happened to us, where we might be, who we might have become if we had not had Rajnimama. He used to come to all my school functions and open evenings. I remember once I was a mouse in a school play and as I said my part I looked right into Rajnimama's face – he was smiling at me and encouraging me to be the best mouse ever . . .

He died so suddenly and I think of him in hospital and know that he must have been so scared, there must have been so many things he wanted to say, worries about his family and his children. He had always been there for me and when he needed us the most, we were not with him. I miss him so much and I never got the chance to tell him how much he has shaped my life. My children will never know him, but I talk to them about him . . . I love him very much and he will always be in my heart.

Her brother Ketan has this to say of Haba:

Rajnimama was the man who built and to a great extent secured our future. I have heard it said that you should never feel obliged towards a member of your family when that person supports you – that's what families are for! However, I cannot subscribe to that view – Rajnimama was there for us right up to the moment of his death. I had never met him before I came here – his only tie to me was that I was his sister's son. The obligation probably stemmed from their time in Nairobi together and their history there. But he never once made me feel that he was doing me a favour. And such was his nature that not once did I feel that I was a burden to him.

Even now if the doorbell rings between 6.30 and 6.45 p.m. I immediately think it'll be Rajnimama and when I go to the door...

He never came empty-handed. He would also from time to time give my mum money to pay the bills. I was at uni at this time and we had no income coming in ... It is ironic that I have not been able to attend the funerals of the two men I have loved the most in my life: my father's as I was too young, and Rajnimama's as I was out of the country. I had told him before I left that he should have a holiday too, and he had replied that locum chemists were hard to find but that he was working on this. I remember him giving me some malaria tablets and I said to him jokingly that if anything went wrong I would hold him personally responsible. He laughed and said 'You won't, because I won't be here ... I'm going on a holiday too...'

Deepa says that Haba 'was a soft touch which meant that I could get away with many things that I couldn't with my mum. He was also possibly one of the first male adults I could hug. This was very important for me in the absence of my own father.' Seema describes him as the 'laughing cavalier' but she also pays tribute to his understated sympathy:

When I came to London in July 1991, it had only been a couple of months since my younger brother Aju had died. I was so raw, and the day I arrived, everyone was gathered for an evening of celebrations preceding Bhavna's wedding day. It was a sad experience for me because I met everyone in the hall, and most people did not know what to say to me, and as an auspicious occasion was under way it probably was not right to bring such things up. But Rajnimama hugged me and let everyone meet me as well. He later sought me out standing on my own, and quietly took my hand in his and held it in his own, not saying anything, but just standing with me looking out at the others. A lot was said in just that gesture...

A couple of years later he proceeded to make enquiries about suitable marriage prospects for me. Each evening, he would come home and take out a post-it sticker from his shirt pocket with exaggerated flare and chant '*shree Ganeshay namah*'. I would describe him as an anchor who held our family boat together through many a troubled and stormy time.

Shyama's memories revolve around special moments of caring when Haba would translate each experience into song. She remembers the weekends she spent with Haba and his family after the death of her father. She would accompany him to the pharmacy on a Saturday morning and he would strike up a Sinatra song in the car, and she would join in with him. They would start discussing what they would have for lunch as soon as they got into the pharmacy, so that by 11.00 a.m. they would have made themselves so hungry that it was time to eat before breakfast had even been digested. Shyama says that he was her second papa and her best friend 'all the way'.

My brother's first memories of Haba are those of a five-year-old, the age he was when Haba came to Baroda bearing packets of Smarties. He is certain that 'the family's destiny' can be directly traced to Haba.

THE FIRST FATHER TO BRITAIN

A maker of the family's destiny; always there for us; he held the family boat together; he was well loved. Why then was he allowed to die so early, his body weary, and so desperately alone that he told no one about the dark cloud of bankruptcy that was looming up over him? A man who had been a father and a mother both, having the gentleness and largesse of active caring which is usually associated with a woman. When anorexia nervosa struck a younger family member, he would sit for an hour or more ladling spoonfuls of lentil soup into a mouth that was too weak to open, coaxing, scolding. He gave and gave and gave; he asked for nothing. Every engagement, wedding, initiation ceremony into male adulthood was celebrated with lavish pomp. He did just give and give and give. 'Self-exploitation', sociologists call it, for he had no one above him to direct his work at the Bij Pharmacy, save himself. Perhaps.

Haba never took any holidays, for locums were expensive to hire. There were growing nieces and nephews to look after, sisters and brothers who needed support. The pharmacy was the family treasure trove. However, he was just not cut out to make money, and he did not do it very well. While he enjoyed working on the prescriptions – chatting to customers as they came in to collect their medications, spending the time of day talking to old people who sat on the chairs placed by the counter – he had not learnt the Great Money Trick at which some are adept, for indeed it is not only in Dupeland that the Field of Miracles is found. Some people just dig a hole in this field, insert a gold piece appropriated from a gullible young boy – and lo and behold! They find a tree laden with as many gold pieces as an ear of corn has grains at harvest time. The alchemy that works this miracle is not visible to the eye, for the Money Trick is granted only to those whose soul is dyed with its colour. Haba's soul was not so dyed.

Haba never made it into the list of Asian millionaires in Britain. The publication entitled Britain's Richest Asian 2000 has pen and picture portraits of playboys and politicos who wield an enormous amount of power over large fiefdoms. The narrative of rags to riches through the setting up of one small pharmacy features prominently in it. This story, of establishing one pharmacy to see it expanding into fifteen ('millionaire!'), has done the rounds within many households. An expansion founded, they say, on hard work and good business acumen, which can enable the achievement of the ambition. 'Becoming bloody rich. That's what I always wanted to be,' reported Vijay Patel, a migrant from Kenya who arrived in Britain in the early 1970s, to Enterprise magazine.[xxvi] Haba was not made of this stuff.

While none of us has gone out to eat this world – we ate him up. We drew from the roots of a tree that bore sweet fruit. Of what use then are eulogies, sung to him when he is no longer here to hear them – or declarations of love? Of course I can write poems, try to ensure that his memory is saved from oblivion, commemorate him in numerous ways. But of what use is this when I know that he was utterly alone at the end of his life? While I am not known for my participation in ritually lavish family celebrations, Haba funded my studies, first at the North London Collegiate School, and later the University of Edinburgh, where I had been classified as an overseas student, the fees being substantial. On my return from research in India in 1989, when my partner and I had been looking for a suitable house in which to welcome the long-awaited baby, Haba had offered to take me to view properties – a generous offer that I had refused. But he had righted my world with his bluntly stated comments: 'Leave aside romantic ideas of living near heath land. With a baby, you will need access to shops and public transport, especially since you are doing evening teaching. We want you to return home safe and in good time. Cannut just live on dreams, you know.'

I left London in 1992 to pursue job opportunities elsewhere, and was not there when he was taken into hospital for a few brief hours in the middle of May 1995. I had not been there for him during those three years in which his health had steadily deteriorated. The signs had been plain to read, but were not picked up except in hindsight: an inward expression when you caught him unaware, which was quickly dispelled by a smile. The breathlessness which overtook him, so that he was no longer able to sing. I had nagged him since the mid-1980s to sell off the pharmacy that was draining him. 'Take up a job in a pharmacy in a small town, Haba. Go and live in Sunderland. You need to relax and rest.' 'I cannut do that, lass. I have responsibilities.'

Haba needed to breathe beauty and music into his life: the

work at the pharmacy, day in, day out, month in, month out, without respite, took its toll on him. Haba and Pushkerkaka both left too early, having borne the burden of settling a very large migratory family in the very heart of Britain. Pushkerkaka, worn out by the long travel to work, and the evening job at the grocer's. Haba, exhausted. There was a strong adherence by family members to the notion of sacrifice. Sacrifice, to them, is when you deny yourself in order to enhance the 'common good' in the family. Those who had lived in Nairobi had done this: those responsible for heading the migration to Britain were expected to do so too. There was no concomitant acknow-ledgement or appreciation within the family culture of the enormous effort which was channelled into making an extended family renew its life cycle. It was simply taken for granted, and Haba was sacrificed on this altar.

Utth
aur utth kar
aag lagaade
phunkde pinjara
pankh jalaade
raakh baboola bankar, pancchi
jaa Saajanke paas,
pancchi kahe haut udaas.

Up
take yourself up
light a fire
blow your cage away
burn your wings
become a whirlwind of ash, winged bird
and go to your Beloved,
winged bird, why keep to sadness?

How many times had I heard him sing this song, and how many times will I continue to listen to this, seeking clues to his life that the words are not able to encompass? I can write a whole tome on the Great Money Trick[xxvii] – exploitation and alienation are so embedded in the very structure of existence that they affect even the gentlest of human beings. But I cannot find the words with which to describe what we did to Haba. My mother and I sit looking at each other over this, dry-eyed, for no tears will come to ease the pain.

Bij Pharmacy in Hendon on the Burroughs was reliant on prescriptions from a general practitioner's surgery on the opposite side of the road, a few yards away. When this surgery moved, the prescription trade dried up. Rising interest rates and exponential rentals on the leasehold leeched him. He was unable to sell the pharmacy: debts accumulated. Then there were two separate incidents in which junkies entered the pharmacy, wielded an axe in his face, and demanded drugs. He had refused, and they had left, uttering threats. It made him anxious in his professional life, exposed as he was in a community pharmacy.

He had had glaucoma for well over two years. His eyesight was badly affected by this, and he was unable to read small print. Driving became difficult. Earlier, when singing had come as easily to him as breathing, he would often sing a *bhajan* composed by the blind saint Surdas, making the very air pulsate with such an aching throb that the stillness that followed it held one in its embrace:

Nayanhinko raah dikha, Prabhu,
Pag pag tthokar khaun mein . . .
chharo aur mere ghor andhera
bhul na jaun dwar tera,
ek baar Prabhu haatth pakad lo,
ek baar Prabhu haatth pakad lo,
manka deep jallaun mein . . .
nayanhinko raah dikha Prabhu.

Show one without sight the path, Lord,
I stumble at each step . . .

Darkness enfolds me on all sides
Lest I forget the way to your door
Hold my hand once, Lord,
Hold my hand,
I light a lamp in my mind...
Show one without sight the path, Lord.

Chiku took Haba into hospital on the night of 12 May 1995 when, for the first time, he had remained at home on a workday, suffering pains in his chest. Darkness enfolded Haba on all sides, and I pray that he was able to light a lamp in his mind as he left this world.

Our First Father to Britain died in the early morning of 13 May, surrounded by family members who were helpless in the face of the ultimate. When I last saw him, he was brought home in a funereal Rolls-Royce, driven by strangers dressed in black. We had all kept vigil in Holland Road, faces contorted because we did not want to see him lying in a coffin. He looked smaller than ever as he lay there dressed in a suit. Gathering around him, we were oblivious of the presence of visitors who had come to pay their respects, as we broke through all proprieties: bending over him, we spoke the words of love which we ought to have said when he was able to hear them. We held Ushakaki, who said he looked so cold and someone bring a blanket ... Written messages were laid beside him, and a collection of compact discs containing the full range of the songs of K. L. Saigal: these turned into a whirlwind of ash and accompanied him to a place where he will have found good rest and warm companionship. In the crematorium, there was one short, high scream after the electric hoist took his body into the inner recess, and a button was pressed. Then silence.

I miss you, Haba. And I wish you were here.

Part Four

SONPARI

LADLI SONBAI

The painting that has the inscription *Sonbai Vanmain Ekli* (Sonbai Alone in the Forest) conjures up a luminous world, filled with watchful speaking birds, guardian tigers and a patrician sun who smiles benevolently on all the creatures of the earth.[i] The trees stand tall and straight in the painting: the child's hands are raised up in both fear and defence. It traverses that dense universe within which a child's experience of dark spaces, large terrors, adult tyranny and vindictive annihilation is both illuminated and flattened (Plate XIX). Khodidasbhai Parmar, a Bhavnagar-based artist, is both a consummate teller of tales, and a painter in Saurashtrian art forms. In this painting he has given visual form to a traditional Saurashtrian story. The bold strokes and bright colours evoke a startled recognition, drawing forth a wondering acknowledgement of the solidity of an immensely familiar tale, captured in brushwork and paints. This particular story is iconic in its representation of a coddled girl-child for Sonbai, as Khodisbhai says, 'exists in the popular culture of Saurashtra as a symbol of every *ladli*, every well-loved daughter. So much so that when a storyteller begins to tell a tale about a young woman, the name that will rise to the lips is Sonbai.' Within this region, Sonbai is Any Daughter, Every Daughter, the Universal Daughter whom Nature tames itself to protect.

This is the story of Sonbai. Once upon a time there was a merchant named Danta Sheth, who had seven sons. Sonbai, born after this munificence, in the mellow twilight of his marital life, was a well-loved child. So much so that her mother and father satisfied her every whim, and the seven sisters-in-law were made to run from pillar to post to please her.

The seven Bhabhis went around the large *delo*, muttering, 'Who does she think she is – no larger than a mustard seed, and yet she rules over us. But wait and see – one day we will crush her between a pestle and a mortar.' It then so happened that the Sheth and Shethani decided to go on a pilgrimage. They called their seven sons and seven daughters-in-law and said: 'We are now entering our last stage in life, and would like to undertake a pilgrimage. Live together in harmony, and take special care to ensure that Sonbai does not want for anything. She has been brought up in great indulgence, and is our *ladli*.' The seven sons and seven daughters-in-law assured the old couple that Sonbai would want for nothing, and the Sheth and Shethani departed on their journey.

As soon as they were out of sight, the seven Bhabhis carved a hole in a pot and sent Sonbai to the riverside, asking her to return soon with a potful of water. Little Sonbai set out, tripping along lightly, smiling at the world. Reaching the edge of the river, she filled the pot and placed it on top of her head. As she did so, the water gushed out and drenched her. Sonbai, realising the trick that had been played on her, understood that she was now bereft in a harsh world. She sat by the river and cried.

A voice asked, 'Sonbai, Sonbai, what is the matter? Why are you crying?' and a bright-eyed frog hopped to her side.

'My Bhabhis sent me to the river with a pot which had a hole in it, to fetch some water ... If I return without water ... My parents are no longer there to protect me...'

The frog was well aware of the cruelty practised by Bhabhis. He puffed himself out to his full breadth, placed himself in the pot, and called: 'You can fill it now.'

The Bhabhis were astonished to see her return home with a pot filled with water, and emptied it in the tank. They then sent her back to the river to wash a large bundle of clothes. Sonbai looked at the clothes dark with soil, and knowing the impossibility of the task, she sat and wept. A flock of herons flew near, settled Sonbai on a stone slab and began washing the clothes ... such washing, such washing, with their wings and beaks and feet − with a *chhab chhab chhab*, and a *dhab, dhab, dhab*. The clothes emerged as white as the herons' wings.

The Bhabhis next set her the task of sorting the chaff from a large basket full of rice, warning that if one grain of rice went missing ...

Sonbai sat, bewildered. Just then, a pair of sparrows flew into the room, and found a perch on the beams. 'Sonbai, Sonbai, you've always had a smile for us: what's happened to you today?'

Sonbai pointed mutely to the basket, and to the voices of the Bhabhis downstairs, who were clapping their hands, one pair against another, gloating about how they were at last going to grind this mustard seed who thought she held such a large space in the world. One of the birds flew out, and gave a loud call. The room was soon full of sparrows, who piled the chaff in one corner with a *chak, chak, chak*, and the grains in the other. Sonbai descended the narrow stairs, and told her Bhabhis that the work had been completed.

'*Arre*, such work ... not a single grain has been broken, nor one missing. Humh, we'll have to think harder.'

The Bhabhis carried Sonbai deep into the heart of a forest while she slept, and left her there. When she woke up, Sonbai gazed in terror around her as the trees rustled and whispered strange tales. Then an animal with luminous eyes, teeth which gleamed white, and sharp talons approached her. This was Tigermama, sovereign of the forest. Tigermama treated Sonbai as he would a favourite niece, and after hearing her story, he gently guided her out of the forest and back to the settlement where Sonbai recognised her *delo*.[ii]

The Bhabhis waited till six of the brothers were out at sea with their trade vessels. Then the Bhabhis sharpened their knives, and with the help of the seventh brother, they killed Sonbai. Sonbai's blood was used to dye the women's saris; it spread dark and red. They buried Sonbai just outside the *delo*, and there, on the very spot which had witnessed the crime, grew two tall, fragrant trees – a *limdi* and a *pipdi*. Sonbai's life stretched out in the branches and leaves to the heavens above.

After some time, the old couple returned from their *jatra*. As they neared the *delo*, the whole household came out to greet them, but there was no Sonbai to be seen. Tired, they rested under the shade of the trees, and called for their beloved daughter. Her voice answered:

> *Kon halaave limdi,*
> *Kon halaave pipdi,*
> *Bhaini maarel bendi,*
> *Bhojaiye rangel chundadi.*

> Who is this who shakes the tree of the *limdi*?
> Who is this who shakes the tree of the *pipad*?
> A sister killed by a brother,
> The Bhabhis dyed their *chundadi* in her blood.

Astonished, they touched the branches of the trees, and again Sonbai's voice answered:

> *Kon halaave limdi,*
> *Kon halaave pipdi...*

Convinced that some dark deed had been committed against Sonbai, the parents dug under the trees. Little Sonbai came out laughing and was enveloped in her parents' arms. The Bhabhis and the brother were saddled upon the backs of donkeys, and driven out of the town. Childhood innocence was vindicated, and so was parental affection.[iii]

The cultural landscape which gave form to the Sonbai tale is splattered with stories of love and blood. Colonial sojourners who arrived in Saurashtra in the nineteenth century to subdue the populace became fascinated by the chivalry of outlaw, by Kathi tales of dashing steeds, of valiant women, the sacrifice of life, and everywhere, the hero-stones.[iv] It is a region that is renowned for its balladeers, fablers and myth-makers as well as its vendettas. It has often witnessed the story of love written in blood, but it also gave birth (unparadoxically) to the best-known philosopher of non-violence in the contemporary world. Gandhi's political fable of love which can win over any enmity, together with the stories of battle and sacrifice, and the magical lore of children's tales traversed continents, carried within the cultures both of those who had lived close to the land and of the merchant migrants. It created a community bound by a specific imaginative landscape.[v]

The cultural landscape is also full of the waters of many rivers and wells, which have swallowed up a Sonbai who could no longer bear domestic servitude within the in-laws' house. Many mothers-in-law who loved their own Sonbai forgot that the daughter-in-law they persecuted daily was someone else's loved one. However, even amidst the terror and the crimes – both of commission and of omission – there grew up many Sonbais who were secure in the knowledge that they were, yes, *ladli*.

Such a Sonbai was born in Nairobi in October 1955, the first child of the third generation, who arrived to the delight of everyone within the extended family. The eleven-year-old Madhu visited the Lady Grigg Asian Maternity Hospital and skipped home with news of the birth. There was rejoicing, though an elderly woman in the communal compound asked: 'Hey, *rand*, are you sure it's a girl? Did you check to see?' *Penda* were distributed. Hasu, Madhu, Bena, Rajni and Pushkar vied to hold her. The young father pretended a dignified distance. The neighbours sniffed.

The first song she lisped was:

Pancchi banu udti phiru mast gagan main.
aaj mein aazad hun duniyaki chaman main.[vi]

Let me be as a bird in the sky
flying freely in the garden of the world.

163

Sonbai roamed her domain, well loved and coddled. Later, she was overheard singing:

Pyar kiya to darna kya,
jab pyar kiya to darna kya,
pyar kiya koi chori nahin ki
chhup chhup aahen bharna kya,
jab pyar kiya to darna kya.[vii]

Why fear to love?
When you love, what is there to fear?
To love is no crime,
why then sigh in secret?
Why fear to love?

Her babbling created great amusement, and she was fondly enjoined to sing one more time. Sonbai performed, holding the gaze of her entire world.

A report produced by the Colonial Office shows that in the year that this Sonbai was born, the government remained concerned by the events that had led to a declaration of a State of Emergency in October 1952. The report stated that while life on the slopes of Mounts Kenya and Aberdare required 'vigilance', the city of Nairobi was quiet. The Save the Children fund that had been launched in Nairobi exactly a year before Sonbai's birth, in October 1954, had seen a total of five hundred children pass through its hands. The School for the Blind in Thika established a wing for African girls. The YWCA initiated monthly meetings for English-speaking 'women of all races'. TB continued to be one of the most worrying public health problems. The Asian Welfare Societies continued their work. And branches of the women's movement, *Maendeleo ya Wanawake*, worked hard to establish themselves, especially in the Emergency areas, where they were aided by Red Cross Workers. The latter found members of the *Maendeleo ya Wanawake* particularly valuable as organisers of children's crèches.[viii]

Sonbai remained ensconced in her world. Rajni danced with Sonbai in his arms, made funny faces, invented rhymes to make her laugh – *habla, habla* ... He became Haba from then on. She was taught to read the Roman script, and she devoured every printed word she could find in the house. Illustrated scriptural texts, English primers, a bound anthology of poems. Words were transfused with spirit, pictures were imbued with life. Sonbai constantly repeated the words that she deciphered from a calendar which showed spectacular mountains: *Sontag, Montag, Dienstag, Mittwoch*. The mountains were arresting, as were the deities on the wall whose eyes followed her everywhere. One day, rummaging for books, she came across a large bound volume of the *Bhagvad Purana*. A particular print depicted a wrongdoer being torn apart by a guardian who was neither man nor animal, with bright red spots of blood dripping off its claws. Sonbai dropped the tome and ran. But she would pore over the illustrations found in the other Gujarati books, unable to decode the script. She pestered Madhu to know what was in one of these; she was read the story of a wooden puppet who was looked after by a blue Pari with golden hair. The volume contained a picture of four rabbits in black suits who arrived at the puppet's bedside, carrying a large black box. Sonbai shivered.

Sonbai accompanied Hasu to Damyanti's house in the afternoons, where she listened to the shared confidences of the two friends. She gave her heart to a trainee teacher who had the same aura as the aunts. The teacher would cut out figures in felt to illustrate the stories that she told: a witch, a fox, a shoe-house. Sonbai received her first lessons in botany from Madhu as she joined her in the search for *bilipatra* and *datura*, which Madhu then offered to the Lord Shiva. Sonbai watched Tara engrossed in her charcoal drawings. She sat quietly while Hasu and Madhu visited Rupama the diviner. Rupama threw grains of *juvar* on the floor, read the signs, and assured the two young women that they would find good husbands soon. The two left the diviner's compound with a faraway look in their eyes. Would He look like the dashing Devanand or the sultry Dilip

Kumar? Would He smile with the charm of Raj Kapoor or of . . . ?

Sonbai's imagination was peopled by the songs, stories and dreams imparted by her aunts. Their departure to new homes meant there was less laughter, no poetry recitations, no dress rehearsals. However, Sonbai knew that she was her father's *ladli*, and she held this conviction deep in her heart.

Ladli: to be loved, beloved. To be sent out into the world, cosseted by the understanding that she was wanted. Her father's house provided Sonbai with light, warmth, illumination. The father channelled his aspirations into Sonbai: while her aunts had delighted in her songs and dances, he nurtured a critical intellect and took pleasure in her independence of mind. He stinted on his own needs to send her to the English-speaking Dr Ribeiro's Goan School, where a large statue of the Virgin graced the main corridor. When her friend Esmeralda told Sonbai of her visits to the confessional box, Sonbai wondered. Next, the recently desegregated secondary school, the Kenya High School, opened up vistas and privileges denied to most young people. Desegregation and a non-apartheid educational system had recently created radical social ruptures. In the previous gen-erations, the dreams and desires of her grandmother, her mother (educated at the Aga Khan School in Moshi) and her four aunts had coursed through the complicated and shifting cultures of the colonial world, while they themselves remained confined within a similarly complicated domesticity. In contrast to this, the aspirations of Sonbai and her sister were suffused by the fraught and seductive charm of intellectual pursuits which broke through the boundaries of home economics and hygiene. Their mouths learnt to repeat Homo sapiens, Homo habilis, Zinzanthropus, Australopithacus with aplomb, while their minds remained awed by the visual display of bones and skeletons. The tools and methods of linguistics, archaeology, palaeontology, palaeology were accepted as scientific procedures, with no whisper of the enormous political contestations going on within these disciplines. And alongside the geometry, algebra, physics and chemistry, there was the incorporation of Cry, the Beloved Country into the English curriculum, as well as change towards identifying migrant groups in the plains of East Africa by the languages they spoke rather than by their racial or tribal affiliations. Over this landscape, the figures of the major African cultural and political figures, Leopold Senghor, Kwame Nkrumah, Julius Nyerere, Patrick Lumumba, Nelson Mandela loomed large, as do towering mountains, while the closer-at-hand Jomo Kenyatta elicited a more sceptical response.

Sonbai drew from the wells of her grandmother's stories too when she sat cross-legged on the bed, absorbed in the story of '*Aapkarmi ke Baapkarmi*'. Her grandmother would pull the fold of her *sadlo* over her head, clear her throat and begin. Once a King put his daughters to the test, secure in the knowledge that they would continue to shine brightly within the constellation of his rule. Answer me, he said: are you *aapkarmi ke baapkarmi* (are you tied to your own destiny or to your father's?) The daughters who were well versed in the art of pleasing their father provided the prompt response: '*baapkarmi.*' But the daughter who was his *ladli* gave the question some thought, and then answered quietly: '*aapkarmi.*'

Baapkarmi – to be bound to the fortunes of the father; to be tied to his actions; to have one's will directed by him; to await his command; to walk in his footprints; to be stamped with his name; to have one's pasts and futures secured to the lineage of his pleasures; filial; vassal; chattel; ward; protégé; charge; dependant.

Aapkarmi – to cut one's own path in life; to stand on the ground of one's own mistakes; to carve out a different genealogy; to take the past and future in one's hands; unfilial; unbiddable; insubordinate; self-willed.

Sonbai, knowing that she was *ladli*, had defined herself as *aapkarmi* early in life. Her move to England in 1972 led to two years of enriching intellectual food at the North London Collegiate School, which continued the best traditions founded by that remarkable educational reformer, Frances Mary Buss. Sonbai left the University of Edinburgh in 1978, aligning herself with other *aapkarmis* who strove to weld the world in an egalitarian mould. The political struggles of the black community involved protests against racial harassment, deportations and virginity tests, and in favour of trade union recognition as well as a just wage. Southall witnessed a takeover by the Special Patrol Group, which defended the right of the National Front to march through a predominantly Asian area in April 1979. In the ensuing violence, a protester, Blair Peach, was killed.[ix] A memorial day was held in his honour. Women, men and children bent in loving homage over the body of the schoolteacher who had given his life to keep the streets safe for them. Later that year, with the lacerating knowledge that the 'community' she defended consistently turned its weapons upon the powerless within its own midst, Sonbai worked to form the Southall Black Sisters group. She joined together with Taro, Parminder, Carmen, Harbhajan, Judith, Navinder, Surinder and Jyoti to create a spectacular bond. Oliver, Wesley, Suresh, Satish and Vishnu supported the sisterhood. A politics was forged which took class, race and gender equally seriously.

Sonbai was chosen in 1980 to run a refuge and resource centre for Asian women in the London Borough of Brent. She gained expertise in the laws relating to immigration, domestic violence and child custody. Children caught in the marital war were coddled and diverted. Reena, Nitchi, Niku, Chotu, Jaimini, Vikram, Rakeshi, Kaka, Bobby – they and many more learnt to walk the terrain of dashed lives while embarking on a new journey. Leena worked quietly and methodically on litigation, rehousing, summer outings, bringing to the process a warmth and largeness of spirit which went above and beyond political commitment. Bharti lent dignity and grace to what were at times raucous proceedings. Anju added laughter. Bindu brought her gifts to providing services for the Asian Elders Group, visiting Mrs Kassam and Mrs Nazarali in a sheltered housing block, completing passport forms, organising activities.

Aapkarmis do not lead easy lives. There is the invigoration of breathing on top of a high mountain, of cutting new clearings.

Then the exhilaration of forging new communities when work and life are staunchly braided. Slowly and ineluctably, there comes the fallout of living in such close proximity. No certainties remained, save the tenacious urge to expose oppression. As women came forward to speak of incest and abuse, of sexualities lived in the shadows and the brutal power of intimate relationships, what was revealed was not simply the fragility of familial ties, but the very brittleness of human innocence. There was a high price to be paid for this loss in the lives both of these first speakers of truth and of those who listened to them, but the price was one that was necessary in order to place the pain high up in the sky, where it remains as a star to light the way.[x]

When Sonbai found watching that star unbearable, and her body buckled, she spent her days rereading, rereading and rereading the story of Magsie: passionate, knowledge-thirsty, large-hearted and dark-haired Maggie, caught between the claims of a wronged father who had always 'taken her part', and the other pulls upon her affection. Maggie Tulliver, who turned back from the prospect of a fulfilled love and a disastrous sea voyage, in order to return to the house on the floss and make amends. Magsie, engulfed within the waters of a flood.[xi]

Sonbai then met and chose as life partner one who shared her inner landscape, and who enjoyed exploring the world with her. But her father, raw from the injuries inflicted on him by a privileged race, rejected his daughter's choice, for the partner was a member of that race. Sonbai, whose father had instilled the respect for and the right to freedom of thought, speech, and action deeply within her, now came up against the limits of these. Sonbai's mother petitioned her: 'Ask his forgiveness,' she urged, 'and everything will be all right.' 'Forgiveness,' said Sonbai, outraged and confused, 'forgiveness for what?' Sonbai had situated her father within the fellowship of free intellects, broad minds and open hearts. She did not then understand that a disappointed affection can take refuge within the walls of a wounded father-love; nor that the security of an avowed socialist and feminist can crumble when the solid foundation of knowing herself to be a *ladli* is removed. Sonbai refused to bow to her father. And he, broken, turned away.

Years later, when the two came face to face on the sunlit veranda of a bungalow in the town of Baroda, where Sonbai was conducting her research, it was not the pain of a daughter's racial transgression, nor the deeply felt injustices of a colonised subject which surfaced, but: 'We had always been open with each other. Why did you not tell me about him yourself? Why did I have to hear from ...?' Sonbai looked down. And then: 'How could I tell you of a journey into the unknown? With what words could I have described the joy, the fear, the holding back, the succumbing?' He nodded. Understood.

While Sonbai's father turned away from her, her mother rallied around in support of her choice and provided asylum. And Ba said, in some astonishment, 'Mira has found her Krishna.' Except that he was not the Dark Lord, and lacked the latter's promiscuous charms. On a research trip to Bhavnagar a curious friend asked, 'Did His family accept you?' The tenor of this question was far removed from the atmosphere of the drawing room of a house in Highbury Terrace in north London, where Sonbai had sat in family gatherings, wine glasses tinkling along to anecdotes and stories of the Calcutta season of 1912, school-days at Bedales, a meeting snatched in Cairo in 1946 (between an officer in the Royal Engineers and a Lieutenant Colonel in the ATS awaiting the landing of his flying boat on the banks of the Nile), London's sewage system, blue bricks found in a skip, gathered up and stored.

Sonbai learnt much from the considerable body of scholarship on the *adivasi* communities which she discovered.[xii] There was also this one critical truth: those communities who were willing to transform themselves in order to meet the demands of a new and brutal age survived to struggle anew. Those who refused to do so died a sometimes spectacular death. One must pause to reflect on this.

Sonbai's father had expected her to excel in the public world, even as she lived an ascetic personal existence, while accepting that his second daughter lived closer to the glossy sheen of her skin. There were other fathers who were more attuned to the messy business of everyday living. Haba. Pushkerkaka. After the two daughters had demonstrated their commitment to a European and an African by garlanding them – no priest, no intrusion by the law, a non-Brahman ceremony which arched across the sky from nineteenth-century Maharashtra to a semi-detached house in Wembley in August 1986 – Pushkerkaka would fight for the two with all the weapons he had at his disposal, when waylaid on Ealing Road by those eager for news of the scandal.

Pushkerkaka: Sonbai poked gentle fun at his inaccurate English and his lack of sophistication, while fiercely protecting his unpolished being, which so easily elicited mockery from English officialdom. Little did she know that while she was defending him from the facile and barbed assertion of power, he was waging an even more fraught battle on her behalf in the inner citadels of the family. In the bleak days of later summer and autumn 1991, in the Central Middlesex Hospital, as Sonbai fought for his life – cajoled, berated, entreated and finally crooned, softly – she realised that he had stood as a shield between the world and her.

Pushkerkaka died on 4 October 1991: a mighty tree, which everyone had considered small, finally fell. Sonbai, who had held the universe in her palm, found flood waters lapping at her feet. The months spent in hospital battling with a Destroyer who had shown no compassion; the pitting of her will against an Almighty who was intent on demonstrating his power; the witnessing of the steady and cruel deterioration of a body unable to give words to its needs; the absolute terror that her first visit to the crematorium inspired as she saw the coffin lifted into an inner cavern from which there was no return – all these things rose up in waves of darkness to envelop her.

Ladli Sonbai, the first child of the third generation, found that while she had been busy tending to Pushkerkaka in hospital, the family tide had turned against her. Long forgotten past hurts of which she herself had no memory were forged into missiles, and these fell like shrapnel shards all around her. 'Who does she think she is? No more than a mustard seed, and yet she rules over us.' 'Just because she has a Ph.D.' '*Bhaneli chhe pan ganeli natthi.*' 'Look how she talks. No respect for her elders.' 'It's only because she is your daughter that we ... Otherwise ...' 'Oh God above, why, why, why, why do I have to hear such words about her? Born of my womb. Carved out of my limbs. Let her ...'

Sonbai was left both bereft and broken. Months later, with her sister Bindu sitting in front of her, the sobs came, torn from her guts, ripping her innards. Bindu rocked her in her arms: 'I didn't know any of this was happening, sitting in Benin. Oh, baby, why was I not there for you? I'm sorry. I'm sorry.'

Choking no breath breathe breathe darkness puff cough vomit water nose mouth blocked. Choking slapping on the back clutching spluttering retching thumping a hand stroking, stroking, stroking on the back. 'Sit up. Don't collapse your lungs. You've loved too much.' 'Cuckoo. Cuckoo. Cuckoo.' 'You're unbending. Love, love – you have to *live*.' 'Cuckoo. Cuckoo. Cuckoo.' 'Go on then, question, question everything: God, scriptures, authority, the limits of each of your actions. See where it's led you.' '*Cuckoo.*'

Sonbai vanmain ekli.
Sonbai vanmain ekli.

The *sarangi* bleeds. The violin weeps. Birdsong plucks the strings, plucks, plucks, plucks. Cuckoo. Cuckoo. The wind whips the sound: the sky amplifies it. The *sarangi* bleeds. The violin weeps. Birdsong plucks the strings, plucks, plucks, plucks. Cuckoo. Cuckoo. Cuckoo.

The music reached a pitch that was so high that no human ear could bear it. Sonbai immersed herself in her work. There were histories that needed to be written, and lives that had to be defended.[xiii] Sonbai was well aware of the history of vendetta making. She saw the shadow of political authoritarianism blight the living space of all those she had written about in her work. As Hindu nationalists in the subcontinent went on the rampage against Muslim minorities, insisting that the fifteenth-century mosque in Ayodhya be torn down as an act of historical restitution, the very freedom to speak up against brute injustice and atrocities was threatened. The poison spread to the diaspora – indeed, the antagonism was in large part fuelled there. When the three domes of the Babri Masjid were turned to rubble by crowds of Hindus who wanted to 'teach the Muslims a lesson' on 6 December 1992,[xiv] Sonbai's entire cosmology, her belief in the totality of all entities and all eternities, was shattered.

The flood rose high. Sonbai entered the dark waters, swirled in them, touched the tiny fleck in the centre of the vortex, emerged holding the knot of lament and life. 'She's a Muslim.' 'No, an atheist. A communist.' 'An academic.' 'Outside the community.'

Sonbai knew that when the fatal fold of an exclusionary Hindu community demands an allegiance which is both disrespectful of difference and genocidal in its attacks on minorities, there is no choice but to say: you do not speak for me. I do not see my face in yours. I draw upon the legacy of those *aapkarmis* who created permeable and open communities by embracing the dispossessed and the destitute.

In the story of '*Aapkarmi ke Baapkarmi*', the daughter who answered '*aapkarmi*' to the question posed by the king was banished from her father's kingdom. She went to live outside the boundaries of his domain. One day, just as the king was embarking on a long sea voyage, he thought of she-who-had-been-his-*ladli*. He paused. Took two steps in her direction. Retraced them. Sent a minion to say that he was travelling to far places, and would she like a gift which would bring a distant horizon near to her? Perhaps he hoped that his daughter would come running and that her face would be the one that would stay with him when his ship left the shore. Aapkarmi, who was busy with the tasks that she had found for herself, replied '*Saboor*' (wait) to the messenger. The father, his face set, sailed off and searched high and low for this wished-for thing. At last, he found an old woman sitting on the streets who had a stone called Saboor. He brought it back for her.

In Aapkarmi's hands, the Saboor-stone cracked, a fan emerged from it and opened out to reveal a handsome prince. Despite this happiness, there followed then a period of grave tribulation for Aapkarmi, as she had to search for a potion to relieve the effects of the poison which the jealous sisters had administered to her lover. Aapkarmi crossed many mountains and the waters of a swelling river before she reached Prince Saboor, carrying the excrement of a speaking bird which had perched on a talking tree. Aapkarmi went to Saboor in the guise of a *vaid*. She used the bird excrement, mixed with her tears, to anoint the prince's poisoned body, and the estranged couple were reunited. Aapkarmi and the prince married – she was then able to demonstrate to the king–father that she was truly a maker of her own destiny, complete with prince, palace, glory.[xv]

While the story of '*Aapkarmi ke Baapkarmi*' ostensibly celebrates the trials and ultimate triumph of a philosophy of action in which a daughter carves out a world by standing on her own sturdy feet, the truth that hovers above this interpretation is the impossibility of mapping out one's destiny in a pure and isolated way. Saboor, after all, was a present bequeathed by the father with some help from a poor old woman. (Some would argue – without necessarily subverting the principle of the story – that destiny would have brought Saboor into Aapkarmi's life in any case, with Nature becoming anthropomorphous in order to accomplish this ending.) The father made a gift to his daughter of a stone, both asked-for and not-asked-for, which inaugurated a sequence of trials and events. This particular life story thus ends with Aapkarmi enthroned in aristocratic splendour, within the very destiny that the father would himself have chosen for her.

Sonbai's father had also bestowed a stone upon her, one which cast her future in colours that are both stronger and more luminous. This stone gives out an ineluctable light which makes clear the truths that hateful vendettas, plucked out of the historical landscape, serve no purpose, and that futures must be built upon a respect for life and the world. The glow reveals that the dark shadows within each person can be made lambent through the nimbus of understanding. It casts an aura which teaches Sonbai that it is not adequate merely to take satisfaction in her own gains, when so many other lives remained thwarted. This stone, iridescent, holds the two of them together, keeps them in the same world.

THE MUSE OF HISTORY,
A WOMAN WRITING

Amidst the political upheavals which turned the world topsy-turvy, and meant that Sonbai could never know who would be the next one captured by the creeping – for some, enticing – authoritarianism, Sonbai clung to her father as her measure of truth. He stood by her, rock solid. He read her writing and provided encouragement: 'Well done, Beta, you should say this strongly. Write. Write. But is writing enough?'

It was not – though for a woman even to be able to write is in itself to exercise an enormous privilege. Across different epochs and societies, the power to remember and to tell history has been held by those who wield authority over both the public realm of dissemination, and the subterranean world of the inner psyche. In Greek mythology, Memory (Mnemosyne) was the mother of the Muse of History (Clio). Mnemosyne also gave birth to Melpomene (Tragedy), Thalia (Comedy), Euterpe (Music), Terpsichore (Dance), Polyhymnia (Sacred Song), Calliope (Epic Poetry), Erato (Lyric Poetry), and Urania (Astronomy). Memory appears to have understood well that many arts were needed to ensure that her own life remained immortal.

In the ancient world, making a female Muse the keeper of

history may or may not have been a device for elevating her on a pedestal, at a time when large numbers of her flesh-and-blood sisters were denied access to the tablet and to knowledge itself. The ancient world, constructed as heroic, is replete with violation of woman after woman, together with the conquest of fabulous shores when the earth itself became an article to be devoured.[xvi] The history of these differing despoliations impinges in curious and not always obvious ways on my writing of the story of a particular family. First of all there is that pressure to insist that this did happen, for it has not yet been accepted in serious measure. There is also that tight and close feeling of being unfree, for how can one write in other ways when this, the supreme act of usurpation of human lives, is veiled both in the eulogy to the Rule of Money and in paeans to Civilization?

We can commemorate the Muse of History, celebrate her, erase her, leave her to rest in peace. Each of these options has implications for the way in which we view history and the keeping of memory. I will not enter into any one of these acts, for each is a simplification. Rather, I will embark on an exploration of two figures – the female Muse of History and a Woman Writing – in order to delineate the complex desires which enter into the urge to write, to tell a story, to preserve memory from oblivion.

Goya's painting, Time, Truth and History, is one cultural representation amongst others of the idea of Woman as History – or more accurately, Woman as the Scribe of History, since to embody all of History in Woman was beyond the imagination of a late eighteenth- or early nineteenth-century painter.[xvii] The sketch shows a woman looking over her shoulder at the past as she inscribes it, in an open book cradled in her bare arm. The woman is comely, with a small, self-contained smile on her face. The woman, History, has an access to knowledge which Time seems anxious both to illuminate, and to surpass, for he cannot pause in one place in any given moment. His wings bear him on. Both Truth and History are female figures whose bodies have not yet been ravaged by the depredation of Time. Both have the supreme confidence which arises from the act of making something manifest. Each has a privileged relationship to Mnemosyne. The question still remains, though: which Mnemosyne, which Truth and whose story does the Muse of History divulge?

There is one particular sculpture that has become iconic as a representation of *A Woman Writing*. It has occupied the cultural imagination of scholars, historians and popular artists from the nineteenth century onwards, for the sculpture is unusual in its foregrounding of the female form absorbed in the act of writing. This particular sculpture was found in the area of Bundelkhand in northern India, within the Khajuraho temple complexes that were built in the tenth and eleventh centuries AD during the dynasty of the Candella kings. These temples display both an aristocratic splendour and decadence, as well as the coiling of power with religious worship and sexual ecstasy. The friezes and sculptures carved on the temples have been much admired for the way in which they glory in the human form. One sculpted figure stands out prominently from the nubile lovemakers and the coupling women and beasts. This is a profile of a woman of statuesque beauty standing on legs which round out into fulsome hips, her left hand cradling a writing tablet underneath a rounded breast while the fingers of her right arm close around a sharp stone flint. (Plate XX)

The woman is scratching with a pen in a substantial book: the stone book reveals several stone pages which bear the mark of her cogitations. These are turned in to the palm of her left hand in order for her to arrive at a fresh page for her writing. The book signifies seriousness. I am covetous of those pages, frustrated by the unyielding nature of their stony materiality.

The long hair of the woman writing is bejewelled and tied in a knot on her back. This leaves her sharply chiselled face, bent towards the book, bare to the eye. The girdle round her unclothed waist accentuates the curves of her flesh. A dwarfed figure stands in her shadow, gazing up in subservient adoration. The statuary is compelling for its dual immersion of Beauty and Knowledge: the boundaries between the two are both tautly contained and dissolved. The long shape of the eye looks both inward to her self and forward to the tablet. The lips shape into a wry smile. It is a look which knows: knows the full import of her written words, knows the all-embracing power of her pen and the plenitude of her poised body. Knows that she is being looked at – by the dwarfed figure, by me, by you – and nonetheless continues scratching with her stone pen, holding these and other knowledges with supreme ease within her figure.

Sonbai's grandmother, mother, and aunts were tutored to be innocent: to not know. To be nice. While sexual innocence was made into an art form – the longing gazes and chasing around manicured parks portrayed in Hindi films gesturing towards play – a heavy stress was simultaneously placed upon an innocence of the public realm, constituted as separate and apart from the domestic world. The latter acted to confine women's aspirations and dreams, while the former world – that of politics – was barred to them, even as its presence seeped in through the cracks in the door, suffusing all endeavours, dyeing all dreams. When Sonbai and her sister reached out beyond the world of domestic innocence into the political movements of the late 1970s and 1980s in Britain, there were pitifully few landmarks to guide them along the way, especially as the women's movement aimed to break out from the overbearing hierarchies of more traditional parties in order to evolve autonomous democratic organisations within which every private thought, each intimate choice became a political battleground. Oh, the tragedy embedded within the innocence which maintained that the world could be transformed through unpicking each personal action. Through placing faith in the power of political groups that worked collectively. Through thinking that the force of reason and the passion of commitment would by themselves convince all those around them. Through putting an unsupportable burden on politicising the personal, while the monster out there renewed and gorged itself by changing shape – enticing some, gobbling others.[xviii]

Innocence is predicated upon not knowing evil. Not naming it. Hiding from it. Not looking at it. Not acknowledging that it exists. Not facing it. Evil – like statecraft, love, kinship structures, law – is always historically situated, locally specific, politically contingent. The knowledge required to face it demands a steely intellect matched with an encompassing heart, lest there be a dissolution, a mirror image strongly resembling the visage that is contemplated. It calls for a hard look at the spectres without and within.

Does the impossibly beautiful figure of the Woman Writing contain the capacity to encompass evil? Does the twin sculpting of Beauty with Knowledge have the space to integrate the dark side of public events that cast their shadow on the intimacy of human relationships? For the fear, of course, was that Knowledge would tarnish Beauty. That it would dethrone her from the pedestal of Innocence upon which she had been elevated. Beauty had then to be protected from Knowledge. Beauty, made female, had to be kept ignorant, innocent. By investing in such a large measure in her innocence, the public face of responsible politics was splintered. It was unable to confront the complex nature of conflict and violence in the private and public realms, nor could it provide adequate justice.[xix]

And the Woman Writing – did she fear that writing unbeautiful truths would tarnish her image? And also, how much would it matter if it did? Did she realise that her beauty was diminished by the lowly placement of an elder transformed into a manikin who was made to stand at such a height below her? That gazing in adoration is an act which demeans the adorer?

Memories are inscribed not solely on the mind, but also on the body: they score the face, furrow the heart, flute the lungs, make ravines of hands whose fingers knot into mounds at each survived collision.

The Woman Writing. Writing prose. Writing knowledgeably. Writing words. Words have a way of reaching out, of binding, of opening up different universes: they can also undo, pierce, rive. Words contain that magic which dissolves the boundary between a hard rock and the ether of the inner eye, and the power to scythe through the tinsel wrappings around the world to reveal the house of poverty and the house of arson – look, there, right at the heart of the globe, where genocide takes many forms.

Central Africa has witnessed violence on a scale so large that the western world has preferred to close its eyes to it, even though governments in Europe have been implicated in the build-up of arms in this region.[xx] In the lands where Kinyarwanda and Kirundi are spoken, they say *zono tua zikidi e nvumbi*: yesterday, we buried the corpse. The word for blood is *menga*; to kill, *vonda*; attack, *tobola*. Hunger has taken its toll on millions, and is an experience which crosses over the different languages spoken. *Noh* (to bite into hungrily), *nh* (to bite into hungrily), *noh noh* (violent hunger), *neen* (hunger), *naj* (to become low), *nol* (bad, worthless, despised), and the Somali cognate which cuts, piercingly – *nash* (fontanelle, dent on a baby's head).

Tutsis were forced off their land in Rwanda in the Hutu uprisings. Hutus were forced to flee from the Congo. The house of the Mussulman went up in flames after the symbolic and absolute destruction of the Babri Masjid in India. The house of the resurgent Hindu, resplendent with the *Jai Shri Ram*, was left intact. The hut of the *adivasi*, marked by the sign of the cross, was razed. The destruction of buildings was accompanied by the brutal raping of women's bodies and the ending of the lives of many men. *Dalit*, woman, *adivasi* – none of these groups has refrained from lighting the fire of revenge. Where then does Innocence reside, save in the infant newly born in this world?

Sonbai, who had been engulfed by the waters of a flood, struggled to reach the shore, her body battered and bruised. She knew that she had to raise herself up from the demolition of cosmologies, dreams, and futures, for her child's face called upon her, insistently, to live once again in this world. Sonbai came up on land, said goodbye to the speaking birds in the forest, and emerged in the clearing. She did not *feng-shui* her home, read tarot cards, or undertake to be reborn. She has made friends with Gautam the Buddha over time, meditated on her violation of the divine law, worn the mantle of a penitent for a while.

Sonbai has lost that wide-eyed look captured by Khodidasbhai Parmar in his painting, and seen on a passport photograph of the seventeen-year-old. Life is no fairy tale. The tiger has turned, snarling, threatening, menacing with his fangs, destroying that most precious of gifts: faith in the ability of those born on this earth to live peaceably, without wreaking vengeance on each other. While hunger stalks the earth, ethnic territorialism has become the sacrificial altar. Syncretic cultures, composite values, hybrid identities, cosmopolitanism – none of these has been able to stem the flow of blood. Once the terror is unleashed, there is no going back to the age of innocence. The sun shines strangely.

What then is left? A quiet voice urging her to do her best. The tenderness with which duties are done. Bindu restitching severed threads. The seven-year-old Sonpari flouting the insubstantial multicultural agenda enshrined in British primary schools, and declaring that the war which preceded the coming of the Festival of Lights was not one between Good and Evil: it was just *bad*. Romila harnessing her formidable intellect against the abuse of history, whereby the past is used to legitimate and justify the violence of the present.[xxi] A fellow *aapkarmi* offering support amidst the spread of totalitarian Hindu movements, saying:

They are ultimately irrelevant to all that is most important in life and living. Yes, they have made everything around us ugly. They embody all those complicated reworkings that were taking place in the late nineteenth and early twentieth centuries, and they have taken this to a new height. But their truth is based on a very shaky foundation. It can't last. Where do I look for beauty? I think in just seeing people go about their everyday lives. I can be in the midst of the most stunning scenery, yet it does not speak to me. But just the ordinariness of ... You have to reach back to your core, slough off all the ...

What would Sonbai look like, stripped of the burden of her personal history, culture, individual yearnings and strife? What tongues would she speak, and what would she wrap around herself? What would remain save the black orbs which gaze out at the world?

THE MAGIC OF A CHILD

There is a hideaway house with a crooked roof that is tucked away from a main road. On a sunny morning in late July, three children sit within a walled garden. They are intent on painting their pictures, heads down, faces concentrated. Occasionally one of them will look up to exchange a few words. The rambling roses hug the red bricks, tendrils clinging to the warmth of the clay. A grapevine meanders across the south-facing wall, laden with bunches of small, sweet grapes. The poppy plants have spent themselves bursting out in one brilliant flame, the delicate petals pressed within pages that lie under the weight of a music system. The Empress of India grows tame in a corner, her red cloak lending a vivid colour to the white of the *solanum album*. Birdsong fills the air and butterflies flitter without rest. A wasp buzzes close to the heads of the three children, and one of them runs inside the house, shrieking. May wasps remain the only terror she knows in her life.

How I had longed for my child's arrival, and how Bindu guards her two! Unlike me, though, Bindu had prayed for them to come into her life, visiting every pir, shaman and saint's shrine in sight, lighting candles at each, while I seem to have thought that the sheer force of my mind's desire would conjure up a girl-child. Sonpari, I call my child – a fairy from the Land of Dreams. She is a September baby, born prematurely when I was completing the writing of my thesis, after I had returned to England, because I wanted my baby to have a large family around to cosset her. One of my first acts when she was placed in my arms was to trace the shape of her hand lying in mine. Ba came to stay with us when my partner and I returned home with her, massaging her body every day before bathing her in a round plastic tub placed in the small living room. When I think of the mornings spent in feeding, massaging and bathing her before swaddling her in for her morning nap, my heart is filled with peace.

There is magic in a child who arrives, drawn by a longing which pulls her to you. There are stories from all over the world of couples who yearn for a child, and whose desires are fulfilled through magic, when little people arrive in their lives, both to conjure up gladness and to test the ability of earthlings to care and nurture.[xxii]

There is enchantment in a child who is growing up beside you: you do not quite believe that she is real and hence you are always reaching out to her to pull, stroke, believe-in – 'Not in public. You're embarrassing me-e-e!' They do say that the cycle of birth and rebirth is predestined, that the baby born tomorrow chooses her future right now, in this life, and that her thoughts, emotions and actions will shape and direct how and where she will find herself in the next life. I know of many attempts to answer the question, 'How did I arrive here?' – and what could be more seductive than this one, whereby the differential chances are explained away with reference to a past, unknowable life, leaving us free to bestow our smiles on the lisping, plump babes around us while we avert our eyes from the uninnocent ones?

I absolutely reject philosophical world views that legitimate social inequalities, however, and as a teenager I often embarrassed the family in Holland Road by arguing with visitors who, having partaken of our hospitality, would turn the conversation to the misfortunes of such and such a family, and they would sigh, shrug their shoulders and then say, 'Pan sun tthay, kain pehla janmana karma hase!' (What is to be done, it must be something they had done in their past life!) However, I still find myself fondling a beautifully illustrated tale, based on the Buddhist dhammapad, which I read to my Sonpari. The writer of this tale, though, has not trodden the well-worn path of karmic reading, and the beauty of the book lies in its exploration of the mystery and glory embedded within the universe when old, familiar stories beckon.

Underneath illustrations which show the starry Milky Way and all the worlds of the universe blazing and spinning like fireworks, Mordicai Gerstein has written of a journey undertaken by a woodcutter after his death, and the choices that faced him on his way. When this woodcutter found himself in a space which was said to be both very dark and very bright at the same time, a voice emerged and said to him that he could be reborn wherever he liked. The woodcutter was dazzled by the galaxies spinning in front of him, but out of all of them, he chose to live on a planet which, from where he sat, looked like a blue-green marble that he had had as a little boy. Later, people speaking a variety of languages danced around him, tempting him with their dishes. This was the hardest choice of all for the woodcutter, who had already had a tussle with himself in deciding what kind of creature he would like to be. (Which would you choose, to be a porpoise and plunge into the depths of the sea where colours shimmer like gems, or to be a bird and soar high up in the sky?) The woodcutter's heart was touched both by the golden people, and by the craggy mountains which appeared to whisper familiar stories to him. He decided to join them. Perhaps it is true that unless we are vigilant, we will always be tugged by the pull of the known. The spirit of the woodcutter then chose a woman and a man as parents, out of a crowd of people who all called out to him: 'Come to us!' But, while Mordicai Gerstein has the woodcutter drawn to an old, well-known place high in the mountains of Tibet, the spirit of the woodcutter also makes a break from the cycle of memory-recognition by deciding to try life next time round as a girl-child. And so a little girl was born. A little girl who loved to fly kites.[xxiii]

The truth contained in this particular story attests to the magic of the universe as well as the mystery of creation. It reminds us that every child who arrives in this world comes on a journey, and that she brings with her a gift of life. Each one requires protection. Each has a right to security, shelter and well-being.[xxiv] I hold my Sonpari to me fast, fearful lest she should dissolve into my imagination. She is forever slipping away from my embraces: '*You're strangling me-e-e-e!*' Some of the closest times have been when we have lain together, close, so close, our eyes held by the lush illustrations in the book in my hand, the words spinning a spell around us. Hiawatha listening to the whispering of the pine trees, the lapping of the water. 'Minnewawa!' said the pine trees. 'Mudway-aushka!' said the water.' Chief Seattle saying: 'How can you buy the sky? How can you own the rain and the wind?' And the big, black cloud, all heavy with rain, that shadowed the ground on Kapiti Plain.[xxv] It is when I am exploring with my Sonpari the universe woven by tales caught in shafts of sunlight that a deep hunger inside me is stilled, and the clamourings inside quieten to a soft murmur.

I remember the evening that I returned home after making a number of social calls to discover a whole packet of *moong-dal* hidden in between the nappies and the water bottle. I screeched and wept: 'My baby, my baby, someone has put a *najar* on her!' My partner circled around me with confusion written all over his face, as I screamed at him to find an incinerator somewhere, anything that would gobble up the *moong-dal*. Later, exhausted, having put my baby to bed, I phoned Leena and told her of my fear. When she informed me that *moong-dal* was a traditional good omen I hissed: 'I don't want any such traditions!'

You become silly with worry when you love a child: I once took my baby to a GP, clutching her close to me all the way up the stairs, and asked that she have a thorough check-up, because I thought she did not have enough appetite. Dr Fernandez had the delicacy not to laugh at me: she simply turned her head to look at the baby on my lap, enabling me to see the rosy cheeks for the first time.

Sonpari's grandfather had constructed an easel for her early on, built in the well-equipped workshop within which he loved to potter. 'John has a Zen personality,' I used to say, even as he voiced his displeasure at the New Age meditators who occupied Highbury Fields on summer mornings. He would spend hours cleaning the surface of a window ledge before applying a coat of paint to it. He had a remarkable ability to find contentment in the moment, a grace which held despite his experience of warfare and carnage. He had been in Algiers in January 1944 when one of the junior officers under his command left a bar late one night in a drunken state, and got behind the wheel of a jeep which he thought belonged to him. Some American soldiers confronted this officer and asked him to get out. He refused, and was shot dead with a pistol held close to his face. John was outraged and took the matter up with the American authorities, who said that the action had been taken while 'defending American property'. John did not like to keep his property locked and gated; he had never drawn the blinds in the homes he created, always inviting onlookers to enjoy the soft glow cast by the lamplight. John spread warmth wherever he went, and he had taken pleasure in his granddaughter (Plates XII and XIII).

Sonpari harrumphs when I try to voice my love: 'That's obvious. You're my mum.' I want to tell her that she is being prosaic, but I don't, accepting the harrumph too as a sign of her embodied materiality. Sonpari – well, what can I say, there are so many hues to the rainbow. She is a generous spirit, bright and quick, turning outwards to the community of people who are there to share her daily joys. She draws and colours in all media – charcoal, oil paints, water and fabric colours: she has a beautiful singing voice which the teacher who conducts the school choir sorely misses on the days that she takes flight; she enjoys writing stories; she has danced with Mrittika Arts in front of a large audience many times now; and she has managed to overcome her mental block about mathematics. She is a good letter writer and keeps up active links with friends and family. She also has a certain way of handling acrimonious issues, bypassing the conflict rather than running straight into it. I wonder where she's learnt this.

Sonpari – from the Land of Dreams. Sucheta Nebiyat – Child of Love and Grace (Plate XVII). Tamrat (Moonie) means 'Child born of a Miracle' in the non-Christian Amharic tradition (Plate XV), and he is and she is and they are. The happiest time of the year is the summer, when my sister Bindu arrives with her two children, Suchi and Moonie, from the various west African capitals where they have lived for the past eleven years, her husband being moved from post to post within the international developmental organisation for which he works. The long summer days are filled with picnics and storytelling and music and play-acting. The three children snuggle amiably into an easy companionship after the initial shy greetings, and it is as if there has been no interruption in their conversation between one year and the next. Bindu and I catch up with each other as we cook and clean and plan the next meal, the air between us suddenly becoming intense and fizzing when we least expect it.

I await Bindu's coming each year, the bottled up ache tumbling out in a rush of words. Bindu says that the annual visits heal her too, for she is able to tell me of the hurts that she has endured from friends and colleagues. Every time that they fly back to west Africa in August, though, I am left with a sense of being incomplete.

The children observe our faces covertly as Bindu and I return from an afternoon spent on the common. Suchi and Sonpari do not say anything, but Moonie is unable to restrain himself. He rushes to stand in front of me, arms akimbo: '*Have you been making my mother cry?*' 'We've both cried,' I answer briefly. The three enjoy gambolling like seal pups in the swimming pool, and Bindu and I leave them to frolic while we sit on the branches of a tree by a stream outside to talk and talk and talk.

The children are always putting on performances. Moonie plays the part of the compère, announcing each act with an extemporised poem in a sing-song voice. Suchi loves dressing up as much as does Sonpari. Suchi's personhood is clearly demarcated, while both Moonie and Sonpari's are more porous. Suchi rarely enters into a quarrel, while Moon and Sonpari will fight it out to the bitter end, worrying and gnawing at each other like two overgrown puppies.[xxvi] Sonpari is proud of the paintings she does and the stories she writes; Moonie of his swift running; Suchi loves fun times and sharing ideas.

They dance and jive to their favourite song: '*Hakuna matata*', their faces lit up, their voices reaching out to a problem-free world. The videotape of *Lion King* 2 has travelled to Benin and back again.

Sonpari snuffles into my mother's body when she stays with my parents. And late at night, she and my father raise the roof with their laughter: '*Mota, tell the story of Doctor Famfooose!*' Famfoo-oo-se! Both my mother and father have the ability to have her in stitches, before she begs them to stop as the laughter is giving her cramp . . . My mother smooths away the child-hurts, stroking her forehead and singing endearments in a voice so liquid it melts Sonpari's heart. My father plies her with treats and gifts. Sonpari visits the Brahma Kumari centre with my mother, sits glued with her to watch the histrionic Hindi soaps on Zee TV, and when everyone is getting ready to go to bed, they both make their way down to the kitchen to snack together. On a trip to the swannery at Abbotsbury one April day, when my mother's arthritis was causing her acute discomfort, Sonpari took her round with great pride in a visitor's wheelchair. And, on a trip up Pavagadh, a mountain which lies fifty kilometres from Baroda, when my parents had taken the cable car, my partner had carried Sonpari up on his back as I kept vigil behind. In 1997, though, while I sat down exhausted in the shade of a Jain temple three quarters of the way up the mountain of Girnar, my Sonpari climbed right up to the peak with her father, squeezing through the small space in a stone formation and coming out unscathed, thus proving to herself that she was no sinner. She ran down to me in triumph, her face flushed from her achievement.

Sonpari has spun fine threads that have bound me to a different way of living, and these have also drawn the larger family around us. She is the next link in the chain, for whom my parents will do anything. My mother has taken her part, always, while my father has watched in astonishment as Sonpari's ankles are adorned in silver bells. Much has changed in all of our lives, and the circle turns, but not on the same axis. There have been times when we have sat together on an evening, aware that the past has slipped away leaving only the murmur of voices in the waters of a river; knowing that the future will be woven in patterns which will bear the legacy of today's dreams and fears: acknowledging that we must act responsibly, in order to wrap the next generation in clothes that will warm it on its journey.

When my sister-in-law gave birth to a baby boy, I named him Hriday, without giving much thought to whether teachers in London schools would be able to pronounce it. Raday, the Kathiawadi maternal family call him, and he revels in their affection. Hriday and Sonpari enjoy being together, and she bestows her smiles on Kishan as she wows the guests at a family wedding dinner where she and her cousin Amisha bustle around offering second helpings of *gulab-jambu*. She watches over the twins, Lily and Jay, who created a panic by arriving in this world ten weeks too early on 28 December 1998, but now Lily stamps her foot to every question and Jay (named after his maternal grandfather) talks non-stop. They twist their tongue around the word 'anemone'. A-ne-mo-ne. Baby Janaki was born on the morning of 11 June 2001, and while her mother stayed with her in the unit for premature babies, her father brought up pictures on his computer that showed the tiny fingers of the baby girl curled up to her side as she opened her mouth in a pursed 'o-o-o' of a yawn.

Sonpari is entranced by Bini skating away on an ice rink, and watches her glide and turn with seemingly effortless grace. She cudgels her brain to work out the kinship network: 'Is Binita my *aunt*, Mum?' 'Sure, yes, your *real* aunt, as is Vibhuti. Both of them are my cousins through ...' But Sonpari is off, talking excitedly about the hours spent with Vibhuti as the latter showed her a work folder containing a full curriculum of activities: history, IT, English, Mathematics, Science. Vipsi attends Grove Park School in Kingsbury, where her best friends are Gertrude and Sarah. The physiotherapy sessions often wear Vipsi out, but

Bharti cajoles her: 'If you do well today, I'll take you straight to a café!' Bharti and Vibhuti have spent many months in Budapest at the Peto Andros Institute for Conductive Education, and I know that Vipsi picks up nuances of tone and gesture as no one else can. She has the power to make me swallow the sharpness in my voice in a way that no other person on this earth has, simply by turning her eyes to me in surprise and wonder.

Every time Sonpari travels to Bombay with us, she appears fulfilled, for the Bharucha household is full of girls amongst whom she flourishes. Perrin and Katie prink and powder her, while Amy outrivals her in dramatics. When their cousins Aoefa and Tehmina arrive from Colaba to join in the play, they all build themselves into a human pyramid with Sonpari at the apex, and when they tumble down and entangle themselves they don't know which arm belongs to which body and which limb is joined where . . .

We did not travel to India during the winter of 1999. John had been very ill, and we wanted to spend Christmas with him. All through the period of John's illness, and at the time that he departed this world in January 2000, Sonpari had been doing a school project on family history. The day we heard that he was no longer with us, one of her friends held her hand in assembly as she cried silently to herself. She won a prize for her project on family history, but there is a vacuum left in her life by the absence of her grandfather.

Bindu and I have both read stories of death and bereavement for the children. Perhaps we have felt that we needed to prepare them for events for which we ourselves had not been prepared, and they seem to have a more accepting attitude towards it than I did. 'My Grandpa and the Sea' remains our favourite story: it is written to honour the memory of a fisherman–grandfather who lived on the island of St Lucia, and who could read the sea and the sky like many of us can read books. On Sundays, rather than accompany Grammy to church, he would tend to his boat called the *Fancy Lady*. Grammy tried to put the fear of God into him, but he would have none of it. Taking his grandchild out into the sea on his fishing boat one day, seeing the sun break over the mountains in colours of a melting gold, he said softly: 'This is God's House.'[xxviii]

Sonpari has spent most of her half-term breaks and Easters at her paternal grandparents' home, where her grandmother has drawn her into the world of gardening and fundraising (for the Save the Children fund, the Women's Institute, the National Association for Adivasi Welfare (Plate XIV)). On Saturday mornings, the two set out for the market held in the centre of Salisbury, Margaret wheeling her bike. They return with the panniers filled with choice cheeses, fruit, vegetables and bird feed. Sonpari enjoys exploring the world with her grandmother, and they have visited Old Sarum, Maiden Castle and the Roman villa in Rockbourne amongst other places. One of Sonpari's Christmas treats from Margaret was a ticket to a performance of the *Nutcracker* at Covent Garden.

Sonpari has inherited her grandma's desk, passed down first to her father and then to her. She also plays her Uncle Andrew's violin. When my partner handed his battered old leather school satchel to her, and I saw how important this legacy was, both in the giving and the receiving. I turned away to hide my pain, for I had nothing tangible to pass on, save my stories. Then I came across a well-worn copy of *Cry, the Beloved Country* which had schoolgirl writing on the inside cover, the only surviving remnant of my life lived elsewhere. We have read this together, following the descriptions of a valley where the cry of the titihoya could be heard no more, and where the soil was red and bare.[xxix]

I find myself zealous in conserving large chunks of my Sonpari's life through storing away mementos: each sweater knitted by her grandmother is folded between mothballs and put away in a box; her first book, building blocks, crayon scribblings and water-colour paintings are carefully preserved; her portfolio is bursting at the seams. When, instead of listening to my imprecations – 'Clean up your room or else!' – she lingers to browse over the past contained in her drawers, I am content.

Do not think I am a walkover. Far from it: I have had to unlearn a certain rigidity of thought and behaviour and divest myself of an inner puritanism in order to enjoy her and to enable her to find a lightness in life. Yes, she has taught me a lot, and I think I am better for this.

Dragons and demons have sometimes risen up in the dark to wreak havoc, but we have taken a leaf out of a storybook and petted them, so that they do not grow even more fearsome. If you refuse to pay attention to the presence of a dragon (as did Billy's mum, declaring 'There's no such thing as a dragon!'[xxx]) it will become bigger and bigger and bigger till it takes over every nook and cranny of the house – and then it will run away with it. All the dragon needs is a pat on the head and a friendly word of acknowledgement. Then it will become kitten-sized and snuggle into your arms.

I have learnt to make *ladva* for my daughter, (who has a sweet tooth) to the delight of my mother and father. For this, you need to make thick, crumbly *bhakhris*, pound them to a fine powder, pour the liquid of heated ghee over it, and add soft earth-brown molasses. You then roll the mixture into round balls, grease some poppy-seeds on your hands and throw the *ladva*. I tell you, when you have sweated and laboured over something that you had sworn you would never, ever, do, just to see the pleasure on your child's face, then you've really made it into the rank of mothers, and girl, does she sleep well on these nights!

I am often asked how Sonpari, as well as Suchi and Moonie, link together the various streams that have gone into their making, and my answer is 'That is just how their life is.' They inhabit it with their whole being. All of it is knitted into their fabric, and they wear it with a light grace. They love the dense texture of life around grandparents and aunts and uncles and cousins, and they keep their antennae out to feel the different temperatures, either turning into each other when it becomes too warm, or slinking up to touch an arm and thus divert the interchange. They have an acute feel for individual sensitivities as well as shared pleasures, and they like nothing better than to be in the thick of these. It is this which has gone into the depths of their being, rather than the cultural mementos that dot their horizons.

Sonpari collects fossils, shells and colouring pens; Suchi collects marbles, stamps and purses; Moonie fossils and stones. They all love the cliffs at Lyme Regis and they have read with avid interest the story of Mary Anning who in 1811, aged twelve, found the fossil there of a great sea monster, the Ichtyosaurus. There is an extra quiet in the air when the taunts that were hurled at Mary by children who laughed at her search for curiosities are read out: 'Stone Girl, Bone Girl. Out on your own Girl!'[xxxi] The Great Wall of China and the volcanic eruption that destroyed Pompeii hold their awe.

On a two-hour journey, I once traced some letters in Gujarati script for Suchi to copy. Bindu, looking back to catch her eyes, gave a laugh of both surprise and appreciation, but Suchi waved it impatiently aside: 'Parimasi, I want to be able to write letters to Ba and Kokilakaki when I leave England. And won't Dada and Bhabhi be surprised!' Moonie makes up poems to describe the foibles of family members, and Sonpari's drawings hang on the walls of many homes.

I believe deeply that it is through the web of relationships that children make sense of the world around them. I have not tried to inculcate my child with my ideas about issues of human worth, multiculturalism, faith and politics in any obvious way. There is, however, one matter about which I have been shrill with the children, where I have been unable to adhere to the conviction that they will understand most from my beliefs being lived but unstated, for I know that they have an uncanny ability to see through the wrappings to the grain.

This is the question of war and violence, and it is probable that the build-up of arms in the world is too large and threatening a phenomenon for me to handle with quiet conviction. Any playing, games or toys concerned with war are banned in my home: once, at my parents' house, when I came across Moonie and Hriday crouched with their right hands curled into fists and their index fingers pointed at each other like guns, I noticed that they froze in this stance at the sight of me, waiting for the storm.

Sonpari flits between the Campaign Against the Arms Trade and the Dogs for the Disabled stall at the peace festival which is held in our town every year. There are fiddlers, drummers and mandolin players at the festival, and we watch the magic of their hands creating music.

Suchi loves Sonpari for her joyfulness and Sonpari loves Suchi's creations. Sonpari shows Hriday new musical notations, and he conspires to keep her close to him. Moonie just loves being with his cousin, and she loves to run to his calling. Summer is a time for restitching threads.

There is a message in the words of a song which perfectly sums up a truth which I hold to be profoundly important in carrying our own lives forward – and those of our children. This is that there is just no point in building a future on the ruins of the past, bestowing a mantle woven from angry hurts to be worn by the coming generations.[xxxii] Our children do belong to us,[xxxiii] deeply and in ways which are often ungraspable. The closer the holding, though, the easier I believe the letting go will be, for when you have touched the brightness of a person you know that it requires a larger space in which to shine, and you will not, I trust, stand as a shadow in its path. It is right to inculcate an abiding respect for the past that has sifted through you, but it is not legitimate to hand down the regrets, the jealousies, the anger and the vendettas, like spears which the children are meant to hold aloft, piercing the sky with the cries of their wounded ancestors. It would blight their lives and nullify their hope.

I look around at the world, and I see children corralled as soldiers into armies: killed for no other reason than that they belonged to a particular ethnic group. Sebastiao Salgado's photographs provide us with images of children living in a detention camp in Vietnam; running around a refugee camp at Sakhi, in

Afghanistan, a country torn apart by invading armies and starvation; playing in the camps which house Palestinians at Ein el-Hilueh and Nahrel-Bared in Lebanon; a little boy rubbing his eyes while the stationary railroad cars containing Bosnian refugees stand behind him; the unspeakable misery of Rwandan refugees making their way to Tanzania, with approximately 350,000 arriving in four days at the camp at Benako, where there was neither adequate shelter nor drinking water. Salgado's book of photographs, *Migrations: Humanity in Transition*,[xxxiv] contains some of the most powerful images we have of the dislocations which have taken place across the globe, as wars, hunger and destruction of the land drive people from their homes. The historical frame crumbles under the weight of these images, and we are left with a view of the contemporary world in which people walk across the earth under a sky darkened by the memory of war and displacement: there are transit camps, camps for displaced peoples, refugee camps, prison camps. Only trees, the earth, tents, railway wagons and makeshift shelters provide a home. This is not a metaphor for our time: this is our time.

Of the children he photographed, Salgado said: 'Emotionally vulnerable, they are unable to understand why they are forced from their homes, why their neighbours have turned against them, why they are now in a slum surrounded by filth or in a refugee camp surrounded by sorrow. With no responsibility for their fates, they are by definition innocent.'[xxxv] This then is the crux of the issue: that children bear the burden of history, politics and community formation at a time when they have no real say in how these should be constituted. They are subjects, not citizens, even amongst citizenless people. However, Salgado's claim that the individual portraits captured the children in the camps that he visited enabled them to say 'I am'[xxxvi] is disingenuous, for the book of photographs contains no names: the captions simply state the location at which the individual child's portrait was taken – a camp, a settlement, a prison. The photographs cannot enable the children to say 'I am' – they are, like all of us, in the process of becoming – except in the simple sense that we know that they existed at a particular moment in time because the camera has captured them there. John Berger perhaps comes closer to the truth (or as near the truth of a child's view as it is possible to reach) through his interpretation of what these images can offer, not to those of us living our secure lives, but to those who are undergoing the pain of this experience. Quoting the philosopher Simone Weil, Berger has said that images such as these can offer the children a story to express their suffering, and that they enable them to find the words (pictures?) to articulate the cry: 'Why am I being hurt?'[xxxvii]

Why? To annihilate hope, refuel the circle of destruction, ignite the flame that will lay waste to all life? My attention is held by a photograph of a child who sits looking out at the world, her eyes deep pools of reflection as she holds her hand to her head, in a gesture of *holding a burden*.[xxxviii] She is sitting in the Benguela Railway Station camp for displaced people in Luena, Alto Zambeze Province in Angola. This is her home. This child is one of the thousands affected by the war in Angola, many of whom have severed limbs from the explosions caused by the landmines that continue to dot this particular region as well as many others. I will not presume to enter her thoughts. They are her own, and she will make sense of the world that she inhabits with the full force of her mind.

I have come to the end of telling this tale. A tale which has intertwined memory traces, life histories and stories to make sense of the lives of those with whom I have shared a close relationship, both spatially and imaginatively. Some who I have loved deeply are no longer on this earth. Perhaps when I have come to the end of living out my own life on this earth, I will be able to trace their footprints in the sand, watch the new hues that will have been streaked in the sky by those who are yet to go out in it. This then is what I have sought to render in words: a history and times of my family as I have lived through it, knowing that others have lived it differently and that the living in the future will be different still.

I love my Sonpari. She will, one day, burst out of the cocoon and fly into the widening horizon. But she will come back to me full of her stories of wonderment, and I will be there for her.

NOTES AND SUGGESTED
READING

PART ONE

i The poet Kalapi (or Surasinhaji) ruled over Lathi between 1895 and 1900. He is best known for being unsuccessful in attaining the love of a maidservant Monghi (or Shobhana) and though he wrote about this evocatively in *Hriday Triputi* (The Trinity of Hearts), he took poison from his wife's hand and died at the age of twenty-six.

ii This history awaits: in the saga of commerce and the evolution of political nationhood, the narrative of women of different communities making important contributions to the forging of a public culture has remained marginal.

iii The midwife Yamunatai was falsely asked by a man to come out to an urgent birth. She was violated by him, and returned to India after this event. No charges were brought against the perpetrator of this crime.

iv For an evocation of this in Kikuyu country, see the novel by Ngugi wa Thio'ngo, *The River Between*.

v 'Speech at Anand', in *The Collected Works of Mahatma Gandhi*, Vol. XLIII, 17 March 1930, page 93.

vi Fiona Mackenzie, 'Gender and Land Rights in Murang'a District, Kenya', in *Journal of Peasant Studies*, 17 (4) 1990. For customary laws relating to pregnancy compensation, matrimonial rights and duties, divorce etc. see Eugene Cotran, *Casebook of Kenya Customary Law*, Nairobi University Press, 1987. For a critical account of the enmeshing of 'customary' marriage laws with the requirements of the colonial economy and polity, see Marjorie Mbilinyi, 'Runaway Wives in Colonial Tanganyika: Forced Labour and Forced Marriage in Rungwe District 1919–1961,' in *International Journal of the Sociology of Law*, 16, 1988. Marjorie Mbilinyi provides a cogent critique of the strand of cultural relativism which defended forced marriages.

vii See Sudhir Chandra, 'Conflicted Beliefs and Men's Consciousness about Women: Widow Marriage in Later Nineteenth-Century Indian Literature', *Economic and Political Weekly*, 31 October 1987 for a discussion on the writings of Bankimchandra Chatterjee and Govardhanram Tripathi.

viii In particular Isvarchandra Vidyasagar.

ix *Ek Punarvivahni Kahani*, by Madhavdas Rugnathdas, first published in 1882, republished in 1984, Kapod and Kapod Mitra, Bombay.

x *Ek Punarvivahni Kahani*, 1984 edition, pages 31–33.

xi Ibid., pages 39–40. The passages quoted from this narrative are in my translations.

xii Ibid., pages 41–42.

xiii The description given of Dhankor's illness, which is categorised variously as 'hysteria' and 'lockjaw', reads more as feverish convulsions, or as an epileptic fit (Ek Punarvivahni Kahani, pages 16, 52–54). The story does not provide information about the course of this malady after her remarriage.

xiv Ibid., page 49.

xv Chandrashankar Bhimanand Shukla, Vidhva Vapan Nished: Etle Vidhvanu Vapan Shastrokta Natthi, Surat, Gujarat Standard Press, 1892, preface, page 3.

xvi Ibid., page 49.

xvii Harikrishna Lalshankar Dave, 'Vidhvavapan Nished' Lakhname Javaab, Ahmadabad, Union Printing Press, 1892, page 6.

xviii The most well-known ones being Isvarchandra Vidyasagar, Rammohun Roy and Jyotirao Phule. For a moving account of the dilemmas facing Vidyasagar, see Sumit Sarkar, 'Vidyasagar and Brahmanical Society', in his Writing Social History, Delhi, Oxford University Press, 1997. On Rammohun Roy, see the articles edited by V. C. Joshi in Rammohun Roy and the Process of Modernisation in India, New Delhi, 1975. See also Rosalind O'Hanlon, Caste, Conflict and Ideology: Mahatma Jyotirao Phule and Low-Caste Protest in Nineteenth-Century India', Cambridge, Cambridge University Press, 1985.

xix 'Position of Widows: Experiences of Widows and Other Girls,' 1911, MSS.EUR. D 346, India Office Library, London. The writings of the two Ambubais can be found on (pencilled page numbers) 5–8 and 18–20, though the whole manuscript is one long cry against both poverty and humiliation.

xx Rewriting History: The Life and Times of Pandita Ramabai, Uma Chakravarty, Delhi, Kali for Women, 1998.

xxi Quoted in Uma Chakravarty op. cit., page 271.

xxii Ibid., page 327.

xxiii For a cogent account of this period of political activity, see chapters 1–3 of Robert G. Gregory's Asian Politics in East Africa, 1900–1967, London, Sangam Books, 1993.

xxiv 'Sir Philip Mitchell' by Fay Carter in Kenya: Historical Biographies, edited by Kenneth King, Nairobi, 1971, page 31.

xxv Ibid.

xxvi Robert G. Gregory, The Rise and Fall of Philanthropy in East Africa: The Asian Experience, New Brunswick, Transaction Publishers, 1992.

xxvii Colonial Annual Reports: Kenya, 1923, page 22.

xxviii Colonial Annual Reports: Kenya, 1948, page 2.

xxix Robert G. Gregory has provided a cogent and comprehensive history of these efforts in his The Rise and Fall of Philanthropy in East Africa: The Asian Contribution, Transaction Publishers, 1992.

xxx John Iliffe, The African Poor: A History, Cambridge University Press, 1987, page 197.

xxxi The elders in my family do not want me to make public the name of this person whose family name has made a consistent appearance in the list of Asian millionaires in Britain published annually since the late 1990s. I have adhered to their wish.

xxxii Female circumcision continued to be practised and contested amongst communities such as the Kikuyu. Jomo Kenyatta (who was to become the first President of independent Kenya) described the violence embedded in clitoridectomy as a 'mere bodily mutilation', without which the continuity of the tribe was unimaginable (J. Kenyatta, Facing Mount Kenya, Secker and

Warburg, 1953, pages 130–133). Female genital mutilation (including infibulation) was reported to have been practised upon sixty per cent of young women in Kenya in 1982, and on fifty per cent of young women in the year 2001. The practice is found in a wide range of communities (Kalenjin, Kamba, Maasai, Pokot, Samburu, Somali) and while it is a clear violation of women's bodies, it also affects the life chances of young women very adversely. A large number of young women are removed from education after undergoing the cut, which announces their entry into 'womanhood'. For the political consequences of this violence against women, see the report by Refugee Women's Resource Project, Asylum Aid, *No Upright Words: The Human Rights of Women in Kenya*, London, February 2001.

xxxiii Romila Thapar, 'Death and the Hero', in volume edited by S. C. Humphreys and Helen King, *Mortality and Immortality: the anthropology and archaelogy of death*, London, Academic Press, 1981.

xxxiv Bindu has reminded me (correctly) that while the publicly articulated world of *bhakti* had Kirshna at its core, Ba's intense personal faith has continued to revolve around Ambaji or Mataji (the Mother). Ambaji is a virgin Mother figure, unlike Parvati, Lakshmi etc. who have a consort.

xxxv Parita Mukta, *Upholding the Common Life: The Community of Mirabai*, Delhi, Oxford University Press, 1997.

xxxvi For the ideological debates that took place in this movement during the late nineteenth and early twentieth centuries in the Punjab, see Madhu Kishwar, 'Arya Samaj and Women's Education: Kanya Mahavidyalaya, Jalandhar', in *Economic and Political Weekly*, Vol. XXI, No. 17, 1986 April 26. The overarching pedagogical configuration of the Arya Samaj in East Africa was heavily circumscribed by this, even as the students in the 'Gujarati stream' were channelled into an engagement with Gujarati society, politics and culture.

xxxvii 'Rishi Dayanand lit a torch both of knowledge, and for the awakening of the race.'

xxxviii For an appreciation of her life, see Khatija Akbar, *Madhubala: Her Life, Her Films*, Delhi, UBS Publishers, 1997.

xxxix A fairly sanitised version of this tale appears in the collection of children's stories by Gijubhai Badheka *Gijubhaini Balvaartaayo*, Lokmilaap Trust, 1991: 24–27. Gijubhai Badheka (1897–1939) was an eminent educationalist in the Gujarat of his times, having made famous his teaching methods through the nursery school he set up in Bhavnagar in 1920. Gijubhai's stories were well publicised in his life-time, through the print media, the establishment of a teaching institute which trained child workers, and the extensive speaking tours he himself undertook between 1920 and 1936 (see *Gijubhainu Jivancharitra: Mucchaadi Ma* by Girishbhai Bhatt, Bhavnagar, 1987). It is possible, of course, that Gijubhai took from already existing oral narratives, and gave them his own stamp. Ba says she remembers this particular story from her own childhood (which was before Gijubhai began writing his stories). I am grateful to Jayantbhai Meghani for bringing this book to my attention.

xl This was to be found in the speeches of the MP Tom Mboya, and can also be glimpsed in some of the writings of Ngugi wa Thiong'o. An account of the boycott of *leso* cloth sold by Indian traders in Mombasa is described in the testimony of Shamsa Muhamad Muhashamy in *Three Swahili Women: Life-Histories from Mombasa, Kenya*, edited by Sarah Mirza and Margaret Strobel, Indiana University Press, 1989, pages 102–5.

xli A description of these events can be found in Esmond Bradley Martin's *Zanzibar: Tradition and Revolution*, Hamish Hamilton, London, 1978, pages 69–

72. The forcible marriages of women from the minority communities to Zanzibari state officials was also given as the main reason for emigration by Zanzibari Asians interviewed by Richa Nagar in 1991–3. See his 'The South Asian Diaspora in Tanzania: A History Retold,' in *Comparative Studies of South Asia, Africa and the Middle East*, Vol. XVI, No. 2, 1996, pages 67–68. A thoughtful account of 'runaway wives' in an earlier period (of colonial Tanganyika) is given by Marjorie Mbilinyi in 'Runaway Wives in Colonial Tanganyika: Forced Labour and Forced Marriage in Rungwe District 1919–1961', found in *International Journal of the Sociology of Law*, 16, 1988. Marjorie Mbilinyi argues here that the colonial state attempted to stop women from moving out of the countryside towards areas of migrant and casual labour, and tried to keep them firmly under the control of local chiefs and male guardians. She compares the plight of runaway wives with that of runaway slaves in nineteenth-century East Africa (page 13). For a story based around the exchange of a young woman for cattle, money and blankets in a Maasai community, see Leteipa Ole Sunkuli, 'They Sold My Sister', in *Tender Memories*, edited by Arthur Luvai et al., Kenya, Heinemann, 1989. Nyamalo's words at parting from her younger sister were, 'Tell Father and Mother that may the wealth they have accepted choke them to death,' page 44. There have been more recent struggles against forced marriages in Britain by organisations such as the Southall Black Sisters.

xlii I had been preparing to enrol myself at the University of Nairobi to study African history.

xliii The Brahma Kumari World Spiritual University has its headquarters on Mount Abu in Rajasthan, and also a large centre in Willesden, North London.

Further Reading and Films

There has been a considerable renaissance in the publishing of women's writings in the past fifteen years. The best presses for these are Kali for Women in Delhi, and Stree in Calcutta. Some of the most well-known stories on widowhood are by the Hindi writer Premchand (1880–1930). Twelve of these appear in *Widows, Wives and Other Heroines*, translated by David Rubin, Delhi, Oxford University Press, 1998. *Phaniyamma*, by M. K. Indira (translation by Tejaswini Niranjana), Delhi, Kali, 1994, is a poignant and muted account of the life of a child-widow who lived from 1840–1952. It was made into a feature film bearing the same title in 1982 (Prema Karanth). Anita Desai's *Feasting, Fasting*, Vintage Books, 2000, minutely observes the world of a high-caste widow in India, and then moves to depicting bulimia in the affluent metropolis. *Rao Saheb* is a moving film by Vijaya Mehta (1986) which depicts very well the limitations of the liberalism of an English-educated landed barrister in Maharashtra in his relationship to the two widows around him. Satyajit Ray's renowned film *Pather Panchali*, (1955), I love most for its detail of the relationship between the young girl Gauri and her very elderly great-aunt, played by Chunibala Devi whose face haunts.

The devotional movement, with its flowering of song-verses and wonderful saint–singers has attracted the attention of both scholars and poets. A. K. Ramanujan's translations of Kannada sayings, *Speaking of Siva*, London, Penguin, 1973 and *Hymns for the Drowning: Poems for Visnu by Nammalvar*, Delhi, Penguin, 1993, contain a beauty of expression which nonetheless does not prettify their rawness. Dilip Chitre's translation of a selection of Tukaram's verses in 'Tukaram: Says Tuka, Delhi, Penguin, 1991, also captures the raw energy of the times. A. J. Alston's *The Devotional Poems of Mirabai*, Delhi, Motilal Banarsidass, 1980, and Swami

Mahadevananda's *Devotional Songs of Narsi Mehta*, Delhi, Motilal Banarasidass, 1985, provide a selection of the range of creativity of these two. For a selected range of the verses of that great weaver–poet, Kabir, who has made the weaving of life immortal, see Charlotte Vaudeville, *A Weaver Named Kabir*, Delhi, Oxford University Press, 1997. See also the articles on Kabir in *The Sants: Studies in a Devotional Tradition of India*, edited by K. Schomer and W. H. McLeod, Delhi, Motilal Banarasidass, 1987. Kabir's songs have been rendered by many major classical singers of our times, Kumar Gandharva being the best known. These are available on audio cassettes and compact discs. The Sabri Brothers' *qawallis* similarly flout orthodox conventions to take pleasure in the truth of the heart. These too are available on compact discs.

The 1950s and 1960s films and songs are often now available for rental hire through local libraries in Britain, in areas where there are settled South Asian communities. Video shops sell them too: Ealing Road in Wembley and the High Street in Southall are good places to begin with.

PART TWO

i For published accounts of this conference, see *History Workshop*, issue 29, 1990.

ii The famine affected Rajasthan, Central Provinces and Bombay Presidency (which included the state of Gujarat). The highest mortality occurred in the districts of Gujarat, 'where the people, long unaccustomed to suffer from scarcity, frequently failed to take advantage of relief measures until the progress of exhaustion had rendered it impossible to save their lives'. *Imperial Gazatteer of India, Provincial Series, Bombay Presidency Vol. 1*, Calcutta, Superintendent of Government Printing, 1909, pages 82–3.

iii T. K. Trivedi, 'Report of the Khedut Debt Inquiry Committee', Bhavnagar State, 1931.

iv T. Sleith 'Report on Trade Conditions in British East Africa, Uganda and Zanzibar,' Cape Town: Union of South Africa Department of Mines and Industries, 1919, quoted in R. D. Wolff, *Britain and Kenya 1870–1930: The Economies of Colonialism*, Nairobi, Transafrica Publishers Limited, 1974, page 130.

v Op. cit., page 131. See also the early part of this history in Chapter Three of Cora Ann Presley, *Kikuyu Women, the Mau Mau Rebellion, and Social Change in Kenya*, Boulder, Westview Press, 1992.

vi *The East African Standard*, 3 February 1923, quoted in Purnima Mehta, Bhatt, dissertation, Howard University 1976.

vii Command paper number 1922, dated 23 July 1923, in *Colonial Reports: Annual. Colony and Protectorate of Kenya*, no. 1227, Report for 1923, pages 5–6.

viii For a song and a story from East Africa which reassures that suffering will be followed by happiness, see that told by Bibi Thecla in *Folk-Tales of East Africa*, Veena Sharma, Delhi, Sterling Publishers, 1987, pages 25–33.

ix Juan Mascaro, *The Bhagavad Gita*, Harmondsworth, Penguin, 1962, pages 103, 112–3.

x Ibid., pages 103–4.

xi Some of the best known of Susan George's books are *How the Other Half Dies: The Real Reasons for World Hunger* (Penguin, 1976), *Ill Fares the Land: Essays on Food, Hunger and Power* (Penguin, 1990), *A Fate Worse Than Debt* (Penguin, 1988). For the best-known writings of Amartya Sen, see his *Hunger and Entitlements*, World Institute for Development Economics Research, Helsinki, 1988; with Jean Dreze *Hunger and Public Action*, Oxford, Clarendon Press, 1989; the three edited volumes with Dreze, *The Political Economy of Hunger*, Volume 1 of which deals with *Entitlement and Well-Being*, Volume 2 with *Famine Prevention*, and Volume 3 with *Endemic Hunger*. Oxford, Clarendon Press, 1990 and 1991.

xii A vivid description of the legend of the 'Panjabi *sharifu*' and his place in the lives of the élite Swahili communities is to be found in the testimony of Bi Kaje (born around 1890) in *Three Swahili Women: Life Histories from Mombasa, Kenya*, edited by S. Mirza and M. Strobel, Indiana University Press, 1989, pages 41–42. Her uncle, Muhamadi bu Rashidi, was an overseer of builders at Kilindini and it appears to be the overseers who were paid in 'lots of rations and small wages'.

xiii Colonial Annual Report, Kenya, 1948, page 4.

xiv Op. cit., pages 11–13.

xv Colonial Annual Report, Kenya, 1949, page 15.

xvi R. G. Gregory in his *South Asians in East Africa: An Economic and Social History, 1890–1980*, Boulder, Westview Press, 1993, is unusually meticulous in the detail he lavishes on the different work sectors. He thus has chapters on the 'clerical service' (within which he includes station masters, baggage masters and ticket sellers) as well as 'crafts and construction', 'law, medicine and teaching', and 'commerce' etc.

xvii Mzee Camelius Kiango of Nandete, quoted in G. C. K. Gwassa and J. Iliffe (eds.), *Records of the Maji Maji Rising: Part One*, Nairobi, East Africa Publishing House, 1967, pages 27–28. These oral testimonies provide some of the most striking details of this rebellion.

xviii Op. cit., page 27.

xix Colonial Annual Report, Kenya, 1955, page 70.

xx Robert G. Gregory, *South Asians in East Africa: An Economic and Social History, 1890–1980*, Boulder, Westview Press, 1993, page 189.

xxi Both of these 'nonsense' phrases are still used by him with delight when he takes a grandchild out for a 'treat'.

xxii For a moving analysis of the ways in which Vidyasagar, a nineteenth-century Bengali reformer, remained tied to ameliorating the lot of poor Brahmins, see Sumit Sarkar, *Writing Social History*, Delhi, Oxford University Press, 1997.

xxiii This is evocatively rendered in the novels by Ngugi wa Thiong'o, *Petals of Blood*, Heinemann, 1977, and *Matigari*, Heinemann, 1987.

xxiv For writings in verse (the stretched hands of 'The Parking Boy,' who cries '*saidia maskini*,' and a father who recognises himself in the face of a street-child and declares in 'Forgive Me, Parking Boy', 'Had I known you were conceived. / Had I known you would end up in the streets / Had I met your mother again … I would have told her to throw you into a pit latrine / That you may never become a living embarrassment / to me and my conscience,' see *Tender Memories*, edited by Arthur Luvai and others, Nairobi, Heinemann, 1989, pages 10 and 16–7.

xxv Don McCullin, *Sleeping with Ghosts: A Life's Work in Photography*, London, Vintage, 1995, pages 16 and 78. Twelve of McCullin's photographs were used by a major newspaper editor to illustrate that the war in Vietnam was 'one of the dirtiest wars in history' (Mark Haworth-Booth, *The Great Photographers: Donald McCullin*, London, Collins, 1983, page 57).

xxvi Ibid., page 79.

xxvii He had been in charge of Britain's National Collection of the Art of Photography.

xxviii Mark Haworth-Booth, op. cit., page 59.

xxix McCullin, op. cit., pages 78 and 138.

xxx For an obituary to Kevin Carter, see Scott MacLeod, 'The Life and Death of

Kevin Carter', in *Time*, 12 September 1994. Arthur and Joan Kleinman have analysed the implications of the 'consuming' of suffering as entertainment in 'The Appeal of Experience; The Dismay of Images: Cultural Appropriations of Suffering in Our Times', in Kleinman et al., *Social Suffering*, Berkeley, University of California Press, 1997. I am grateful to Gauri Raje for bringing the Kleinmann essay to my notice, and to Anita Noguera for discussions of this particular image.

xxxi Alula Pankhurst, *Resettlement and Famine in Ethiopia: The Villager's Experience*, Manchester University Press, 1992, page 24.

xxxii Ibid., page 25.

xxxiii See Joanna Macrae and Anthony Zwi, *War and Hunger: Rethinking International Responses to Complex Emergencies*, London, Zed Books, 1994.

xxxiv E. P. Thompson, 'Custom and Culture', in his *Customs in Common*, London, Penguin, 1991, page 15.

xxxv The story moves from plenty to want again, the *dabli* being discovered and confiscated by the snooping stepsister. The *dosima* puts in another appearance, makes a gift of a second *dabli*, and the story ends with a handsome prince carrying off the beautiful and good maiden. I have been unable to trace the source of this story outside the words and imagination of my grandmother and aunts. It is likely to be a variant of a folk story.

xxxvi A high literary variant of this story appears in R. M. Dorson, *Folktales Told Around the World*, University of Chicago Press, 1975. See 'The Mother Serpent (Gujarati)', pages 181–187; see also 'The Serpent Mother' in A. K. Ramanujan, *Folk-Tales of India*, Pantheon Books, 1991, 212–219.) This story is part of a ritual fast undertaken on *Naag-Panchmi*, a Day of Serpent-Worship, where women paint a representation of the Serpent by the cool of the water pots and make food offerings to it.

xxxvii Alan Travis in the *Guardian*, 15 March 2000.

xxxviii The Asylum Aid 2000 report, *Only Crooked Words: Home Office Decisions on Kenyan Women's Asylum Claims*, Refugee Women's Resource Project, Asylum Aid, February 2001, provides vivid details of the brutal repression facing political activists in Kenya and of Home Office procrastination on their cases in Britain.

xxxix Bindu has a large family of in-laws in Addis.

xl Pierre Bourdieu's analysis of the notion of 'taste' which exists amongst the different social groups in France is now a classic. See his *Distinction: A Social Critique of the Judgment of Taste*, London, Routledge Kegan Paul, 1986.

Further Reading and Films

The literature on the settlement of South Asian communities in East Africa is now fairly substantial, this being for the most part related to well-known male politicians, trade unionists and industrialists. Robert Gregory's economic and social history, cited above, as well as his *Quest for Equality*, London, Sangam Books, 1993, will provide the interested reader with a comprehensive bibliography. A history of the rise of the Indian merchants appears in Claude Markovits, *The Global World of Indian Merchants, 1750–1947*, Cambridge University Press, 2000. For a eulogy to 'people of wealth ... power and influence', see Ram Gidoomal's *The UK Maharajahs: Inside the Southern Asian Success Story*, London, Nicholas Brealey, 1997. Yasmin Alibhai-Brown's *No Place Like Home: An Autobiography*, London, Virago, 1997, is an account of her life in Uganda prior to the expulsion, which at the same time seeks to answer why there was such hostility felt and directed towards the

'Asian community' there. It is one of the few women's narratives to emerge out of this era, and is at its best when detailing family, neighbourhood and school life. Mira Kamdar's *Motiba's Tattoos: A Granddaughter's Journey into her Indian Family's Past*, New York, Public Affairs, 2000, travels to the villages of Saurashtra as well as to Burma and captures some of the shifts in diasporic family life well.

Rohinton Mistry's novel *A Fine Balance*, Toronto, McClelland and Stewart, 1997, is an unsurpassed epic of the lives of migrants in the Bombay of the mid-1970s. If you have not done so already, read this. Lan Samantha Chan's *Hunger: A Novella and Short Stories*, London, Phoenix House, 1998, also stands in a league of its own for the extraordinary texture of words which tell of the lives and hungers of Chinese migrants to America. Kunal Basu's *The Opium Clerk*, London, Phoenix House, 2001, depicts well the ambience of clerical life in nineteenth-century Calcutta, the heartland of imperial rule. Bessie Head's writings remain exemplary in knitting together the hardship of life in twentieth century southern Africa with the yearnings and pain of marginal women. Bessie Head, *Tales of Tenderness and Power*, 1990; *Maru*, 1995; *Collector of Treasures*, 1992; *When Rain Clouds Gather*, 1995. All are published by Heinemann Press. E. P. Thompson's *Protest and Survive*, edited with Dan Smith, New York, Monthly Review Press, 1981, as well as his edited volume of *Star Wars*, Harmondsworth, Penguin, 1985, both provide a cogently argued case for nuclear disarmament. James Scott has a good analysis of the 'subsistence ethic' of the peasantry in *The Moral Economy of the Peasant: Rebellion and Subsistence in Southeast Asia*, New Haven, Yale, 1976. Satyajit Ray's film *Ashani Sanket*, (Distant Thunder), is a close portrayal of village life during the 1943 Bengal famine.

For the railways in East Africa, see M. F. Hill, *The Permanent Way: The Story of the Kenya and Uganda Railway, Volume 1*, and *The Story of the Tanganyika Railways* Nairobi, East African Railways and Harbours, 1945 and 1947. For an analysis of the place of railways within nineteenth-century western consciousness, see Wolfgang Schivelbusch's *The Railway Journey: The Industrialisation of Time and Space in the Nineteenth Century*, Leamington Spa, Berg, 1986. *Le Tombeau d'Alexandre*, or *The Last Bolshevik*, (written and edited by Chris Marker, produced by Michael Kustov, Epidemy, 1993) has some wonderful clippings of the 'film-train' used by the film-maker Alexander Ivanovich Medvedkin, who had been a railway man in his youth; also of Soviet Russia's 'agitprop trains' which carried books, posters and party materials throughout the land. For a history of Auschwitz (trains being central for transportation to the place of genocide), see Robert Jan van Pelt and Deborah Dwork, *Auschwitz 1270 to the Present*, New Haven, Yale University Press, 1996. Khushwant Singh's *Train to Pakistan*, London, Chatto and Windus, 1956, remains the most well known of the partition accounts.

Further Contacts

Barbed Wire Britain is an organisation that is seeking to end detention of asylum seekers, their treatment as criminals, and the government's flouting of their civil liberties. It can be contacted at 40, Richmond Terrace, Oxford, OX1 2JJ. Tel: 01865 558145. Most major cities in Europe have seen concerned citizens coming together to provide a welcome to asylum seekers. There will be one such organisation where you live. If there is not, you could consider setting one up.

PART THREE

i John Macbeth.

ii Heather Thakkar.

iii Ashwin Thakkar.

iv Geoffrey E. Milburn and Stuart T. Miller (eds.), *Sunderland: River, Town and People, A History from the 1780s*, Sunderland Borough Council, 1990 provides a good overview; *Sunderland in Old Photographs*, collected by Stuart Miller and Billy Bell, Stroud, Alan Sutton, 1991, contains black-and-white photographs of Grangetown, Roker, as well as the harbour and river area; and *I Remember ... the North-East: Recollections of Yesteryear*, Durham, Pentland Press, 1993, has tales of life in this region.

v Peter Fryer, *Staying Power: Black People in Britain since 1504*, New Jersey, Humanities Press, 1984; see in particular section titled 'Racism as Riot: 1919,' pages 298–316.

vi 'Winter Song' by Lindisfarne, written by Alan Hull, Chappell Music Ltd., in *The Best of Lindisfarne*, Virgin CD VIP 103.

vii 'Bury My Body', arranged by Alan Price, Dash Music Ltd., in EMI CD *The Complete Animals*, CD 79 46131.

viii 'Gonna Send You Back to Walker', written by Matthews/Hammond Jnr. Renleigh Music Inc./MCPC. In *The Complete Animals*, as above. Walker is a dock area of Newcastle-upon-Tyne.

ix 'The Fog on the Tyne', written by Alan Hull, Charisma Music Pub. Co. Ltd., in *The Best of Lindisfarne*.

x This song verse is part of the oral tradition, familiar to all who are from this cultural region.

xi *Our Kate*, Macdonald and C, London, first published in 1969, 1990 edition, page 15. See also Carolyn Steedman: 'I see now that I have spent all my life resisting the account of class formation that I was given in that teaching, not because it excludes women, but because it is a heroic tale, which most experiences do not fit' (which even most of the experiences of the men named in the epic, do not fit.) C. Steedman, 'The Price of Experience: Women and the Making of the English Working Class,' in *Radical History Review*, 59, 1994, p. 108–119.

xii Catherine Cookson, *Colour Blind*, Corgi Books, London, 1968.

xiii *Colour Blind*, page 155.

xiv This may well be another reason for the popularity of Cookson's writings (the propounding of the 'ordinary' working person's views, as opposed to the politicised one). It would however be important to assess the impact of Cookson's work in creating this very 'ordinary' world view. For a more 'radical' reading of the events see David Byrne, 'The 1930 "Arab riot" in South Shields: a race riot that never was', in *Race and Class*, XVIII, 3 (1977), pages 261–277.

xv David Byrne, op. cit., page 276.

xvi It is worth remembering here the earlier history of Shahpurji Saklatvala, who started his political career in London by forming the Workers' Welfare League of India in 1916, which initially represented Indian seamen. Saklatvala worked tirelessly throughout the depression years and was charged with sedition for a speech in Hyde Park during the General Strike of 1926, when he urged soldiers to refrain from firing on workers. Saklatvala, a cardholding member of the Communist Party, had come from an affluent anglicised Parsi family in Bombay. He married his maid Sarah in Battersea and they had five children.

xvii Sydney F. Collins: 'The Social Position of White and "Half-Caste" Women in Colored Groupings in Britain', in *American Sociological Review*, Vol. XVI, no. 6, 1951, pages 796–802.

xviii The term 'Geordie' refers to Tyneside speech. Sunderland peoples refer to themselves as 'Mak 'ems' but this term is scarcely heard of outside the north-east.

xix It was a solution that Cookson adhered to in her own life. See the book by Cliff Goodwin *To Be a Lady: The Story of Catherine Cookson*, London, Century, 1994. Cookson described how she had carried within her from an early age the picture of a big house full of ladies and gentlemen who were surrounded by horses and servants: she had always envisaged herself 'in [this] picture, dead centre' (page 12). Catherine Cookson received the Order of the British Empire in 1985, and was made a Dame of the British Empire in 1993.

xx See also her books, *The Mallen Streak* (1973), *The Mallen Girl* (1974), and *The Mallen Litter* (1974).

xxi For a cogent analysis of the politics of 'colour blind' see the first of the 1997 Reith Lectures entitled 'The Emperor's New Clothes' by Patricia J. Williams, published as *Seeing a Colour-Blind Future: The Paradox of Race*, London, Virago, 1997, where she argues that the essence of integrity is never having to split into a well-maintained 'front' and a closely-guarded 'inside' (page 4).

xxii Beatrix Campbell, *Goliath: Britain's Dangerous Places*, Methuen, 1993, page 61, Part IV ('The challenges of lawless masculinity') and page 303.

xxiii For a hagiography see K. L. Saigal: *The Pilgrim of the Swara*, by Raghava R. Menon, Hind Pocket Books, 1989.

xxiv Mrinalini Sinha, *Colonial Masculinity: the 'manly Englishman' and the 'effeminate Bengali'*, Manchester University Press, 1995.

xxv Nabendu Ghose, scriptwriter for Bimal Roy in *Bimal Roy: A Man of Silence*, by Rinki Bhattacharya, Delhi, Indus, 1994, page 168.

xxvi *Devdas and Other Stories by Sarat Chabdra Chatterjee*, selected and translated by V. S. Naravane, Delhi, Lotus Collections, 1996, page 67.

xxvii *Britain's Richest Asian 2000*, London, Ethnic Media Group, 1999, part 16.

xxviii For this, see *The Ragged Trousered Philanthropists*, by Robert Tressel, London, Panther Books, 1980, chapter 21.

Further Reading/Films/Songs

Amber Film Productions, set up in 1969 'with the aim of documenting working-class life in the North-East of England,' have made some wonderful films: *Tyne Lives*, *Seacoal*, *In Fading Light*, *Dream On* and *The Scar* are some of these. You can buy videos of films made by Amber. Bloodaxe is a publishing house based in the north-east which publishes some excellent poetry. L. S. Lowry used to holiday in Sunderland (as did many working families), and his paintings of the area can be found in *Lowry in the North-East*, edited by Juliet Horsley, Tyne and Wear Museum Services, 1989.

Some of the best known of the films in which K. L. Saigal acted (apart from *Devdas*) are *Tansen*, *Street Singer*, *Crorepati*, *Meri Bahen*, *President*, *Shah Jehan*, *Bhakta Surdas*. I would recommend these, though I have not been lucky enough to obtain a copy of either *Bhakta Surdas*, or *Chandidas*. K. L. Saigal's collection of songs are available on audio cassette, as well as on CDs. The latter can be found in four volumes, produced by Hindusthan Musical Company Limited, as *Hits of K. L. Saigal*. Try and encourage your local library to build up a collection of these films as well as the songs. Haba's favourite from the Pankaj Mullick songs were 'Yeh Kaun Aaj Aaya

Sawere Sawere,' 'Piya Milanko Jaana,' and 'Tere Mandirka Hoon Deepak Jal Rahaa.' All of these can be found in *Piya Milan Ko Jana: Hits of Pankaj Mullick*, CDF 132107 AAD, Gramophone Company of India Limited.

John Stratton Hawley's *Sur Das: Poet, Singer, Saint*, is an accessibly written text on the blind saint, Delhi, Oxford University Press, 1984. Surdas' song are on the lips of every blind singer on the subcontinent, and some of them can be found in the K. L. Saigal collections.

For details of the work of the Community Pharmacy Action Group, which is seeking to ensure that a vital local health service is not wiped out of localities in Britain, telephone 020 7831 3839.

PART FOUR

i Reproduced in colour by the Lalit Kala Academy, New Delhi in 1970 under the English title *Sonabai and Tiger*.

ii For an eighteenth-century English variant (in which the parents of the lost girl 'saw their sleeping child, / Among Tygers wild', and the poet is able to demonstrate that in the future 'the desart wild / Become a garden mild'), see William Blake 'The Little Girl Lost' and the 'The Little Girl Found', in *Songs of Innocence and of Experience: Shewing the Two Contrary States of the Human Soul, 1789–1794*, London, Rupert Hart-Davis Limited, 1967, pages 34, 35 and 36 (with the poems facing the plates).

iii I have put this story together through my memory of it, and from hearing Khodisbhai narrate it to me when I visited him at his home in December 1997.

iv Alexander Kinloch Forbes published *Ras Mala or, Hindoo Annals of the Province of Goozerat in Western India*, in 1856. He asked for the post of Political Agent of Kathiawar in 1859, for he 'found the Mahratta country tame and uninteresting after Goozerat'. By March 1860 he had quelled the rebellious Waghers of the Okhamandal area ('Memoir of the Author' by A. K. Nairne, Esq., BCS, in *Ras Mala*, London, Richardson and Co., 1878, pages xv–xvi).

v For a wonderfully evocative fictional account of the cultural syncretism of early South Asian settlers in East Africa, see M. G. Vassanji *The Gunny Sack*, Oxford, Heinemann African Writers Series, 1989.

vi From the film *Chori Chori* (1955) starring Nargis as the self-willed, runaway daughter of a millionaire who learns to enjoy eating roasted maize-on-the-cob in the company of an impoverished journalist (Raj Kapoor).

vii From the film *Mughal-e-Azam*, where Anarkali (a palace slave) dances in the Sheesh-Mahal in front of the Mughal Emperor and declares her love for Prince Salim with the famous lines, *pardah nahin jab ko Khudase, Bandose pardah karna kya … jab pyar kiya to darna kya* (When there is no veil [i.e. concealment] from God, why conceal from men … To love is no crime).

viii *Report on the Colony and Protectorate of Kenya for the Year 1955*, London, Colonial Office, Her Majesty's Stationery Office.

ix *Southall, 23 April 1979: the Report of the Unofficial Committee of Enquiry*, London, National Council for Civil Liberties, 1980.

x For some literature on this period, see Amrit Wilson, *Finding a Voice*, London, Virago, 1978, Beverley Bryan, et al *The Heart of the Race*, London, Virago, 1984, *Charting the Journey: Writings by Black and Third World Women*, London, Sheba Press, 1988, *All the Women are White, all the Blacks are Men, but some of us are Brave*, Old Westbury, NY Feminist Press, 1982.

xi George Eliot, *The Mill on the Floss*, first published in 1860.

xii David Hardiman, *The Coming of the Devi: Adivasi Assertion in Western India*, Delhi, Oxford University Press, 1987, and 'The Bhils and Shahukars of Eastern India', in *Subaltern Studies V: Writings on South Asian History and Society*, Delhi, Oxford University Press, 1987.

xiii See Parita Mukta, 'Ramjanmabhoomi Comes to Milton Keynes', in *Economic and Political Weekly*, Vol. XXIV, Nos. 44 and 45, 4–11 November 4–11 November 1989; and 'Worshipping Inequalities', *Economic and Political Weekly*, Vol. XXV, No. 41, 13 October 1990, for a foretelling of the clouds that were looming. 'Lament and Power: the Subversion and Appropriation of Grief', in *Studies in History*, 13: 2, 1997 for an exploration of the relationship between the rise of political authoritarianism and the rejection of real, lived grief.

xiv For a discussion of the bitter struggle over Babr Masjid, and the violence that was unleashed by the contemporary Hindu nationalist movement against Muslim minorities in India after the symbolic demolition of a mosque in December 1992 (violence which was later extended to impoverished Christians in the *adivasi* belt of Gujarat) see Sarvepalli Gopal (ed.), *Anatomy of a Confrontation*, India, Penguin, 1991 and also K. N. Pannikar (ed.) *The Concerned Indian's Guide to Communism*, Delhi, Viking, 1999. The terrible violence unleashed by the Shiv Sena against citizens of the Muslim faith in the city of Bombay has been documented in a report which came out in 1993. The full report of the Justice Shrikrishna Commission can be read in *Damning Verdict* by Sabrang Communications and Publishing Pvt. Ltd, which can be obtained from sabrang@bom2.vsnl.net.in.

The public theatre of violence (in the fullest sense of this term) has made for a marked aggression within the heart of Hindu culture. For this, see Paola Baccheta, 'All our Goddesses are Armed: Religion, Resistance and Revenge in the Life of a Militant Hindu Nationalist Woman', in Amrita Basu (ed.), 'Women and Religious Nationalism in India,' special issue of *The Bulletin of Concerned Asian Scholars*, 25: 4, 1993 and Lise McKean *Divine Enterprise: Gurus and the Hindu Nationalist Movement*, Chicago, University of Chicago Press, 1996. For women's central involvement in the militantly anti-Muslim movement, see Tanika Sarkar and Urvashi Butalia (eds), *Women and the Hindu Right*, London, Zed Press, 1995 and Kumari Jayawardena and Malathi de Alwis (eds.), *Embodied Violence: Communalising Women's Sexuality in South Asia*, Delhi, Kali, 1996. The rise of religious nationalism has blighted the lives of all in the subcontinent. The Islamic Hudood Ordinances were promulgated in Pakistan in 1979 and have led to grave violations of women's rights. The controversy over Taslima Nasreen's book, which led to the author having to flee Bangladesh, is also a mark of the times. Taslima Nasreen, *Lajja: Shame*, translated by Tutul Gupta, Penguin, 1993. For the diasporic linkages which made Hindu nationalism a global phenomenon, see the contributions to the special issue of the journal *Ethnic and Racial Studies*, edited by Parita Mukta and Chetan Bhatt, 23: 3, May 2000, and Chetan Bhatt, *Liberation and Purity*, London, UCL Press, 1997.

xv For a close variant of this story, see *Folk-Tales from India: a selection of oral tales from twenty-two languages*, selected and edited by A. K. Ramanujan, New York, Pantheon Books, 1991, pages 159–168. Source: Putlibai D. H. Wadia, *The Indian Antiquary*, 'Prince Sabar', vol. 16, no. 202, November 1887, pages 322–27.

xvi See Roberto Calasso, *The Marriage of Cadmus and Harmony*, Vintage, 1994, in particular the argument on pages 355–359.

xvii Just as he was unable to go beyond the racialisation of the 'savage' in some of his paintings. I am grateful to Carolyn Steedman for bringing the print of *Time, Truth and History* to my notice, in *Truth and Fantasy: Goya, the Small Paintings*, London, Royal Academy of Arts, 1994, pages 222–225. For a vivid analysis of Goya's depiction of old women in his paintings (so different from the woman marked as 'History') see Jutta Veld, 'Between Bourgeois Enlightenment and Popular Culture: Goya's Festivals, Old Women, Monsters and Blind Men', in *History Workshop Journal*, Spring 1987, issue no. 23.

xviii For some accounts of these times, see Sheila Rowbotham *The Past is Before Us: Feminism in Action since the 1960s*, London, Pandora, 1989; and, with Hilary Wainwright, *Beyond the Fragments: Feminism and the Making of Socialism*, London, Merlin, 1980. For accounts which raise uncomfortable questions, see Beatrix Campbell, *The Iron Ladies: why do women vote Tory?* London, Virago, 1987, and Carolyn Steedman's *Landscape for a Good Woman: A Story of Two Lives*, London, Virago, 1986, which raises questions on the experiencing of class, gender and 'race'.

xix See endnotes xiii and xviii above, as well as Beatrix Campbell, *Stolen Voices: an exposure of the campaign to discredit childhood testimony*, London, Women's Press, 1988, and Helena Kennedy, *Eve was Framed: Women and British Justice*, London, Chatto and Windus, 1992.

xx There are now very detailed writings on the genocide in Rwanda. Some of the most telling accounts are in *Rwanda: Death, Despair and Defiance*, London, Africa Rights, 1995, and Philip Gourevitch, *We wish to inform you that tomorrow we will be killed with our families . . .* London, Picador, 1999. Also Bridget Byrne, *Gender, Conflict and Development, Vol. 2*, Brighton, Institute of Development Studies, 1996.

xxi Some of Romila Thapar's more recent writings include *Sakuntala: Texts, Readings, Histories*, Delhi, Kali for Women, 1999, *History and Beyond*, Delhi, Oxford University Press, 2000, *India: Another Millennium*, India, Viking, 2000. Her 'Somanatha: narratives of a history', in *Seminar* 475, March 1999, is an immensely important scholarly article which throws the Hindu nationalist discourse of the raiding of this temple by Mahmud of Ghazni into disarray.

xxii For published tales which go beyond the 'Tom Thumb' genre see *Bimwili and the Zimwi: A Tale from Zanzibar*, retold by Verna Aardema, pictures by Susan Meddaugh, London, Pan Macmillan Children's Books, 1992, which tells of Bimwili being captured by an itinerant singer who travelled from village to village carrying his drum; *The Changeling*, by Selma Lagerlof, translated from the Swedish by Susanna Stevens, New York, Alfred A. Knopf, 1992, which tells of a troll-crone who exchanged her boar-bristled child for a human baby; and *Catkin*, by Antonia Barber, illustrated by P. J. Lynch, London, Walker Books, 1996 which tells of the yearning of the childless Dark Lord and Lady who lived under the green hills.

xxiii *The Mountains of Tibet: A Child's Journey through Living and Dying*, by Mordicai Gerstein, introduced by Sogyal Rinpoche, Bristol, Barefoot Books, 1987. The *New York Times* judged it as the best illustrated book of 1987.

xxiv UNICEF documents provide more than adequate evidence that these 'rights' are yet to be realised for large numbers of children on this globe; the practice of sex determination of foetuses is also a highly damaging one.

xxv *Hiawatha's Childhood*, Henry Wadsworth Longfellow, illustrated by Erroll Le Cain, London, Puffin Books, 1984, *Brother Eagle, Sister Sky, a message from Chief Seattle*, paintings by Susan Jeffers, New York, Puffin Books, 1991, *Bringing the Rain to Kapiti Plain*, by Verna Aardema, illustrated by Beatriz Vidal, London, Macmillan Children's Books, 1991.

xxvi Moonie wants you to know that the two of them do not quarrel any more.

xxvii From *The Lion King*, vocal Nathan Lane and Ernie Sabella with Jason Weaver and Joseph Williams, music by Elton John/Tim Rice, 1994.

xxviii *My Grandpa and the Sea*, Katherine Orr, Minneapolis, First Avenue Editions, 1990.

xxix *Cry, the Beloved Country*, Alan Paton, London, Longman, 1970.

xxx THERE'S NO SUCH THING AS A **DRAGON**, story and pictures by Jack Kent, London, Blackie and Son Limited, 1984.

xxxi *Stone Girl, Bone Girl*, by Lawrence Anholt, illustrated by Sheila Moxley, London, Doubleday, 1999.

xxxii Lyric by Paul Brady, sung by Dolores Keane on an audio cassette entitled *A Woman's Heart*, Darte C 158, marketed by Dolphin Traders, Dublin.

xxxiii The poetical assertions of Khalil Gibran notwithstanding.

xxxiv Sebastiao Salgado, *Migrations: Humanity in Transition*, Paris, Amazonas Images, 2000.

xxxv Sebastiao Salgado, *The Children: Refugees and Migrants*, Paris, Amazonas Images, 2000, page 7.

xxxvi Ibid., page 9.

xxxvii John Berger introducing the work of Sebastiao Salgado in the *Guardian*, 28 May 2001, page 10.

xxxviii Salgado, op. cit., page 109.

Further Reading

Toni Morrison's *Beloved*, Vintage, 1997, is an exemplary writing of the story of a ladli (which the author insists is not one to be passed on – pages 274–5). Anna Grimshaw has written a beautiful text of her time spent amongst Buddhist nuns at Julichang, who lived a life of daily hardship in subordination to the hierarchy of monks (Grimshaw, *The Servants of the Buddha: Winter in a Himalayan Convent*, London, Open Letters, 1992). Tanika Sarkar's *Words to Win, The Making of Amar Jiban: A Modern Autobiography*, Delhi, Kali, 1997, provides a moving and cogent portrayal of the yearning to write by an upper-caste Bengali woman in the nineteenth century. Rashsundari taught herself to read and write in secret in the confines of her home, and succeeded in writing an autobiography.

These are some of the books the children, Bindu and I have all loved reading together: *The Mousehole Cat*, by Antonia Barber, illustrated by Nicola Bayley, London, Walker Books, 1993; *Snowy*, by Berlie Doherty, illustrated by Keith Bowen, London, Harper Collins, 1993; *Lali and Bablu's Mango Tree*, Rupa Gupta, Delhi, Children's Book Trust, 1989; *The Man who wanted to Live Forever*, retold by Selina Hastings, illustrated by Reg Cartwright, London, Walker Books, 1991; *Once in a Village*, H. C. Madan, illustrated by Nina Bahl, Delhi, National Book Trust, 1988; *Shaker Lane*, Alice and Amrtin Provensen, London, Viking Penguin, 1987; *The People who Hugged the Trees*, adapted by Deborah Lee Rose, with pictures by Birgitta Saflund, Colorado, Roberts Rhinehart Inc. Publishers, 199-; *Grandmother's Song*, written by Barbara Soros, illustrated by Jackie Morris, Bristol, Barefoot Books, 1998. The last is an excellent publishing house for children's books.

GLOSSARY

AARDOOSI medicinal plant, *adhatoda vasika*

BHAJAN devotional song

BHAKHRI thick, crumbly chapatti

BHAKTA devotee

BILIPATRA leaves of the tree *eagle marmaloss*

CHULA stove

CHUNDALDI outer, upper garment; symbol for the human form

DAHI yogurt

DALIT empowering term for the oppressed, 'untouchables'

DARGAH enshrined tomb

DATURA *datura* plant

DOSIMA an old woman, considered useless to society

DUKHIARI unhappy

GANTTHIA fried savouries made from gram flour

GAUD-DHANA jaggery with popped grain

HARAMBEE 'pull together', a work song turned into a state call

KHARETO a *sari* with a special design on it

LADLI beloved

MAHAL land area

MBARI patrilineal sub-clan

MEHNDI henna

MOONG DAL pulse

MULA long white radish

NAJAR evil eye

NIMKI savouries

OBAD cow dung, stacked up with strips of wood for fuel

OSHIADA ROTLA *rotla* for which one is indebted

PALLAV the edge of a *sadlo*. Also 'shelter, support'

PALLAVU connoting caring as in 'to bring up, nourish'

PANCHANG lunar calendar

PATTER VELIA *bhajias* made of green *advi* leaves

PENDO a sweet, made of milk, sugar and almonds

PITRU male ancestors

PRASAD sanctified food

PUJA acts of worship

PURAN PODI chapatti stuffed with sweet lentils

ROTLA millet bread

ROTLI chapatti wheat

SADLO cotton *sari* that is worn draped over the right shoulder

SAL MUBAARAK happy new year

SARANGI string instrument

SATYAGRAHI non co-operator, standing up for the truth

SHAK cooked vegetables

SHAMBA plot of agricultural land

SHRIKHAND yogurt delicacy, fragranced with saffron

SUKSHMA subtle

TAPURIA little ones

TTHALI tin, steel plate

VAID medicine man

VRATTA-KATTHA stories accompanying ritual observances